ALWAYS THE BRIDE

A Biography of Elsa Lanchester

ALWAYS THE BRIDE

A Biography of Elsa Lanchester

By Victoria Worsley

Published in the United States of America by:

BearManor Media
1317 Edgewater Dr #110
Orlando FL 32804
bearmanormedia.com

Printed in the United States.

All photos used with permission.

Typesetting and layout by DataSmith Solutions

Cover by DataSmith Solutions

ISBN — 978-1-62933-809-5

For Anamika and Li

Contents

Introduction: Best Supporting Actress

As the Monster's Mate in *Bride of Frankenstein* (1935), Elsa Lanchester has become a horror icon, instantly recognizable by many, although few perhaps would know the actress's name. It is not how she would have chosen to be remembered, although toward the end of her life she accepted this curious fame with good grace.

My aim in writing this book is to give Elsa Lanchester the leading role, the top billing, the moment alone in the spotlight that she was repeatedly denied in life. Elsa was the ultimate supporting actress, always cast alongside bigger, more bankable stars, and frequently stealing the scenes from under their noses. Reviewers bemoaned that her talents were wasted in such small roles, but the Hollywood studios struggled to fit her quirky appearance and character into any of their generic "types." Even in her career-defining *Bride of Frankenstein*, she has less than fifteen minutes on the screen, and that includes her time playing Mary Shelley in the film's frequently cut prologue.

But it was not just in the movies that Elsa was stuck in a supporting role. Married for over thirty years to Oscar-winning actor Charles Laughton, Elsa was overshadowed by her husband's greater fame, to the extent that one headline for her obituary, twenty-four years after Charles's death, read "Widow of Charles Laughton had many talents."[1] Perhaps if the marriage had been a happy one, this might not have rankled so much, but her early discovery and reluctant acceptance of Charles's gay identity led to mistrust and resentment that festered over the years. Elsa and Charles seemed to love and loath each other in equal amounts, and their relationship was marked by decades of mutually wrought emotional damage.

As I researched this book it seemed like all the major players in Elsa's life had been the subject of biographies—even her unassuming puppeteer brother, Waldo—and in these books, Elsa is again a supporting character, providing a witty anecdote or cutting remark before disappearing from view.

Perhaps in an attempt to rectify matters, Elsa wrote several accounts of her life. The first was *Charles Laughton and I*, published in 1938, which is in-

---

1. *Los Angeles Times*, December 27, 1986.

teresting for the detail it provides about the couple's homes but is limited by the necessity of promoting them as the ideal couple, with no mention of his sexual orientation. After Charles's death, Elsa authorized Charles Higham to write *Charles Laughton: An Intimate Biography*, which was published in 1976, and in which Charles's sexuality was addressed. Elsa wrote the introduction for this book. More than that, though, she was deeply involved in its construction, with Higham writing: "She would read through my bad typing . . . with quiet patience, sharpening a phrase here, cutting another there, suggesting additional material. . . . She did not want her name on the book, except as author of the introduction. Yet much of the book owes its existence and nature to her attentiveness and her influence."[2] Indeed, when the book was published, it was she who was criticized for allowing Charles's secret sexuality to become public knowledge.

Even Elsa's autobiography—*Elsa Lanchester, Herself*, published in 1983—features Charles and his career heavily, often to the exclusion of Elsa's own achievements. That is not the book's only problem, although it is a wonderful book to read, and I would encourage everyone to seek it out. As reviewer Peter Hepple wrote, "Few books can have more misspellings and errors of fact than this one, but all are readily forgivable in a story that is quite enthralling in its scope."[3] Such errors are doubtlessly due to Elsa's admittedly bad memory rather than intentional misrepresentation; she told one reporter that "the secret to long life is a faulty memory and the constitution of an ox, both of which I'm glad to say I possess!"[4] What is harder for a modern reader to comprehend or forgive is Elsa's self-effacement: she dedicates several pages to Charles's speaking tours, for example, but omits entirely any mention of her own Oscar nominations. An autobiography is a poor container for such modesty.

What her writings do provide, if not a true picture of Elsa's career and achievements, is a glimpse into Elsa's complicated personality, which is more interesting than any part she played on stage or screen. Her writings demonstrate moments of breathtaking cruelty and a sense of devastating isolation, but she also had a sharp sense of humor and a charming sense of the ridiculous, and she never took herself too seriously. This book aims to keep that mischievous, caustic, witty personality in mind always, while amending mistakes and providing details that previous writings left out. It is time to resurrect Elsa Lanchester in all her flawed glory, so that readers of today can fully appreciate this extraordinary woman.

---

2.   Higham, *Charles Laughton*, xvii.

3.   *The Stage*, March 15, 1984.

4.   Hadleigh, *Leading Ladies*, 90 (interview from 1976).

1   The Woman Who Didn't

Elsa Lanchester never suffered from a want of personality. Reading her two autobiographical works—*Charles Laughton and I* (1938) and *Elsa Lanchester, Herself* (1983)—leaves one with the impression of a woman who was, perhaps, difficult to like. Her literary self-portraits have no softness, subtlety, or rounded edges. She is strident, opinionated, and biting, both clever and cruel. A friend of hers commented that Elsa was "the quickest, wittiest, most mercurial *bitch* you could ever hope to meet. She couldn't help herself. The darts just flew out of her mouth."[1] In the grand old English tradition of self-deprecation, she saves several of her choicest comments for herself.

Her cutting directness—both a character flaw and a demonstration of strength of character—is a trait that Elsa inherited undiluted from her mother, Biddy. If Elsa's was to be an unconventional life, she had been primed from childhood to embrace her otherness, indeed to declare it with pride and hang the consequences.

One such point of pride was Elsa's status as a bastard. That her parents were unmarried at the time of her birth in 1902 was considered shocking. The stigma attached to illegitimacy was so deeply engrained in society in the early twentieth century that Elsa did not mention it in her first autobiographical work. However, by the time of *Elsa Lanchester, Herself* (1983), social convention had relaxed to the extent that Elsa could admit she found it "rather glamorous" to be a bastard.[2] Indeed, the circumstances of her bastardy make compelling reading.

Although Elsa's maternal grandparents, Henry and Octavia Lanchester, were progressive enough to provide a good education for all eight of their children, including their three daughters, there would prove to be limits on how forward-thinking they were prepared to be.[3] The family was upwardly mobile—father

---

1. Quoted in Callow, *Charles Laughton*, 282 (emphasis in original). The friend is not named.

2. Lanchester, *Elsa Lanchester, Herself*, 14.

3. More details of the Lanchester family can be found in Cockayne, *Master of the Marionettes*, 2–7.

1

EDITH LANCHESTER.

Edith "Biddy" Lanchester, Elsa's formidable mother.

Henry was an architect, and three of the sons would later form the Lanchester Motor Company—and people of this middling, aspirational class in the twilight years of nineteenth-century England were not generally disposed to disrupting social conventions and mores. Henry and Octavia's daughter Edith, who was always known as Biddy, did not inherit such delicacy.

Born in Hove in 1871 (her mother's date of birth is the first of many factual errors Elsa makes in her autobiography), Edith Lanchester matriculated at London University with "honors in every single subject," including zoology and political economy.[4] She then took up a post at the Maria Grey teacher training school, the first such establishment for women in the country. Presumably such a career path would have been pleasing to her parents, as teaching was considered a respectable profession for a single woman.

However, Biddy's time at the Maria Grey institution—and as a respectable single woman—was to be brief. She became a passionate member of the Social Democratic Federation, speaking out frequently at meetings about freedom, equality, and the division of wealth. Such opinions, and the volume at which they were voiced, proved "rather too strong" for the school, and she was asked to leave.[5] A course in shorthand and typing followed, leading to work as a clerk for the Cardiff Gold Mining Company in London. She was set up for continued progress along the path of middle-class respectability, despite her unconventional political leanings.

That "progress" would come to halt, however, when she met James "Shamus" Sullivan, who was considered to be Biddy's social inferior by all those who were concerned about such matters. He was the son of an Irish policeman, worked in a factory, and spoke with a strong Cockney accent. But Biddy's passion for equality enabled her to see beyond such circumstances to his intelligence, ambition, and socialist values. They fell in love despite the obstacles in their path, and then they proceeded to create even more obstacles for themselves.

In 1895, a book called *The Woman Who Did* scandalized polite society. Written by Grant Allen, it was published as part of a series to promote the idea of the New Woman, which was just beginning to emerge on both sides of the Atlantic. The New Woman was educated and independent (she was also usually upper class, as few in society's lower echelons could afford such radical ideals). In *The Woman Who Did*, the heroine of the novel seeks independence from her parents, so she moves out of their house and begins working as a teacher. When she falls in love, she insists that they live together without getting married.

This opposition to marriage on the grounds of independence and New Womanhood was to strike a resounding chord with Biddy Lanchester. In October 1895, declaring that she was not and never would be a man's "chattel," she coolly informed her parents that she and Shamus Sullivan were setting up

---

4. Lanchester, *Elsa Lanchester, Herself*, 1.
5. *Lloyd's Weekly News*, October 27, 1895.

house together, and that they had no intention of becoming husband and wife legally, as they did not believe in marriage. (Actually, according to several sources, Shamus was quite keen on the idea of getting married, but he was never one to stand up to the force of nature that was Biddy.)

Henry and Octavia Lanchester were astounded, not least because they had believed their daughter to have been engaged to be married for the past two years. That they were devastated by such developments is understandable, given the era. The way they reacted to the situation, however, shows that the dramatic, stubborn, and cruel streak was active in the family bloodline several generations before Elsa Lanchester set out to pen her memoirs.

It began when Octavia visited her daughter's lodgings in Battersea in order to enlist the help of Biddy's landlady, Mrs. Mary Gray, in persuading Biddy to change her mind. During this conversation Octavia allegedly said she would rather see her daughter dead than disgraced in such a manner. Over the days that followed, Biddy's siblings and other relations stopped by and added their pleas to Octavia's, but to no avail. This continued for five days, with Biddy digging her heels in further each time. Desperate times had arrived; desperate measures were to follow.

On the morning of Friday, October 25, 1895, Biddy was eating breakfast with Mary Gray and Mary's daughter Florence. As had by now become routine, one of Biddy's brothers called round and attempted to "talk sense" into her, and was met by the usual response. But this time, unbeknown to Biddy, things would be different. After a few minutes, Biddy's father and two more of her brothers arrived, accompanied by Doctor G. Fielding Blandford; they demanded to talk to Biddy alone. When Biddy refused once again to change her stance, she was presented with an Urgency Order—a certificate of insanity. The cause of her insanity was given as "over-education."[6] They had come, they told her, to take her away.

Biddy, unsurprisingly, did not go quietly. She screamed repeatedly for her landlady, who ran to her aid but was thrust back. Mrs. Gray shouted to Florence to go for the police, but the girl was prevented from doing so by one of Biddy's brothers, who held on to her. Biddy was removed forcibly from the house and bundled into a waiting brougham; her wrists were tied with rope, and the men held her legs, although it was later reported that Biddy kicked out a window of the carriage.[7] Blinds drawn, the brougham raced away, and a frantic Mrs. Gray, nursing a black eye from the altercation, rushed off in search of Shamus Sullivan.

And so began what was to be known as the "Lanchester kidnapping case," a cause célèbre that was chronicled in reams of newsprint around the world. Shamus Sullivan began his frantic search at the police court, from where he was sent to the high court, with every sentence he spoke appearing in the newspapers

6.   Lanchester, *Elsa Lanchester, Herself*, 2.

7.   Lanchester, 2.

shortly afterward. He told the magistrate, "her parents and her brothers have, I believe, carried her off by violence, and now I am given to understand she is . . . detained in a madhouse."[8]

He was right. The carriage had taken the struggling young woman to Roehampton Asylum in South West London. The hospital, a stately mansion with ivory Gothic façade, had been converted from a private residence in 1872. (Still open today, it is now called the Priory Hospital, Roehampton, and has counted among its celebrity patients such folks as Amy Winehouse and Johnny Depp.) Biddy Lanchester was to provide the institution with its first taste of life in the headlines; her experience was reported in *The Times* as follows:

> She was seen on arrival by Dr. Chambers. She then asked to see him alone, and the doctor directed her brothers and her father to retire. She explained matters fully to the doctor, who replied that he had a certificate and was obliged to receive her. She was well treated. On Sunday morning she was given a separate sitting room. On Monday evening two Commissioners in Lunacy called. After talking with her for more than half an hour they had a consultation with Dr. Chambers and his assistant, and then they informed her that they could not honestly detain her, as they considered her perfectly sane, but somewhat foolish.[9]

The commissioners wrote an order for Biddy to be discharged on November 1, but after further pressure from member of Parliament (MP) John Burns, she was released on October 29.

While she had been detained, members of the Social Democratic Federation clustered outside the walls of the asylum, singing their anthem, "The People's Flag." Upon her release, participants and spectators from both sides of the debate spoke out in the press. Dr. Blandford, who had written the original certificate that got Biddy committed, defended his actions, saying, "I was informed that there was insanity in her family, the grandmother and an uncle having been insane; that she had always been eccentric and had lately taken up with Socialists of the most advanced order. She seemed quite unable to see that the step she was about to take meant utter ruin. If she had said that she contemplated suicide a certificate might have been signed without question. I considered I was equally justified in signing one when she expressed her determination to commit this social suicide." He further commented that she was a "monomaniac on the subject of marriage" and was "quite unfit to take care of herself."[10]

Biddy's father, Henry Lanchester, condemned the commissioners for releasing her, and wrote an open letter to the press. In it, he stated: "My opinion, and that of the family, is that the girl is, for the time being, not of sound mind, and that the effects of overstudy have predisposed her naturally impressionable

8. *Lloyd's Weekly News*, October 27, 1895.

9. *The Times*, October 30, 1895.

10. *Tenbury Wells Advertiser*, November 5, 1895.

temperament, to be abnormally acted upon by her self-imposed surroundings."[11] An article sympathetic to Mr. Lanchester opined that "Miss Lanchester as a school girl worked far too hard for her comparatively slight physical reserve," and Mrs. Fenwick-Miller, writing in the Ladies' Column of *The Times*, thought it was "quite easy to understand and sympathise with the anguish of Miss Lanchester's parents, who see their daughter about to place herself in a position which will undoubtedly taint and harm her entire future."[12]

Elsa was later to discover that her mother had kept a box of newspaper clippings from these years, and the extracts she quotes in her autobiography demonstrate the feelings of the day: "I think Mr. Lanchester has acted towards his daughter as every British father should do"; "Should she have children she will learn the disgrace which she deliberately assigns to them."[13] However, there were also some voices raised in support of her stance, including those of fellow socialists such as J. W. Wood, who wrote in the *Clarion*, "Edith Lanchester has dared to assert her right to live her own life. . . . Socialists believe that a woman has perfect right to do what she likes with her own body."[14] The Marquis of Queensbury offered Biddy and Shamus one hundred pounds to go through a wedding ceremony and then denounce their vows.

The general tone of both press and public seemed to be the same as that taken by the lunacy commissioners: Biddy was "perfectly sane, but somewhat foolish."

She may have been perfectly sane, but upon her release from Roehampton Asylum, Biddy Lanchester was utterly furious. She told the press that she had previously been willing to go abroad with Shamus Sullivan in order to spare her family any shame (the couple had been thinking of Australia), but, given the way she had been treated, she was no longer willing to do so. Nowhere is it stated what Shamus thought; after his initial heroic dash to the police court, he is something of a silent figure in the whole affair.

The outcomes of this entire exhilarating episode are somewhat disappointing. Although Social Democratic Federation branches across the country held meetings to discuss any legal action that might result from the situation, the light of public attention dimmed quickly. By December 1895, less than two months after Biddy's release, it was reported that:

> We all thought we had heard the last of the "woman who didn't." Apparently, however, we were all wrong and the matter is not to be allowed to drop if the clique by which Miss Lanchester is surrounded can help it. Anyhow, they have decided to hold a meeting . . . nominally to protest against the abuse of the Lunacy Laws,

---

11. *Beverly and East Riding Recording*, November 2, 1895.
12. *Musselburgh News*, November 8, 1895; *The Times*, October 30, 1895, quoted in Lanchester, *Elsa Lanchester, Herself*, 4.
13. Quoted in Lanchester, *Elsa Lanchester, Herself*, 13.
14. Letter from J. W. Wood, *Clarion*, November 2, 1895.

but virtually to try and revive public interest in the case. . . . [We] are informed that there will be no charge for admission. It is, perhaps, as well that there is not, for otherwise the speakers might have it all to themselves, for there is little doubt that all interest has now died out, and, if anything, public sympathy is now with Miss Lanchester's parents rather than with that young lady herself. In fact her best friends are counselling her now to let the matter drop. Let us hope she will take their advice.[15]

She did not take their advice, if indeed any were offering such. In January 1896, a deputation waited on the Lunacy Commission to demand a prosecution against Dr. Blandford. Biddy gave evidence to a panel of commissioners, headed by Charles D. Bagot, but there was to be no dramatic showdown or day in court; the commissioners agreed that the doctor had been mistaken, but they would take the matter no further as they could see no evidence of a corrupt motive. Biddy was referred to in the press as "a nine days' wonder,"[16] and those nine days were up.

The lasting legacy of the Lanchester kidnapping case was that Biddy never again spoke to her father, and he would play no part in Elsa's life. Additionally, perhaps even more tragically, the affair created for Biddy Lanchester and Shamus Sullivan a tie even more binding than marriage vows could ever have been. They were forever ensnared on each other, held fast by Biddy's stubbornness, to the detriment of their individual happiness. Elsa wrote: "They were held in a grip by their early strike for freedom. In defying convention they were chained by it."[17]

For better or worse, richer or poorer, stay together they did. Their son, Waldo Sullivan Lanchester, was born in 1897, the image of his father with a head full of black curls. Prior to his birth, Biddy had been employed as secretary to Eleanor Marx—socialist, author, and daughter of Karl Marx—and the two women developed a close friendship. Biddy's pregnancy with Waldo was difficult, made harder by social pressure and lack of family support. Eleanor played a key role after the baby was born; she wrote to a friend that Biddy was "very ill after her confinement" and so was "coming to me for a few weeks' nursing," and, as her biographer notes, she "looked after Edith and protected her, James and the baby from Edith's family and social opprobrium."[18]

Eleanor Marx was in need of some care and protection herself. She had been in a relationship with fellow socialist Edward Aveling for many years, but suffered frequently as a result of his infidelities and bouts of ill health, through which she often nursed him. In early 1898—less than a year after she had opened her home to Biddy—Eleanor discovered that not only was Aveling's

15. *Bristol Times and Mirror*, December 19, 1895.

16. *Woman's Signal*, January 16, 1896.

17. Lanchester, *Elsa Lanchester, Herself*, 316.

18. Kapp, *Eleanor Marx*, 5; Holmes, *Eleanor Marx*, 412.

illness thought to be terminal, but he had betrayed her and married a young actress, Eva Frye, in June of the previous year.

Deeply depressed, Eleanor Marx committed suicide at the age of forty-three by swallowing poison. Although the coroner's verdict of "suicide while in a state of temporary insanity" technically absolved Aveling of any legal accountability, he was widely considered to be responsible for her death, to the extent that when he died four months later, of kidney disease, no representatives of the socialist groups with which he was associated attended his funeral.

Elsa Lanchester would learn the story of Eleanor Marx during her childhood in a way that seems a fitting introduction to Biddy's peculiar parenting style, not to mention her signature unemotiveness, which Elsa would inherit. Biddy told her young daughter, "If a person must commit suicide . . . Eleanor Marx did it very well. She had a bath and cleaned herself thoroughly inside and out, wrapped herself in a sheet and took prussic acid." Elsa reports, without judgment, that her mother "thought this very fine—'not at all messy.'"[19] Once again, her father's opinion on the matter is not recorded.

---

19. Lanchester, *Elsa Lanchester, Herself*, 16.

2 Sufficiently Odd to Be Interesting

In 1938, when her husband was at the height of his Hollywood success and had just set up his own film production company, Elsa Lanchester wrote a curious book entitled *Charles Laughton and I*. Although publicized as a biography, it is at least half an autobiography, and critics at the time felt that Elsa focused too much on herself, although they praised the book overall. It was, after all, the name in the title that sold the book, not the name of the author. Elsa was aware of her husband's greater fame—it was impossible for her not to be—and she is almost apologetic when introducing the section of the book that discusses her own early years. Almost, but not quite.

"The tendencies of Charles's youth are of interest because of the fame which he has achieved," she writes after a six-page account of Laughton's boyhood. "Although my own childhood does not arouse the same curiosity, it was sufficiently odd to be interesting, and since I am writing about Charles and myself it is necessary to add a few lines to the picture of the narrator who at least plays a large role in the life of the principal."[20] These "few lines" then take up the next seven pages.

Condensing her highly unusual upbringing into only seven pages required leaving out several choice episodes and reducing others to mere anecdotes. She would expand greatly on this material in her 1983 autobiography *Elsa Lanchester, Herself.*

Elsa Sullivan Lanchester was born on October 28, 1902, in Lewisham, London. The earliest photograph that I have been able to find was published in a "When We Were Very Young" feature in *The Sketch.*[21] In the picture, Elsa looks to be about a year old, but even at such a young age, she is clearly recognizable. Although her wispy hair has not yet blossomed into its full riot of red curls, the cleft in her chin and her wide, slightly protruding eyes are very much in evidence, as she stares directly into the camera with a slightly startled expression. She had cause to look wary; from her earliest years life was unsettled, unconventional, and unhealthy. Her mother, Biddy, may have won the argument about the marriage

---

20. Lanchester, *Charles Laughton and I*, 26.
21. *The Sketch*, May 24, 1933.

Elsa's father, James 'Shamus' Sullivan.

question, but there was still plenty of fight in her, and being a parent did not slow her down at all. In fact, her children were to prove useful weapons in her battles against pretty much anyone she perceived to be in a position of authority.

In November 1903, around the time the picture of Elsa was taken, Biddy was summoned to Penge Magistrates' Court to answer for Waldo's erratic school attendance. She told the magistrate that she was educating the six-year-old Waldo at home—apparently her brief time at the Maria Grey teacher training academy was to prove useful after all. However, she was willing to admit that there were some aspects of Waldo's development that required her to send him to school occasionally, and she told the court: "I believe it is good and healthful for him to mix with others, and, therefore I send him to school in the morning in order that he may have companionship. But for that I would not let him go to school at all."[22] She was informed that schooling could not be conducted in such a manner, and that Waldo must be educated either solely at home or solely

22. *Londonderry Sentinel,* November 10, 1903.

at school, whereupon Biddy chose to continue teaching him at home. Later she would send him to a small boys' school in Clapham run by a fellow socialist, Frederick Kettle.

By the time Elsa reached the age of five—the legal age for children to begin attending school—Biddy had decided once again to educate her child at home. Although she managed to keep up such an arrangement for a while, helped in large part by the family's frequent changes of lodging, another showdown with the authorities was inevitable. This time Biddy was informed in no uncertain terms that she was not permitted to teach her child at home, and so, at the age of six and a half, Elsa Sullivan Lanchester was enrolled in the local council school.

Her experience at the school was not easy. As both her parents were atheists, Elsa did not join in with morning prayers but was kept outside, where she watched the other children through the glass. Biddy had also failed to prepare her daughter academically for conventional schooling, as Elsa later explained: "I knew all about wild flowers, why women ought to get the vote and where children came from, but I did not know the Lord's Prayer or how to spell APPLE."[23] When asked by her teacher how many pennies were in a pound—a significantly more difficult question in those pre-decimal days than today—the little girl burst into tears and ran home. A London County Council inspector came to the flat to investigate the incident, and Elsa countered with a peaceful protest, lying motionless and silent on the floor, and refusing to answer any questions. She repeated this performance whenever the inspector called.

The solution to the problem of Elsa's education came from an unexpected source. Frederick Kettle, headmaster of the Boys' Public Day School that Waldo attended, suggested that Elsa become a pupil there as well. Elsa thus became the only girl at an all-boys school—a status that she would retain, barring a few interruptions, for the next seven years. If life was a movie, then it seemed that Elsa had already been typecast as someone who never quite fit in, the perennial odd-one-out. She was not yet seven years old.

Mr. Kettle's school did little to add any discipline or structure to Elsa's hectic life. Rather than following any set curriculum, the children began each day by reading the newspapers, following which, according to Elsa, "We more or less chose the day's work for ourselves and did as we liked, as long as we did *something*." She was later to say that her schooldays were "divinely happy."[24]

The same could not always be said of her home life at this time. During these years the Lanchester-Sullivan family was making do on Shamus's salary as a commercial clerk, "constantly moving from one depressing home in

---

23. Lanchester, *Charles Laughton and I*, 27.

24. Lanchester, *Elsa Lanchester, Herself*, 9 (emphasis in original); Lanchester, *Charles Laughton and I*, 28.

Clapham Common to another," moving its belongings under cover of darkness in a greengrocer's van.[25] The reasons for these night flights, known as "shooting the moon," were occasionally financial, but more often than not they were a means of evading authority. Six moves were made early in Elsa's life in an attempt to avoid having her vaccinated, and more followed as the family dodged the education inspectors and more than one angry landlady. The houses and flats the family occupied were dirty and small, and family life centered on the kitchen, where comrades would drink endless cups of tea and debate the virtues of Marxism and communism until the early hours. The children learned to sleep through the noise. Elsa remembers not wanting her friends to visit her at home because she was ashamed of their poverty: the house "had that cabbage smell that goes with no money."[26]

One of the many causes espoused by her mother was vegetarianism, and where Biddy went so did the rest of the family, willingly or not. On this cause, Biddy was alone. Shamus occasionally managed to convince Biddy that he needed meat for health reasons—he suffered from rheumatism—whereupon he was grudgingly given half a pig's head boiled in vinegar or some salted smoked fish known as bloaters. Biddy would be sure to make her disapproval known on such occasions, with an acidic "Hope you're enjoying your corpse," while the children watched their father's small disobedience in wonder. Elsa also craved meat, and she spent her pocket money on stock cubes, which she would chew on her way home. She later recalled, "The smell of frying bacon coming from houses on the way to school made me start to think that maybe my mother was a bit evil."[27]

In Elsa's memory, her father was passionate but passive, a hearty follower; although he never spoke out at the endless socialist meetings the family attended, he was vocal in his support of those who did speak. She admitted that she never understood Shamus, "I didn't know him. As I remember him, his fire had gone out."[28] Certainly, while Biddy's antics leap off the page, Shamus appears as a character to whom things happen, but not someone with any hand in creating events, "an almost invisible presence in the household."[29] Elsa presented her brother, Waldo, in much the same way, describing him as "an inactivist, and many a punch in the stomach I gave him for being that way."[30]

However, one incident perhaps proves that Shamus was not quite the pushover his daughter thought he was. On census night, April 2, 1911, enumerators

25. Higham, *Charles Laughton*, 11.

26. Lanchester, *Elsa Lanchester, Herself*, 12.

27. Lanchester, 11.

28. Lanchester, 314.

29. Cockayne, *Master of the Marionettes*, 26.

30. Lanchester, *Elsa Lanchester, Herself*, 10.

visited houses across the country to collect details of the residents. This census is famous for being the one where campaigners for women's suffrage determined that "if women don't count, neither shall they be counted," with women spoiling their forms by writing slogans on them or refusing to write information. One suffragette filled in the name of a male servant, and then added "no other persons, but many women"; another wrote "no vote—no census."[31]

Another form of protest was evading the census by staying away from home on the night in question. This was the method chosen by Biddy, who was a member of the Women's Social and Political Union. She had determined that neither she nor her children would be counted, and so she left Shamus home alone while she took Elsa and Waldo to camp out in the Surrey woods.

One can imagine Biddy boasting of her cleverness at avoiding the enumerators, and perhaps our imagination can stretch to Shamus giving a small, secret smile beneath his enormous black mustache: a glance at the 1911 census return for 32A Rudloe Road, Clapham Park (made available to the public in 2009) shows that although Shamus respected Biddy's wishes not to be counted, he did fill in the details for his children. A small victory.

According to Elsa, her mother was once arrested as a suffragette and spent a day and a night in prison, picking oakum and pulling rags apart. She recalls attending suffragette marches and protests in Trafalgar Square with her parents, which often became violent. On one occasion she remembers Biddy and Shamus screaming at her to keep her arms down, because if she reached up her arms may get broken by the surging crowd that raged around them. Another time was even more frightening for the young girl: "The police all had truncheons and were banging women on the head. I screamed a lot, I think, but the whole thing is now oddly a still picture with no sound at all. Shock, I suppose—a blank in time memory."[32]

These years before the outbreak of World War I saw suffragette activity increase in frequency and intensity; that Biddy only got arrested once perhaps shows that she did not participate in this cause as fully as she did in her socialist activities. She did, however, attend the funeral of Emily Davison, the first martyr to the suffragette cause, and so did Elsa. Davison had died from injuries she sustained in a protest at the Epsom Derby in June 1913, when she ran out onto the track as the race was in progress, clutching her suffragette banners, and was hit by Anmer, the king's horse. Her funeral on June 14, 1913, saw a procession of five thousand women marching in ranks, wearing the suffragette colors of white and purple. Newspapers described the event as having "something of the deliberate brilliance of a military funeral."[33] Even so, the sense of occasion was lost on Elsa,

---

31. Castelow, "No Vote, No Census."

32. Lanchester, *Elsa Lanchester, Herself,* 17.

33. *Manchester Guardian,* June 16, 1913.

then just ten years old, who recalled, "we walked for miles, it seemed . . . I was so tired I was just dragged along."[34]

Something that did catch Elsa's imagination around this time and was to develop into a lifelong passion was music hall. The English traditional music hall—similar in style and content to American vaudeville—originated in saloon bars and retained its rowdy, risqué nature until it was overtaken by the more polished, family-friendly variety show after the First World War. Audiences, seated at tables, could drink and smoke while watching the acts, and so performers had to work hard to keep attention from wandering. Elsa remembers watching comedians such as George Robey, and male impersonators including Vesta Tilley and Ella Shields. But the artist who was to have by far the greatest influence on her as a performer was the so-called Queen of the Music Hall, Marie Lloyd.

Victorian England was divided as to whether Marie Lloyd was a national treasure or a vulgar embarrassment, but she topped the bill with her performances of songs such as "When You Wink the Other Eye" and "She'd Never Had Her Ticket Punched Before." Observers noted that even when the lyrics were entirely innocent, with a wink or a gesture, Marie could fill each phrase with innuendo. Elsa was to showcase a similar skill during her residency at Hollywood's Turnabout Theatre in the 1940s. "The art of selling the *double entendre* is to make the members of an audience feel almost guilty that such strange thoughts should pass through their minds," she later recalled. "I am told that my innocent expression prior to my knowing smile is my number one weapon."[35] Although she was unaware of it at the time, Elsa was learning her craft by watching a master at work.

Such bawdy fun was not limited to the music hall. On a rare family seaside holiday to Clacton-on-Sea—made possible by Biddy's withholding rent payments because of unsanitary living conditions—Elsa was fascinated by the entertainments on offer, including a comedian who specialized in the kind of jokes that drew the appreciation of adults but that went over the heads of younger audience members. There was also a talent competition for the children. Elsa was not yet ready to take part, claiming that a combination of pride and shyness kept her from the stage, but she did commit many of the songs to heart, and would later practice them when alone at home.

Ultimately, however, it was to be as a dancer that Elsa Lanchester took her first steps into the spotlight. Her inspiration in this direction began when she was taken to see the Russian prima ballerina Anna Pavlova dance *The Dying Swan*. Elsa wrote in her autobiography, "I shall never forget her and I was never the same after that. I rumbled with ambition."[36] Other, different styles of dancing also had an impact on Elsa, particularly free dance, as practiced by artistes such as

---

34. Lanchester, *Elsa Lanchester, Herself*, 18.

35. Lanchester and Brown, *A Gamut of Girls*, 18.

36. Lanchester, *Elsa Lanchester, Herself*, 19.

Maud Allan, Loie Fuller, and Isadora Duncan. This style was a rebellion against the formality and constraints of classical ballet, and its practitioners performed barefoot, draped in loose layers of chiffon. Maud Allan and Isadora Duncan were accused of having morals as loose as their clothing and frequently had their exploits detailed in the newspapers. Such rebellious behavior and disregard for convention could only endear them to the Lanchester women, and so when the opportunity arose for Elsa to study dance with Isadora Duncan in France, both mother and daughter leapt at the chance.

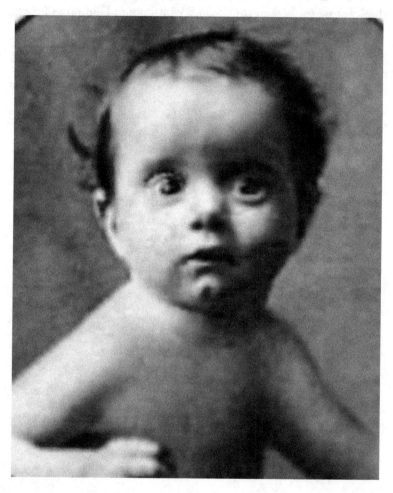

From Elsa's earliest years, her life was unsettled, unconventional, and unhealthy.

3   Never Trust Anyone

Raymond Duncan, Isadora Duncan's brother and a dancer in his own right, was the first to see talent in the young Elsa Lanchester. Originally from America, Raymond arrived in London in 1912 and caused quite a sensation, not least because he always dressed in the fashions of ancient Greece, as did his wife and child. A photograph from the time shows him clad in toga and sandals, all home-made, with his long hair hanging in his face in a manner that must have scandalized Edwardian London. Upon his arrival in the city, Raymond was interviewed by eager newspapermen, to whom he explained his lofty ambition of creating "an open house for every new effort in theatre, literature, music and art."[37]

What transpired was a series of free classes held at Crosby Hall in Chelsea, which included spinning, weaving, and sandal-making. Biddy and Elsa embraced Raymond Duncan's philosophy wholeheartedly and were soon hard at work soaking leather to make their own sandals. Elsa, who had previously enjoyed skating to school, even went so far as to ditch her roller skates; the skates could not be worn over her sandals and therefore had to go. Her eagerness to emulate the ancient Greeks may have partly resulted from a schoolgirl crush on the unusual American visitor—she describes him as "attractive" and "sensual-lipped."[38] Coming from Elsa, who was far more renowned for her acidic putdowns than for her compliments, this was praise indeed.

The opportunity to study with Isadora Duncan came about when Raymond recommended Elsa to his sister after seeing her in a dance class at Crosby Hall. In late 1913, Isadora opened an elite school in Paris, where she intended to train a small brood of handpicked children from around the world—the aim being nothing less than "to teach the world to dance"—and Elsa was to be one of the chosen few. Rather to the eleven-year-old's chagrin, however, she wasn't to have her adventure unaccompanied. Biddy "rather pushily" came too, even going so far as to get a part-time job at the school in order to remain at the heart of the action.[39]

---

37. Raymond Duncan biographical notes, c. 1948. Raymond Duncan Collection, Syracuse University Special Collections Research Center.

38. Lanchester, *Elsa Lanchester, Herself*, 19.

39. Lanchester, 27.

No mention is made in Elsa's writings of what Shamus and Waldo thought about the whole Raymond Duncan fascination, or of what they did when the women of the family decamped to Paris, although it is perhaps acceptable to assume that they enjoyed a bit of peace and quiet, and perhaps a bacon sandwich or two.

There would be little quiet to be found in Paris, for Isadora Duncan's whirlwind life to this point made Biddy's seem almost staid. A bisexual atheist who had sworn never to marry, Isadora had two children out of wedlock by two different (married) men—theater designer Edward Gordon Craig (himself the illegitimate son of actress Ellen Terry) and philanthropist Paris Singer, scion of the Singer sewing machine family. However, the year 1913 would prove to be a horrific one for Isadora; in April both of her children died, along with their nanny, when the car they were traveling in ran into the Seine. Her daughter was six, and her son was just three years old.

The story made headlines all over the world. To avoid a collision with a taxi, the chauffeur had applied the brakes suddenly, at which point the engine stopped. What happened next would haunt Isadora for the rest of her life.

> The chauffer got down from his seat to crank his engine when the car leaped forward as he was still bending over the starting handle. He was unable to jump to the steering wheel in time to stop the car and it headed for the Seine with the chauffer in pursuit.
>
> At this point there is no parapet to the river, and the motor rushed up a slope of about fifteen feet before it toppled over into the water. The nurse and children shouted frantically as the car tore up the bank, but their screams ended abruptly as with a great splash the car disappeared into the Seine.[40]

Overwrought, Isadora went abroad to recuperate. According to her autobiography, she craved a child so badly that she begged the young sculptor Romano Romanelli—whom she barely knew—to sleep with her. By the time Elsa arrived in France in early 1914, Isadora was pregnant with Romanelli's baby. Romanelli, having served his purpose, was not present.

The school was situated in a former hotel that Isadora had been given by her onetime lover Paris Singer. Known as Bellevue, the building was resplendent with two hundred rooms, including eighty bathrooms, all with the original luxurious furniture and furnishings, and it was set on a hill that overlooked Paris. Its grounds included sloping gardens and a disused funicular railway. Elsa described it as a "miniature Versailles" and marveled over the decor, describing the brass bedsteads and vast tiled bathrooms complete with bidets—this was a world away from the roach-infested walls of the family flat on Rudloe Road.[41] Elsa also men-

---

40. *Berks and Oxon Advertiser*, April 25, 1913.
41. Lanchester, *Elsa Lanchester, Herself*, 28.

tions that they were fed on the finest French cuisine, but she does not disclose whether vegetarians were catered for.

There were no school fees, and all expenses were paid, including the children's clothing. The classes were witnessed by the great and good of the age; rumor has it that Auguste Rodin made several of his famous watercolor sketches in the Bellevue salon. When the children were taken out into the city, they traveled in Rolls-Royce cars and visited the Louvre and Versailles. "We were shepherded around Paris like valuable Pekinese," Elsa recalled—an observation she liked so much that she used it in both her autobiographical works and in her 1950s nightclub act, as well as in talk show interviews in the 1970s.[42]

Ultimately, despite the luxury and the glamour, despite the honor of being chosen, and despite the fame of her teacher, Elsa Lanchester was nothing but dismissive when recalling her time at Bellevue (which lasted only three months, given the looming war). She disliked Duncan's teaching style especially. "I soon learned that all Isadora could do was to teach us to run away from or toward an enemy or to become an autumn leaf," Elsa recalled. "As a matter of fact, she had no technique of her own that she could pass on to others."[43]

It seems that the dislike was mutual. Each day began with the children lining up to kiss their teacher's hand and bid her good morning, a practice that was so at odds with Elsa's egalitarian upbringing that the hypocrisy of taking part manifested in a physical repellence. As Elsa later described, "the retching, almost vomiting child was not very popular with the veiled, gilt-sandalled cocoon posed on a large white divan at the end of the salon."[44]

Elsa sets Isadora Duncan up as a figure of fun: a has-been, portly woman gesturing vaguely from beneath her layers of chiffon, pointing at falling rose petals and crying out "they dance, now you dance." It's an amusing caricature, but also a cold rendering of a woman who was still deep in mourning. Elsa tells the story with a child's cruelty, never tempering her observations with any adult feelings of sympathy, even when recounting that two of the children at the school were only there because of their resemblance to Deirdre and Patrick, the children Isadora had lost. As one of Duncan's biographers remarked: "While Duncan's flamboyant lifestyle, financial difficulties, and above all, her utter lack of practicality undermined her effort to sustain these schools, her passion for educating the young child, particularly the children of impoverished workers and from lower classes, never waned throughout her life, and in some sense, became her reason to live and survive after the death of her children."[45]

42. Lanchester, *Charles Laughton and I*, 20; *Elsa Lanchester, Herself*, 28; *The Dick Cavett Show*, August 11, 1970.
43. Lanchester, *Elsa Lanchester, Herself*, 28.
44. Lanchester, *Charles Laughton and I*, 29.
45. Mantell-Seidel, *Isadora Duncan in the 21st Century*, 17.

Isadora Duncan gave birth to a son on August 1, 1914, but the child died within a few hours of being born. She wrote, "I believe that in that moment I reached the height of any suffering that can come to me on earth."[46] The years that followed were not kind either, as her career floundered and she took to drinking. Elsa pointedly but accurately remarked that aging was "the most ungraceful thing she ever did."[47] Isadora died in 1927 when the silk scarf she was wearing got caught in the wheels and axle of the car she was being driven in, pulling her from the open-top vehicle and breaking her neck. She was fifty years old.

The episode with Isadora Duncan marks the beginning of a curious period in Elsa's life that was to last about the same length of time as the war. During these crucial adolescent years, been the ages of eleven and sixteen, Elsa seems to have found herself in a world dominated by older women, each of whom she rebelled against in the way she had learned from watching her mother—who, in an inevitable thrust of irony, was to be the person Elsa ultimately rejected.

Charles Higham, who sat for hours with Elsa in the 1970s when researching his biography of Charles Laughton, said of her: "She had been selected for Isadora Duncan's free school of dancing in Paris; her refusal to be impressed by Miss Duncan's posturings made her unpopular there. Already, as a child, she had developed a deeply irreverent attitude toward pretentiousness, pomposity, self-importance, and complacency—sitting targets for her accurate satires in later years."[48]

Her satires may have been accurate, but a lot of Elsa's criticism is based on the unappealing physical aspects of these older women rather than on deeper character analyses. Her Aunt Mary is "not very attractive" and "nothing to write home about"; headmistress Miss Coombs "had a rather cruel face and looked like a current bun"; dance instructor Rose Benton was "a dark, quite muscular spinster with a beak of a nose—a strict, dehydrated, noncompanionable lady"; and music hall performer Ida Barr was "an enormous woman with paper-white puffy flesh and hennaed hair . . . I couldn't stand dressing in the same room with this corseted white barrel who had no modesty."[49]

Another theme of these years is Elsa's venturing out into the world, only to find it not to her liking, upon which she would return home to her mother's condescending "Oh, you're back." Her first such adventure was with her maiden aunt, her mother's sister Mary Lanchester, who had been commissioned shortly before the war to write and illustrate a book called *The River Severn from Source to Mouth*.[50] Mary planned to travel by bicycle, camping and painting along the way, and Elsa was to come along to help out, which mainly consisted of carrying

46. Duncan, *My Life*, quoted in O'Connor, *Barefoot Dancer*, 69.

47. Lanchester, *Elsa Lanchester, Herself*, 31.

48. Higham, *Charles Laughton*, 11.

49. Lanchester, *Elsa Lanchester, Herself*, 32, 36, 38, 40, 45.

50. This book was published by Thomas Murby in 1920.

supplies and cycling ahead to open the gates along the route so Mary could pass through them without stopping. Then Elsa would close the gate and ride quickly to overtake her aunt before stopping to open the next gate. She was also required to cut bracken for their pillows, and to find and strip saplings to hold the tent. Elsa was exhausted and indignant, and after nine days of such rural servitude she had had enough. Elsa informed her aunt that she was going home, where her parents "seemed surprised to see me and yet seemed to half expect me, too."[51]

Her next venture out of the nest was to boarding school. Mr. Kettle's school closed with the outbreak of war, when Elsa was twelve, and as she was legally obliged to pursue education until the age of fourteen, she was found a place at a school in Kings Langley, where she would teach dancing in exchange for her school fees. Here she made a friend of Ian Rorie Hay Stewart-Richardson, the son of yet another free dancer, Lady Constance Stewart-Richardson. Lady Constance had been banned from Court in 1910 by Edward VII for dancing onstage semi-clothed and was an aficionado of Isadora and Raymond Duncan, so the unusual Elsa probably seemed quite normal to the young boy. However, nothing else at the school suited Elsa's personality or temperament. She couldn't eat the food, she couldn't sleep in the dormitory, she didn't get on with the other children, she lacked the academic knowledge to participate in the lessons, and the headmistress was cruel to her. After ten days, she packed her wicker case, fastened it with a leather strap, and returned home. "Oh," said Biddy when Elsa arrived, "you didn't like it there?"[52]

Next came a lecture tour with Miss Rose Benton, where Elsa would demonstrate the moves that Miss Benton—another Raymond Duncan devotee—would describe. Once again Elsa left home, this time traveling as far as Scotland. But after a while the tour "fizzled out," and she was back again.[53]

One place where Elsa *was* happy, at least at first, was Margaret Morris's school in Chelsea, where she studied dancing and—thanks to her time with Isadora Duncan—progressed quickly to becoming a student teacher. Morris was a free spirit who had developed a system of movement based on the work of Raymond Duncan. She was attractive, earthy, ambitious, successful, and young, and in her Elsa thought she had found somebody she could "envy, admire, and not dislike too much."[54]

During her time at the school, Elsa made the acquaintance of the Baddeley sisters, Angela and Hermione, who would also become character actresses and appear alongside Elsa in various shows and films over the years. Angela Baddeley became Elsa's first real female friend at this time, helping her with such rites of passage as removing her underarm hair. In her autobiography, Hermione

---

51. Lanchester, *Elsa Lanchester, Herself*, 36.

52. Lanchester, 39.

53. Lanchester, 40.

54. Lanchester, 41.

Baddeley recalled Elsa's Raymond Duncan–inspired attire, writing that she wore "only handwoven Greek tunics and barefoot sandals even when the snow lay thick on the ground, and she was never without a filet around her brow."[55] Hermione and Elsa would appear onscreen together in *Mary Poppins* many decades later, in 1964.

Wartime London was no place to be if one could help it. During raids, Elsa hid in the coal cellar with her mother and brother, while her father stubbornly remained upstairs in the dark. "He only does it to annoy," snipped Biddy.[56] When the offer came to go and teach in Margaret Morris's summer school on the Isle of Wight, Elsa was delighted to escape both the raids and the ever-present family tensions.

Things began well. With her friend Angela as a roommate, Elsa enjoyed her classes and on one occasion stole the show from Margaret Morris herself by performing a "Maori Dance" of her own composition. However, events were to transpire that had a significant effect on the teenager. At a party, Morris danced a tango with Elsa that "frightened me out of my wits. Her body thrust forward at the hips, and with her thighs gripping me I felt trapped . . . I made some excuse and ran." This is not the only time in her writing that Elsa describes herself as the victim of unwanted attention from women—there is mention of a girl in Edinburgh who insisted on washing Elsa's hair and kept edging closer to her in bed, and a married employer who made a pass.[57]

Although there is nothing further in the records to suggest that Margaret Morris was ever suspected of any improper sexual activity with her students, there is no doubt that Elsa felt that their dancing had been inappropriate. Her sexual education had been surprisingly Victorian considering how free thinking her parents were in other matters. It seems that Biddy had explained things in a way that "was agony to her" and left Elsa "with a disgust about how I must have been created."[58] Perhaps, in her confusion—after all she was only fourteen years old—she voiced some concerns to somebody at the school. Elsa's recounting of the events that followed is worth quoting at length because it reveals the uncertainty and emotional turmoil that she felt at this point in her life:

> Then the gossip began about Margaret Morris. Two or three mothers got together to talk and then blamed each other for possibly libelous remarks. In the end they decided that a red-headed girl had not only started the rumors but must now be saved. One night after dinner I was called into a conference and they gave me the third degree. I was mystified by what they were talking about, completely. Finally I said that I didn't like dancing with Margaret Morris, Yes, I thought it was disgust-

---

55. Baddeley, *The Unsinkable Hermione Baddeley*, 22.

56. Lanchester, *Elsa Lanchester, Herself*, 42.

57. Lanchester, 40, 44, 58.

58. Lanchester, 35.

ing. Apparently she had danced with them all—*like that*. I was sent outside to walk on the beach. I was full of hatred and felt wronged from an unknown direction. I will never know what really happened, but it seems now that I had become a scapegoat for idle gossips.

. . . There and then I realized that in the future I would never trust anyone, no matter who. I was being wronged by these adult friends, without any redress. . . . I was sent back to London the next day. When I got home to Leathwaite Road, I was greeted with the usual "Oh, you're back". . . I never saw Miss Morris . . . again.[59]

What really happened at that summer school on the Isle of Wight can only be guessed at now, with such temporal distance and lack of clear evidence. However, that Elsa emerged from the experience more brittle and less trusting is without question.

The London that she returned to was battle damaged and weary, and talk everywhere was of war. In March 1916, because of the dwindling numbers of voluntary army recruits and growing number of casualties, the Military Service Act came into effect, stating that all single men aged between eighteen and forty-one were "deemed to be enlisted for the period of the war." Elsa's forty-eight-year-old father was spared, but her nineteen-year-old brother, Waldo, was right in the line of fire.

The attitude in the family flat on Leathwaite Road was "violently anti-war, of course, and pacifism roared through the Kitchen."[60] It was decided that Waldo would appeal his conscription by becoming a conscientious objector—a decision that Elsa lays entirely at Biddy's door, giving Waldo no option or opinion in the matter. Waldo's biographer agrees, saying that "his political stance probably owed more to his mother's convictions than his own."[61]

Conscientious objectors were a new phenomenon in England at this time. They were permitted by the Military Service Act to serve in a noncombatant role, provided that they could convince a tribunal of their reasons for objecting. Those doing work considered "of national importance," such as farming, were permitted exemption, as were those who objected for religious reasons. Waldo had been an apprentice to a maker of scientific instruments, but that had ended, and as he had been raised an atheist, there would be no help from that corner either.

Waldo was arrested at Camberwell Public Baths on July 17, 1917, as an absentee under the Military Service Act. Public opinion that conscientious objectors were lazy, cowardly, and ungrateful meant that tribunals were notoriously harsh and unpleasant. Elsa, who attended her brother's tribunal, remembered Waldo being asked questions such as "If you were attacked by a German, would you fight back?" and "What would you do if a Prussian soldier raped your sister?" To each question, Waldo calmly replied "No" or "I don't know." Elsa later recalled:

---

59. Lanchester, 44 (emphasis in original).

60. Lanchester, 37.

61. Cockayne, *Master of the Marionettes*, 22.

"The judge was a happy beast, enjoying his work. I like to remember him as frothing at the mouth."[62]

Waldo was not granted exemption. He was sentenced to two years' hard labor in the infamous Wormwood Scrubs prison. His biographer says that this was "an appallingly difficult time for him. Conscientious objectors in prison were the victims of constant bullying and abuse, not only from their fellow inmates, but from the prison authorities too. They were kept in solitary confinement and were forbidden to speak to one another, even during exercise periods."[63] Released and recommitted several times, he was eventually discharged on March 31, 1920. Elsa visited her brother in prison but felt conflicted about his reasons for being there, and admitted missing one visit due to a period of "jingoism."

Despite her disappointment and heartbreak at the way her time at the Margaret Morris school had ended, Elsa was still keen to pursue a career in dancing, and during the war years she studied different styles and techniques. To her repertoire of free dance she added a course of Dalcroze eurhythmics, which taught her about musical phrasing and structure; and lessons in Eastern dancing, during which she discovered that she was double jointed. Her unique flexibility enabled her to perform complex moves, such as bending over backward until her head touched the floor, and to gyrate her hips and move her head while keeping her torso completely still in what was referred to as "snake dancing." Although the meaning of this term was confusing to Elsa, she nevertheless mastered the art quickly: "I don't know whether a snake dancer is supposed to be imitating a snake or mesmerizing a snake, but I was very snaky and supple."[64]

This skill would lead to Elsa's first performing job, when she answered an ad in May 1917 for an "Aerobatic Dancer, to join young lady; view to dancing scena."[65] Hired on the spot by comedienne and singer Ida Barr, Elsa danced—barefoot and in a skimpy costume—while Ida played the clarinet. It was an inauspicious beginning to a life in the theater; Elsa found the whole experience sordid and left after just a week, refusing Ida's offer of a job touring with her.

---

62. Lanchester, *Elsa Lanchester, Herself*, 48.

63. Cockayne, *Master of the Marionettes*, 20.

64. Lanchester, *Elsa Lanchester, Herself*, 41.

65. *The Era*, May 2, 1917.

4 This Must Be Fame

It is tempting to argue that the 1920s were the happiest years of Elsa's life. She gained her freedom when she turned eighteen, at the beginning of the decade, and her marriage in 1929 could be seen as an end to this period of independence and autonomy. During this time she established herself in bohemian London society, became a cabaret star and a West End performer, and owned her own nightclub. She inspired artists and writers including Jacob Epstein, H. G. Wells, Doris Zinkeisen, Evelyn Waugh, Reginald Grenville Eves, and John Armstrong. She worked as a professional "other woman" in divorce cases, posed naked for photographers, and enjoyed casual love affairs.

As society loosened its corsets and raised its hemlines, Elsa Lanchester became something of a cult figure in London. Her unconventional beauty inspired journalists to wax lyrical. In 1925, for example, one journalist wrote: "She is child and imp, innocence and well—the reverse. Angular. The lines of her arms and legs and waist run into Cubist and Post-Impressionist forms. But a dash of real genius; unmistakable."[1] This was the decade that saw Elsa at her finest: young and beautiful, certainly, but also joyful and fearless, surrounded by like-minded friends. Her youthful cruelty had developed into a dry cynicism that was witty but not yet overly bitter.

After the war ended, Elsa performed where she could while making money as a dance instructor. Still very much a part of her parents' activist world at this point, she performed at a social and dance held by the Southwark branch of the British Socialist Party, at the Old Cockney Fair, which raised money for the Workers' Socialist Federation, and at an event organized by the Women's Freedom League.[2]

Such appearances, coupled with her striking looks, unusual attire, and fantastic self-confidence, started to attract attention and an air of local celebrity. Elsa recalled, "My hand-woven clothes, home-made sandals, hatless red head

---

1. *Yorkshire Post and Leeds Intelligencer*, January 23, 1925.
2. *Call*, May 30, 1918; *Workers' Dreadnought*, December 14, 1918; *The Vote*, February 20, 1920.

Elsa with her brother Waldo, who would go on to become 'master of the marionettes', and the subject of a 2018 biography. The siblings were not close.

and fanatically self-satisfied expression must have been one of the more colourful sights of Clapham. I was delighted once when a journalist approached me on the Common and asked to photograph my sandalled feet . . . this, I thought must be fame."[3] It was only the beginning.

Around the time she was appearing in support of her mother's causes, Elsa was also cutting the apron strings. She got a job teaching dancing once a week at a large school, Bedales, which paid £2 a week, just enough for rent and gas for a room off Baker Street. At the age of sixteen, Elsa left home for good.

Despite Biddy's preaching of the importance of independence, when the time came she found it hard to let go, and Elsa was impatient with what she viewed as her mother's hypocrisy. Neither woman had sufficient emotional maturity to handle the situation well. Elsa said: "Since my whole upbringing had conditioned me toward self-sufficiency, Biddy did not have any valid argument, so she was tentative in her criticism of me—whimpering and, of course, quietly sarcastic."[4] Biddy, it may be argued, had truly created a monster in her own image.

---

3.   Lanchester, *Charles Laughton and I*, 31–32.

4.   Lanchester, *Elsa Lanchester, Herself*, 63.

In addition to working at Bedales, Elsa volunteered two evenings a week at her local Children's Happy Evenings Association, run by Lady Florence "Firenza" Montagu. The Happy Evenings program was one of the earliest providers of after-school play using school buildings, and it offered a mixture of performing arts, sports, and quiet recreational activities such as board games. At the school in Soho, Elsa taught dancing and movement to the thirty or so children who attended, most of whom were from immigrant, Jewish backgrounds, and all of whom were from poverty-stricken families.

By way of contrast, she also taught Lady Montagu's children (for a fee) and stayed at their Surrey home once a week, the very house where J. M. Barrie wrote *Peter Pan*. Seeing such luxury made her realize that the finer things—good food, well-apportioned rooms, and beautiful clothes—were perhaps not to be sneered at, as she had previously been taught.

However, Elsa's heart was less with the privileged Montagu children and more with her free Soho pupils. She worried about what would happen to them during the summer, when Lady Montagu went away for a long family holiday and there were no Happy Evenings activities to occupy them. With that in mind, she rented a small hall at 107 Charlotte Street, Soho, and set to work forming what would come to be known as the Children's Theatre. Her partner in this endeavor was the young man who played the piano at her Happy Evenings dance classes. He was also to become Elsa's first serious love interest and a major player in her personal and professional life during the early 1920s.

Harold Scott was born in 1891, and so he was twenty-nine to Elsa's seventeen when they started the Children's Theatre together around 1920.[5] They first met a year earlier when Harold formed the People's Theatre Society with author Douglas Goldring and some other friends. Intending to stage D. H. Lawrence's *The Widowing of Mrs. Holroyd*, the new drama society interviewed "a number of stage aspirants." As Goldring would later recall in his chronicle of the era, "Among them was a girl of about sixteen, with flaming red-gold hair, who had learnt dancing in Paris."[6] Although the Lawrence production never developed further, the encounter led to an artistic and romantic partnership for Harold and Elsa, even though Harold was married when they met. His wife was the fantastically named Raymonde Blanche Augustine Marie Gaspard-Michel, a French singer who performed under the name Raymonde Collignon and was a favorite of Ezra Pound. Harold and Raymonde had married in 1915, but their union was brief, and they were divorced in 1921. Elsa was a virgin when she began her relationship with Harold, although she later claimed that she nearly lost her virginity in the flat of the actor Miles Malleson, "when he and Harold Scott combed my hair until I nearly swooned."[7]

---

5.   Some sources date Scott's birth to 1890.

6.   Goldring, *The Nineteen Twenties*, 147.

7.   Lanchester, *Elsa Lanchester, Herself*, 73.

Activist and writer Freda Utley, who knew Harold and Elsa as a couple, described Harold as "one of those small, slight, blond, blue-eyed types who never look their age."[8] While Elsa, with her customary lack of flattery, records that he was "blond, with a rather overpink face," Utley offers a fuller portrait: "Strange that although I never knew him well or liked him much, I can today still vividly remember Harold Scott dressed in grey flannel trousers and a worn tweed jacket, his high forehead surmounted by scanty golden hair and his long, thin nose slightly red at the tip above his full lipped mouth, strumming on the piano and singing a long forgotten song."[9] Harold was bohemian, artistic, and creative; he was unconventional and intelligent (later in life he would write a history of the traditional music hall, which is well worth seeking out); and he and Elsa had a lot in common. But despite the fact that he had been a conscientious objector during the war and was a member of the 1917 Club, a socialist organization in London, Elsa's mother disapproved of the relationship, telling her daughter, "He's not the type I'd have hoped for you at all." Again, Biddy's seeming hypocrisy rankled, and Elsa remarked, "I was annoyed because I should have thought he *was* the type. Apart from his talent, he was erudite and certainly continued my education where Mr. Kettle's school left off."[10] When Biddy committed the grave sin of reading one of Elsa's love letters from Harold, Elsa was incandescent. That Elsa continued to see Harold despite her mother's disapproval is no surprise whatsoever—just another case of history repeating. However, that she sought her approval at all is significant. Although Elsa was steadily breaking away from her family during this period, she was still young and inexperienced.

Biddy definitely approved of the Children's Theatre, which had its first performance at King George's Hall, Tottenham Court Road, on October 14, 1920. An article in *The Vote*—the newspaper of the Women's Freedom League—described what audiences could expect: "The children . . . drawn from the many nationalities represented in Soho, will dance, and will present a play from Hans Anderson, adapted by Mr. Harold Scott . . . , who shares responsibility for the Children's Theatre with Miss Elsa Lanchester. Miss Lanchester will appear in solo dances."[11]

The play would have been either *The Nightingale* or *The Emperor's New Clothes*, both of which the Children's Theatre performed multiple times over the years. Other pieces in its repertoire included *Tom Thumb* and Jane Austen's *Love and Freindship* (the misspelling was Austen's). The children—and Elsa—performed at functions that raised money for socialist and feminist causes, and they donated any profits from their own shows to Save the Children, except when funds were needed closer to home.

---

8. Utley, *Odyssey of a Liberal*, 52.

9. Lanchester, *Elsa Lanchester, Herself*, 55; Utley, *Odyssey of a Liberal*, 52.

10. Lanchester, *Elsa Lanchester, Herself*, 56 (emphasis in original).

11. *The Vote*, October 8, 1920.

The members of the Children's Theatre also contributed to the program when Elsa gave "a highly successful exhibit of dancing" at the Steinway Hall in 1921. *The Era* praised Elsa's work as "highly interesting and individual, her supple form, excellent command of movement, and obviously artistic temperament all combining to render her interpretation full of significance and devoid of monotony."[12] It was her first real review, and it was a rave.

A curious observation about Elsa's autobiographical works is what she leaves out. This is far more obvious when she discusses her later career, when a reader can't help but notice that not only does she barely mention *Witness for the Prosecution* (1957), for which she was nominated for an Oscar, but that she doesn't discuss her Oscar nominations at all. It is not so easy to discern the missing pieces in her accounts of her early career. In *Charles Laughton and I*, Elsa states that her first stage part was in *The Insect Play* in 1923. While this was her professional debut in a full-length play (albeit an episodic one), and also her first experience of a longer-running play—it played forty-two performances—her first professional acting role actually occurred a year earlier, in April 1922.[13]

The Playwrights' Theatre at the Kingsway presented plays by new authors, and Elsa appeared in two of the three one-act plays presented on April 2, 1922— *Girl in the City*, as an extra, and *Thirty Minutes in a Street*, as Second Shop Girl.[14] Both plays were written by Beatrice Mayor. The first was critically panned, and given that it was "largely a monologue," Elsa's role was likely miniscule.[15] *Thirty Minutes in a Street*, however, was a different matter. The *Pall Mall Gazette* described it as a "wild blend of harlequinade farce and pungent satire" and opined that it "had the benefit of the most distinguished cast that has appeared in a one-act play by a new author in quite some time."[16] While such praise seems overly conditional, the cast certainly was exceptional, led as it was by Sybil Thorndike and her brother Russell. Edith Craig was the director, and the author Virginia Woolf attended rehearsals and wrote about them in her diary.[17]

Although it might be assumed that the brevity of this endeavor—a single performance—is the reason Elsa leaves it out of her memoirs, this explanation is not entirely satisfactory, and not only because the evening merits a mention as her first professional acting experience. Her association with Sybil Thorndike, almost certainly cultivated at this time, was to lead to Elsa's taking on Thorndike's two daughters as private pupils. Mary and Ann Casson were apparently eager to follow in their mother's profession, and to this end they were set to appear in a

---

12. *The Era*, June 8, 1921.

13. Lanchester, *Charles Laughton and I*, 53; Wearing, *The London Stage*, 225.

14. Wearing, *The London Stage*, 158.

15. *The Scotsman*, April 3, 1922.

16. *Pall Mall Gazette*, April 3, 1922.

17. Cockin, *Edith Craig and the Theatre of Art*, 234.

series of plays organized by the British Drama League. It was reported in the press in early 1923 that "Miss Elsa Lanchester, the nineteen-year-old actress who runs the Children's Theatre for Soho kiddies is arranging one of the dances and is coaching the two Thorndike-Casson children."[18]

All good things must come to an end, however, and eventually the Children's Theatre became a victim of its own success. The shows began to make money and attract attention, which was all very well until those paying attention were working for the authorities. "The London County Council stepped in with its red tape and regulations," Elsa remembered, "and said that I was exploiting children, and quoted the Child Slave Act to me."[19] The council forbade her from giving the planned performance of Jane Austen's *Love and Freindship*, which was to be interspersed with songs and dances. In the finest Lanchester tradition, Elsa told them, "Nevertheless I will give it—arrest me after the performance if you wish."[20]

The performance took place as planned on Sunday, March 4, 1923, at the rehearsal premises on Charlotte Street. The full house of 150 people included Lady Maud Warrender, as well as "Mariegold," a columnist for *The Sketch*. The latter wrote in her column, Mariegold Again, that "the little Soho girls who wander into Miss Elsa Lanchester's free classes on Saturday mornings . . . have caught her freedom of expression, her sense of humour, and much of the beauty of her very distinctive dancing, so that every item, from the old songs to the burlesque music hall ditties and the scenes from Jane Austen's 'Love and Friendship' [*sic*], was a joyous success."[21] The council inspectors also attended the performance but took no action against Elsa as she had managed at the last minute to turn the performance into a fundraiser for Save the Children by means of inserts in the programs. Elsa remarked that now her mother "wasn't the only one who could crow over the London County Council. She admired me for tricking her old enemy the Law."[22]

Although the Children's Theatre continued meeting and rehearsing for a while after this, there were to be no more performances. Never still for a second, Elsa was already moving on to her next adventure. Less than a month after attending that final performance on Charlotte Street, Mariegold was back on the premises for a very different kind of evening entertainment: "the latest Soho rendezvous . . . is a little hall in that dingy Charlotte Street, and all kinds of people go to dance—tissue frocks, fancy dress, and coats-and-skirts all cheek by jowl, so to speak. Amusing little cabaret show too, with Elsa Lanchester doing top-

---

18. *Hull Daily Mail*, January 8, 1923.
19. Lanchester, *Charles Laughton and I*, 47–48. See also Lanchester, *Elsa Lanchester, Herself*, 52–53, for nearly identical text.
20. Lanchester, *Charles Laughton and I*, 48.
21. *The Sketch*, March 7, 1923.
22. Lanchester, *Elsa Lanchester, Herself*, 53.

ping burlesque dances. Nigel Playfair was there, and Cyril Asquith and his pretty wife."[23] This was the Cave of Harmony, and it, more than anything else, was responsible for Elsa's elevation in artistic and bohemian London society. "Night club was hardly the word for this new scheme," wrote Elsa in 1938, before going on to use that exact term repeatedly in her later work. Indeed, to call the Cave of Harmony a nightclub would be to confuse the modern reader, for whom the term has a rather fixed meaning. Although there was a dance floor, there was no alcohol available, and the coffee stall sold sandwiches for sixpence. "We gave old and modern plays and cabaret turns at midnight, and never had a drink licence—it was more like a midnight play production club."[24] The name "Cave of Harmony" was a suggestion from the poet Sylvia Townsend Warner, who later wrote a poem with the same title.[25]

Although the club moved premises over the years—from Charlotte Street in Soho, to Gower Street in Bloomsbury, then on to the Old Grapes Inn in Seven Dials—descriptions of it remain consistent, with walls and woodwork painted pink, yellow, and green, rich velvet curtains of red, and a small booth "about the size of a Punch and Judy show,"[26] where artist John Armstrong sold mushroom sandwiches and trifle. When the shows were performed, the audience members sat on the dance floor to watch, and one of the people they came to see was Elsa Lanchester.

She and Harold Scott—her partner in the Cave of Harmony as he had been in the Children's Theatre—shared an interest in old music hall numbers, and researched them at the British Library. As Harold would later relate:

> By the end of the European war of 1914 the Music Hall was already half-dead. . . . But in the relaxed atmosphere of the first post-war years—that well-remembered decade of "let's-have-fun-at-all-costs-and-be-madly-sophisticated-about-it"— some elements of entertainment connected with the Music Hall reappeared in the form of pastiche. This, as can be understood, occurred first among a small coterie, but the taste grew, and penetrated later into some London theatres. Elsa Lanchester and I were, perhaps, mainly responsible for this.[27]

In a crepe paper ballet dress with bare legs, high heels, and a top hat, years before Marlene Dietrich, Elsa would lend her naughty smile to songs such as "The Ratcatcher's Daughter" and "Please Sell No More Drink to My Father." Angela

---

23. *The Sketch*, April 6, 1923.

24. Lanchester, *Charles Laughton and I*, 49. For examples of her referring to the Cave of Harmony as a nightclub, see Lanchester, *Elsa Lanchester, Herself*, 54, and Lanchester and Brown, *A Gamut of Girls*, 13.

25. Scott, *The Early Doors*, 266.

26. Lanchester, *Charles Laughton and I*, 51.

27. Scott, *The Early Doors*, 226.

Baddeley, whom Elsa had known since her days with Margaret Morris, joined her for a regular skit where they played charladies Mrs. Bricketts and Mrs. Du Bellamy. Angela's sister, Hermione, later recalled that the Cave had a reputation as a "rather curious and risqué place."[28]

Word spread quickly, and soon writers, performers, authors, and artists of all descriptions were sat on the dance floor, "the overlapping of London's *haute bohème* and artistic intelligentsia with the West End's flamboyant theatre crowd": H. G. Wells, James Whale, Evelyn Waugh, Aldous Huxley, and Arnold Bennett, among so many others.[29] Some even say that a certain Charles Laughton was in the audience, although this seems unlikely in the early days.[30] Elsa would end up making films with Wells, Whale, and Waugh, as well as being painted and sculpted by several of the artists who were inspired by her offbeat beauty.

In April 1923, not long after the Cave of Harmony first opened its doors, a newspaper reported that Elsa had been cast in *The Insect Play*. The article draws attention to Elsa's "astonishing versatility": along with rehearsing for her West End role, she was "arranging the dances for a Royal matinee play by Lady Margaret Sackville, . . . rehearsing her Children's Theatre, . . . and in addition is being 'sculptured' by no less an artist than Jacob Epstein. This remarkable young woman, moreover, is 'managing' the 'Cave of Harmony,' one of London's cabarets, and has undertaken to appear in a dance of her own designing at next Saturday's all-night show, which begins at midnight and continues until six."[31]

According to Elsa, the Epstein commission came about when he requested she sit for him after a brief encounter in the street. Although acknowledging that the artist (whose most famous work at that point was Oscar Wilde's tomb in Père Lachaise Cemetery) "had a scandalous reputation and was credited with having wild times with his models," Elsa found her morning sittings in his house to be relatively uneventful. Epstein's wife provided refreshments, and his young daughter Peggy played under the table—at least until Elsa's time with Epstein was drawing to a close, when, Elsa wrote, "that horrid child . . . forced my hat down the w.c. and blocked the plumbing."[32]

When the sculpture was put on display in Epstein's exhibition at the Leicester Galleries, Leicester Square, in January 1924, the *Illustrated London News* featured pictures of several of the busts, including the one of Elsa. The accompanying text describes the "rugged power" of Epstein's work, but expresses concern that "it is an art that is obviously more suited to the gnarled and masculine type

28. Baddeley, *The Unsinkable Hermione Baddeley*, 22.
29. Witchard, "Sink Street," 225.
30. Baddeley, *The Unsinkable Hermione Baddeley*, 22.
31. *Belfast Telegraph*, April 30, 1923.
32. Lanchester, *Elsa Lanchester, Herself*, 68.

in portraiture. Some might think that, in the treatment of feminine subjects, a little concession to natural smoothness might not detract from its strength or impair its beauty."[33] Certainly Elsa is rendered with each feature amplified: her eyes bug out, her nose is blunted, her chin cleft is severe. She meets the observer's gaze head on. It is a fierce and powerful sculpture that captures the essence of Elsa's personality during these years.

---

33. *Illustrated London News*, January 19, 1924.

Elsa's status as an outsider began in her childhood, when she attended an all-boys school run by socialists.

5   Even in Bed, She Is Busy

While Elsa's performance in *The Insect Play* would lead to a rich career in film and theater, eventually allowing her to support herself through acting, she had to rely on several different sorts of employment during these early years.

First, Elsa posed for artists and sculptors, but also for "artistic" photographers—which, then as now, meant that she was often photographed naked. The pictures were sometimes displayed in the window of an art store near the Ritz hotel, and Elsa reports that she would occasionally reward "some dear old admirer who had given me lunch" with a trip to view the photographs. On a sadder note, she also writes that her mother went to see the pictures whenever she was nearby. "It was probably the only way she could see how I was developing physically."[1] Many actresses of Elsa's time who posed nude before they were famous lived in fear of the pictures surfacing again. As far as I can ascertain, none of these pictures of Elsa surfaced to embarrass her during her lifetime, although searching for evidence of them on the internet is certainly an eye-opening experience.

Less glamorous was Elsa's job cleaning houses—but as was typical for her, even in such a mundane occupation, she found some mischief. Her employers in this instance were Edmund and Yvonne Kapp. Edmund, a well-known caricaturist, and Yvonne, a journalist, were good friends of Elsa's and frequent guests at the Cave of Harmony, even sometimes participating in the performances by playing their recorders. In a curious coincidence, Elsa's onetime employer Yvonne Kapp would later write a biography of Elsa's mother's onetime employer Eleanor Marx. Elsa's time cleaning for the Kapps ended when, according to her autobiography, "they *both* made a pass at me. I was very shocked, especially by hers. I was curious enough to try anything once—but not *that*."[2]

Elsa's clumsy insistence on her heterosexuality seems at odds with her otherwise tolerant and liberal ideals; that she is once again presenting female (homo) sexuality as threatening and unnatural seems even more so. Of course, there have been those who claim that this is a case of the lady protesting too much, but the

---

1.   Lanchester, *Elsa Lanchester, Herself*, 56.
2.   Lanchester, 58 (emphasis in original).

"evidence" offered by authors such as Boze Hadleigh—"some friends say she is [a lesbian], and Laughton's brother said so"—cannot be verified in any way.[3] What is perhaps more likely is the position taken by a 2018 article discussing the reissue of Elsa's 1983 autobiography: Elsa was "pretty much born to defy heteronormality," and her "story makes no claim to sexual identity, barely traces three or four almost passions with male friends, adding up to possible asexuality."[4]

Whatever the truth of Elsa's sexual preferences, she was active socially during this period and gained something of a reputation as a good-time girl. Aiding this may have been another of her avenues of income: working as a divorce co-respondent. Best known now as the plot driver in the Fred Astaire–Ginger Rogers movie *The Gay Divorcee* (1934), co-respondents were often necessary in the British legal system as a means of securing a divorce. Infidelity was one of the few grounds for divorce that was accepted by law, and so couples who wished to legally part would sometimes hire a co-respondent to make it appear as if one party was being unfaithful. Elsa's job would have been to spend the night with the married gentleman in a hotel room, before being "caught" in the morning by a detective. It was all very innocent, and Elsa regarded this unusual occupation as an extension of her acting ambitions. Her friend Douglas Goldring was to benefit from Elsa's services in this way, although most of her engagements were with strangers and arranged through a lawyer.

Aside from her irregular and extracurricular methods of employment, Elsa also made her living on the stage. Producer and director Nigel Playfair was a regular at the Cave of Harmony, and he spotted Elsa's potential quickly, casting her and Angela Baddeley in several of his plays, the first of which was *The Insect Play*, which opened at the Regent on May 5, 1923. The play was adapted by Playfair and Clifford Bax from a translation of the original Czech-language script by the Brothers Čapek (Karel and Josef), and it was heavy-going stuff—"a sharp satire on contemporary morals, in which the vices and foibles of humanity are shown through the corrupt and immoral behaviour of butterflies, beetles, flies, ants and snails."[5] Actor and director John Gielgud was also in the cast. Nineteen years old at the time (*The Insect Play* was his first professional production), he wrote in a letter that the cast was "nearly all young and inexperienced. . . . However, it is all so fantastic and unlike anything else that even the old stagers in the cast seem to find the same difficulty in dealing with it."[6] Other members of the cast included another future Universal monster, Claude Rains (*The Invisible Man*, 1933), as well as the leggy Noelle Sonning, who would later find fame as children's author Noel Streatfeild.

3.   Hadleigh, *Hollywood Lesbians*.

4.   Loudermilk, "Elsa Lanchester Was Born to Defy Heteronormativity."

5.   Croall, *John Gielgud*, 45.

6.   Croall, 45–46.

The action was split between three acts, and many cast members played multiple roles. Elsa made up the numbers in the first and third acts (as a butterfly and a mayfly respectively), but her moment in the spotlight came in the "tiny but pivotal" role of the Larva in Act 2.[7] Elsa was costumed in a padded minidress, a design of Doris Zinkeisen's that resembles what the Michelin Man might wear if he were feeling cheeky. Her stocking-clad legs, topped with visible suspenders, caught the eye of the *Times* reviewer, who sniped, "We have not studied the *Larva* of the ichneumon fly; but doubt if it wears, as it did on Saturday (and flaunted before the public eye), a set of garish 'suspenders.'"[8] Although this critic was perhaps missing the point, the costuming was the least bizarre thing about this production, as a brief description of one of Elsa's scenes makes clear:

> A cricket couple (Mrs. Cricket was played by Angela Baddeley) is stabbed by an ichneumon fly, which feeds their body fluids to its larva (played by Elsa Lanchester as "a huge, sluggish and also Cockney child"). The larva is devoured in turn by Parasite, played by [Claude] Rains. The feasting took place discreetly off stage. Rains returned to reveal the parasite, hiccupping, "with Elsa inside me."[9]

Elsa wrote that this part was "one of the jammiest in the world" and "ninny-proof," and that "any actress who fails as this *enfant terrible* should be put under a stone and forgotten,"[10] although to a modern reader it certainly appears to have presented its share of challenges. Such downplaying is typical of Elsa, who never claimed for herself any great talent. Indeed, she said of *The Insect Play*, "I was staggered when I walked off with rave reviews. . . . I knew it was the part itself and not really me. I didn't understand the power of the printed word or why the reviews would cause the slightly cold shoulder from some of my fellow actors."[11] Such innocence of theatrical jealousy is, perhaps, a little hard to believe, even for a newcomer.

After *The Insect Play* closed on June 28, 1923—after forty-two performances and mostly unenthusiastic reviews—Elsa didn't appear in a professional show again until February 1924, when she was cast in another Nigel Playfair production, *The Way of the World*. But this did not stop her from attracting attention in the theatrical world. In September 1923 she attended the premiere of James Elroy Flecker's *Hassan* as the guest of Douglas Goldring. Goldring later recalled of the occasion that Elsa was "then scarcely out of her teens. Her flaming red-gold hair and *gamine* appearance had—much to my amusement—a startling effect on all the stuffed shirts who beheld her. 'Who's that girl?' I heard people murmur-

---

7.   Lanchester, *Elsa Lanchester, Herself*, 75.

8.   *The Times*, May 7, 1923.

9.   Skal and Rains, *Claude Rains*, 49.

10. Lanchester, *Charles Laughton and I*, 53 (italics in original).

11. Lanchester, *Elsa Lanchester, Herself*, 75.

ing in the entr'acte. Shortly afterwards Elsa made a hit in Kavel Capek's 'Insect Play.'"[12] Although he misremembers the order of events, *The Insect Play* having occurred some months previously, the incident—and Elsa's youthful beauty—clearly made a lasting impression on Goldring.

The Insect Play provided good publicity for Elsa; pictures of her in costume appeared in illustrated newspapers and magazines, and costume designer Doris Zinkeisen would later paint her portrait. Zinkeisen—who was at this point engaged to future *Bride of Frankenstein* director James Whale—would also design the costumes for Elsa's next stage outing, *The Way of the World*, which starred Edith Evans and also featured performances from Harold Scott and Nigel Playfair himself.[13] This performance garnered for Elsa even greater press plaudits than did *The Insect Play*. Reviewers singled her out for praise—"A word should be said for the grotesque dance in the fourth act of Miss Elsa Lanchester, which brought down the house," "Miss Elsa Lanchester's dance is too clever to be spared"—and a full-page colored photograph of her in costume as the Shrimp Girl" appeared in *The Sketch*. Text accompanying the picture described her as a "well-known figure in artistic London."[14]

The Way of the World played for 158 performances at the Lyric Hammersmith, but Elsa did not appear in all of these. When she was absent, her part was played by Beatrix Lehmann, sister of the novelist Rosamond. Beatrix's mother was concerned that her daughter would be influenced by worldly actresses such as Elsa and Tallulah Bankhead, who was also a regular on the London theater scene at this time. This prompted Rosamond to write in a letter to her mother, "I don't think you ought to worry about her friendship with Elsa. The fact that Elsa has lovers will no more incline Peg to want to emulate her than the fact of, say, Elsa's marriage would make her want to marry." She also dismissed Tallulah's reputation as "mostly only talk."[15] Later Beatrix would become an author, and dedicate her book *Rumour of Heaven* (1934) to Elsa.

Elsa's name was clearly well known, if not, in some circles, well respected. Her rapidly growing celebrity is apparent in the way that her absence from *The Way of the World* was explained and discussed at length in the press:

> Elsa Lanchester . . . has had temporarily to leave the caste [*sic*] to undergo a slight operation on her throat. At the moment she is rapidly recovering in a private ward at the Charing Cross Hospital, where she holds something of a Court, sympathetic enquirers waiting in queues for a few minutes with her. Even in bed, she is busy, and has been perfecting the plans of a new Sunday club, which is to meet in Gower Street. It is to be only for those really interested in the modern theatre, and no one

12. Goldring, *The Nineteen Twenties*, 230.
13. Curtis, *James Whale*, 31.
14. *Truth*, February 13, 1924; *The Sphere*, February 23, 1924; *The Sketch*, March 5, 1924.
15. Quoted in Hastings, *Rosamond Lehmann*.

can become a member except by invitation. The club is to have no name, but the evening entertainments are to be called "Elsa Lanchester's Select Evenings," a title in which the young promoter takes the keenest joy.[16]

This "club with no name" was the Cave of Harmony's clumsy attempt at discretion in its new Bloomsbury lodgings. As Elsa later remarked, although the club used the Gower Street property for about two years, "the dance music in a residential district was never welcome."[17] The secrecy as to its name and new location didn't last long, but while it did, E. P. Leigh-Bennett wrote an article for *The Bystander* about a Sunday night at the club, which he described as "a lesser light of a distinctly interesting kind. To it flock the all and sundries of the art and literary world. There are more brains and talent packed into this studio on a Sunday night than probably any other of its size in greater London."[18] Leigh-Bennett claimed to have enjoyed his evening—singling Elsa's performance out for particular praise—although he admitted that some of the entertainment, such as the one-act play performed by three unnamed actors, was beyond his comprehension, commenting "I am not clever enough." For the uneducated Elsa, this high-minded entertainment and lofty company must have meant a steep learning curve.

One of the intellectuals who frequented the Cave of Harmony around this time was Evelyn Waugh, although at this point he was not the successful writer that he later became, but rather a wild and debauched young man, fresh out of Oxford University, who was usually "half drunk," according to Elsa. Evelyn had been introduced to Elsa by his older brother Alec, and by summer 1924 he had developed a crush on her. The feeling was not reciprocated: Elsa was unimpressed with the younger Waugh's appearance, saying that he "was not at all attractive looking. Not very tall, he had a pink face. That is, not all over pink, pink in patches as if he had a bad cold. Therefore the features were not well-defined and the bitter-witty-cruel mind shone through the pinkness."[19] They did, however, attend at least one party together, which Waugh later wrote about in his diary, saying that it was attended by "pansies, prostitutes and journalists and struggling actors all quite drunk and in patches lusty."[20]

However lacking in personal appeal he was, Waugh was to play a part in Elsa's career development around this time. In summer 1924, Royal Academy of Dramatic Art (RADA) student Terence Greenidge had an idea for an amateur silent movie called *The Scarlet Woman*. He persuaded his brother and several friends, including Waugh, to contribute to the cost of purchasing a camera. Waugh committed himself wholeheartedly to the venture: "He wrote the sce-

16. *Hull Daily Mail*, April 15, 1924.
17. Lanchester, *Charles Laughton and I*, 50.
18. Leigh-Bennett, "Lesser Lights."
19. Lanchester, *Elsa Lanchester, Herself*, 56–57.
20. Wilson, *Evelyn Waugh*, 19.

nario, played two of the parts, recruited [his brother] Alec to play another (in drag) and got his father's eager permission to shoot scenes at [the family home] Underhill."[21] He also persuaded Elsa to take a part as the cocaine-addled "cabaret-queen" Beatrice de Carolle. Amazingly, the film—which makes for amusing, albeit confusing, viewing—has survived the near century since it was made.[22] "The quintessentially undergraduate character of *The Scarlet Woman* is indicated by its plot," wrote Waugh's biographer. "The Pope has decided to bring about the immediate conversion of England to Rome by enforcing the conversion of the Prince of Wales by means of a seductress."[23]

To see Elsa at this early stage of her career is a treat. She is gawky and jarring, overacting and wildly gesticulating, but not out of step with the style of the silent era, although her bohemian dress and wild, untamed hair make her seem more modern, more like us, than the bow-lipped, marcelled flappers often associated with the mid-1920s. Her eyes flash under over-plucked eyebrows, and when she snarls and bares her teeth in her close-up, her beauty wavers on the very edge of grotesque in a way more fully developed in *Bride of Frankenstein* a decade later. In a scene when she attempts suicide by jumping from a bridge, her every gesture shows her to be a dancer. Elsa would sum up the experience of her first onscreen appearance by saying "the film was awful though we laughed hysterically."[24]

Back on the stage, Elsa's next performance was *The Pleasure Garden*, the first full-length play from writer Beatrice Mayor, which was presented by the Stage Society at the Regent for two performances on June 29 and 30, 1924. Elsa played "1st factory girl" and a "pert and ebullient" housemaid who "went into tantrums" when she did not get her own way.[25] This was followed by another Nigel Playfair production, the comic opera *The Duenna*, which opened at the Lyric Hammersmith in October 1924, and in which Elsa and Angela Baddeley played pages Sancho and Lewis, "who did just about everything," including a dance number with Nigel Playfair. *The Tatler* described them as "clever and attractive in a deliberately bizarre kind of way."[26]

Elsa was featured heavily in the press around this time, even garnering a full-page photograph in *The Bystander* entitled "A dancer with personality," and the front cover of *The Sketch*, where she was described as a "brilliantly clever dancer."[27] But with such scrutiny came her first criticism. In January 1925, during the run

21. Wykes, *Evelyn Waugh*, 39.

22. The film is available to UK-based audiences through the website of the British Film Institute, https://player.bfi.org.uk/free/film/watch-the-scarlet-woman-1924-online.

23. Wykes, *Evelyn Waugh*, 39.

24. Lanchester, *Elsa Lanchester, Herself*, 57.

25. *Illustrated London News*, July 12, 1924.

26. Lanchester, *Elsa Lanchester, Herself*, 75; *The Tatler*, November 12, 1924.

27. *The Bystander*, December 10, 1924; *The Sketch*, October 29, 1924.

of *The Duenna*, Elsa and Harold Scott took some of the turns from the Cave of Harmony and presented them as a variety show at the Court Theatre; this featured performances by Elsa, Harold, and Nigel Playfair, among others, and a short play by Aldous Huxley. In a lengthy review—which can be summarized as saying that what works in a small space does not necessarily transfer well to a larger stage—*Sketch* critic J. T. Grein did not hold back:

> Miss Elsa Lanchester has reached that phase in her career that most young artists of marked individuality have entered—and left. She should beware—that is to say, if she wants to get beyond the cabaret . . . Miss Lanchester is at present relying on tricks . . . [she] contributed a great variety of dance items to the programme; but the variety began and ended with the titles and the music—the dancer never varied her methods. With her demure knee-length skirts, and her face of a wicked little sprite, Miss Lanchester is content to be cornery and cubistic when she might, with her brains and her talent, be a true comedienne of the dance.[28]

Perhaps this was not the most auspicious start to the year, but Elsa kept busy in 1925. In addition to her work at the Cave of Harmony, she appeared again in *The Duenna* after it moved to the Golders Green Hippodrome, played the Moon in *The Rehearsal* at the Regent, took over the role of Sophie Binner from Jane Ellis in *Cobra* at the Garrick, and appeared in *Doctor Faustus* at the New Oxford. Although she attracted little critical attention for these roles, she was learning her craft in an attempt, perhaps, to "get beyond the cabaret."

---

28. *The Sketch*, January 28, 1925.

Elsa (far left) with Harold Scott, Philip Godfrey, and Helen Egli, dressed for one of their turns at the Cave of Harmony.

6   A Genius for the Grotesque

By the mid-1920s, Elsa's social circle was fast becoming a who's who of the great and good—not to mention the decadent and debauched—of London's offbeat artistic scene. Some of their names have echoed down the ages, but others have been forgotten with the passing of time. If Evelyn Waugh, say, counts among the former, then author Mary Butts falls into the latter category, although some publications about her in the 1990s speak to a small resurgence of interest. Elsa discusses Butts at some length in *Elsa Lanchester, Herself*, having rented a room from her at Forty-Three Belsize Park Gardens after her relationship with Harold Scott ended. In typical Elsa fashion, we are given no details about the break-up— we were given precious few about the relationship—but Harold Scott and Elsa continued their professional partnership until around 1927/28.

Elsa does wax lyrical for a couple of paragraphs about her attitude toward close romantic relationships around this time: "Many of my friends who might have thought to be lovers were just friends, and here and there a friend was a lover. Distance had to be planted at the very beginning. . . . Ties were something I was always running away from."[1] Indeed, many of Elsa's acquaintances at this time were just that: shallow and fleeting relationships. Her lifestyle, combined with her cruel sense of humor and fear of getting hurt, did not encourage the formation of deep and lasting friendships. The artist John Armstrong was an exception—once Elsa had rejected his romantic advances—and another was film critic Iris Barry, whom Elsa would describe, with none of her usual acidic humor, as an "amazing woman" and "like family."[2]

In contrast to Elsa's boarded-up emotions and self-protection, Iris "lived with her heart and her heart was often broken."[3] When Elsa met her in the early 1920s, Iris had borne two children out of wedlock by painter and writer Wyndham Lewis. The children were adopted by Iris's mother and grew up unaware of their parentage for many years. Despite Elsa's assertion that her friend never got

---

1.   Lanchester, *Elsa Lanchester, Herself*, 64.

2.   Lanchester, 74, 283.

3.   Lanchester, 74.

over Lewis, Iris married fellow writer Alan Porter in 1923, the same year that she became the first female film critic in the country, writing for *The Spectator* and the *Daily Mail*.[4]

Through Iris, Elsa met the future media baron Sidney Bernstein—with whom Iris set up the London Film Society—and the three of them would sometimes go out to dinner together. Bernstein, also wary of commitment, apparently found safety in numbers, and Elsa and Iris appreciated the free meal. However, as Elsa tells it, although Bernstein came from a wealthy family, "when he took us back in a taxi, he always fumbled in his pockets for change. He never had any. So Iris and I always had to pay out more than the price of a cheap meal. How we laughed at him."[5] Iris's warm, good-humored, and uncomplicated friendship would provide support for Elsa at several key points in her life.

The household of Mary Butts, that Elsa escaped to after her relationship with Harold Scott ended, was wild enough to be considered shocking even a century later. Nudity, black magic, partner swapping, devil worship, drug abuse, and free love—before anyone thought to call it that—were regular occurrences. Mary Butts had ties to the infamous occultist Aleister Crowley, who was considered by many at this time to be "the wickedest man in the world."[6] His crimes against polite society included devil worship, sexual experimentation, and drug misuse that led him to battle addictions to heroin and cocaine; Butts also struggled with similar addiction issues. Elsa claimed to have met Crowley once, when he came to Belsize Park to seek out one of the tenants, whom Elsa refers to only as the "Lady in Red." Despite Crowley's fearsome reputation, Elsa treats the encounter with the lack of reverence common throughout her writings: "He had a bicycle and his head was shaved. He was wearing a yellow kilt. Apparently he was always an odd dresser. . . . I helped him find The Lady in Red. She was down in the kitchen stirring a large pot on the stove. It could have been stew or dirty washing."[7]

Another sometime resident of Belsize Park Gardens was the author Douglas Goldring, by now a good friend of Elsa's. His memoirs mention that Mary Butts wrote to him from abroad, asking, "If I hear from you, please include a little gossip—Harold and Elsa for instance."[8] It's clear that Butts was for a while something of a mother figure to Elsa, although a less likely mother figure is hard to imagine. Elsa recalls that Butts introduced her to the work of Richard Freiherr von Krafft-Ebing "for laughs"; this author's work about sexual pathologies and perversions apparently made Elsa feel "ready for anything."[9] In the end, though,

4.   Sicherman and Green, *Notable American Women*, 57.
5.   Lanchester, *Elsa Lanchester, Herself*, 74.
6.   *John Bull*, March 24, 1923.
7.   Lanchester, 66–67.
8.   Goldring, *The Nineteen Twenties*, 211.
9.   Lanchester, *Elsa Lanchester, Herself*, 65.

she wasn't quite ready for the free love atmosphere that existed in the household. Butts at the time was living with Cecil Maitland, a man Elsa found frightening, and with good reason—during tea one day in Butts's study, Maitland grabbed Elsa and pulled her onto the bed. Repelled, she retaliated with a knee to his groin, and he ceased his attack. Eventually Elsa concluded that "Mary and her lover Cecil were sometimes very odd, and I went in to visit them at teatime less and less often."[10] Elsa moved out and for a while lived in the balcony room at the Cave of Harmony, then in its Gower Street location, before moving into a ground-floor flat on Doughty Street, Bloomsbury.

Douglas Goldring later presented Mary Butts as a victim of the excesses of the decade, which "proved too much for her originally robust condition" and led to her death in 1937, at the age of forty-four. He goes on to say that Butts and others like her "were 'period' figures, products of an upheaval which first liberated and then destroyed them."[11]

In Bloomsbury, Elsa's new neighbors included economist John Maynard Keynes, theater critic James Agate, and actor and singer Paul Robeson. For Elsa, "the very air of Bloomsbury was so thick with the past, present and future that I almost choked with excitement half the time."[12] Friends that she had around this time would be in her life for many years; besides Goldring, Iris Barry, and John Armstrong, these included theater critic Alan Dent and actor and director James Whale. Armstrong and Goldring were also connected to the 1917 Club, to which Harold Scott had introduced Elsa some years earlier. Goldring described the club premises on Gerrard Street, Soho, as having "all the squalor and dinginess associated in the popular imagination with a conspiratorial den of Bolsheviks and thieves."[13] Armstrong was even less flattering. Seeking out Elsa, whom he had a crush on, at the club, Armstrong was sufficiently unimpressed to write the following poem about the place:

> In nineteen seventeen they founded a club,
> Partly as brothel and partly as pub.
> The members were all of them horrible bores,
> Except for the girl in Giotto-pink drawers.[14]

Golding commented in 1945 that "the colour of Elsa's alleged 'drawers' was an innocent club joke, the point of which I have forgotten," and Elsa in 1983 added,

---

10. Lanchester, 66, 67.

11. Goldring, *The Nineteen Twenties*, 219.

12. Lanchester, *Elsa Lanchester, Herself*, 73.

13. Goldring, *The Nineteen Twenties*, 145.

14. Quoted in Goldring, 146. Elsa amends it slightly in Lanchester, *Elsa Lanchester, Herself*, 62, but the meaning is the same: "In nineteen one seven they founded a Club / Partly as brothel & partly as a pub / With a membership mainly of literary bores / Redeemed by a girl in Giotto-pink drawers."

"I have forgotten too. I don't recall having any pink drawers, being more partial to white. But the principal in a 'legend' is the last person to know its causes."[15]

John Armstrong would be a good friend of Elsa's, and their careers would often intertwine. He ran the coffee stall and made food at the Cave of Harmony, and he would later design costumes for some of her films. He and Harold Scott were both involved in her next stage venture, which would prove to be her biggest success so far.

Opening in April 1926 at the Lyric Hammersmith, *Riverside Nights* was a revue by A. P. Herbert and Nigel Playfair: "a grab bag of music, dance, and comedy that would become the surprise hit of the summer."[16] *Riverside Nights* was considered more highbrow that the average revue, featuring work by English poets, composers, and dramatists dating back to the sixteenth century. In addition to two complete operas and a three-act historical drama, the show featured Victorian music hall numbers performed by Elsa and Harold Scott. Elsa sang several of her songs from the Cave of Harmony in a similar costume, although her paper ballet dress was replaced by one made of silk, designed by John Armstrong. James Whale and Nigel Playfair were also in the cast.

Although, as Elsa remarked, "no member of the cast was really the 'lead,'" no one thought to inform the press of that, and Elsa's reviews were exceptional.[17] In his column for *The Sphere*, Herbert Farjeon wrote: "Miss Elsa Lanchester had a genius for the grotesque, and specialises in the songs that delighted some of our grandfathers. 'Please Sell No More Drink to My Father' and 'The Grecian Bend' . . . are little gems of execution."[18] J. T. Grein, who—as noted in the previous chapter—had previously criticized Elsa's variety work as lacking in variety now changed his tune, reporting, "I don't know who is the cleverer of the two: Miss Lanchester, who has the funniest, liveliest, prettiest legs on the stage and works them as if they were run on wire; or Mr. Harold Scott, who is the *beau-ideal* of the old-world comedian of *basso profundo* and beer in his voice."[19] When the script and lyrics were published in book form, a portrait of Elsa by John Armstrong was on the front cover.

Such reviews led to more opportunities for Elsa to perform these songs. While appearing in matinee and evening performances of *Riverside Nights*, which ran for eight months, she also picked up work singing in the Chez Nous night show at the Cavour Restaurant, as well as on radio broadcasts of the British Broadcasting Corporation (BBC) and at private parties. These last paid much better than theater work, but they could sometimes be a degrading experience for the proud performer: "It was typical of the snobbery of the period that Elsa was

---

15. Goldring, *The Nineteen Twenties*, 147; Lanchester, *Elsa Lanchester, Herself*, 62.
16. Curtis, *James Whale*, 42.
17. Lanchester, *Elsa Lanchester, Herself*, 76.
18. *The Sphere*, April 24, 1926.
19. *The Sketch*, April 21, 1926.

not treated like a guest at these aristocratic soirées," wrote Charles Higham, "but often was given her meals on a tray in a secretary's room."[20] The run of *Riverside Nights* overlapped with that of Playfair's version of *Midnight Follies* at the Metropole Hotel. Although many of the *Riverside Nights* cast also appeared in the *Follies*, the latter was much less successful: "the show disgusted the regular clientele of the Metropole and attendance fell with amazing swiftness."[21]

Once again, Elsa divided opinion. In "a letter from London" that was published in the regional press, an anonymous journalist neatly summarizes the discomfort that Elsa seemed to provoke in this era:

> Elsa Lanchester is not for every taste. She brings something to dancing and acting that Mr. Epstein brings to sculpture. I believe she has had mixed reviews at the Metropole, although she has been one of the outstanding successes of "Riverside Nights." She would make her fortune in Paris—she will one day, no doubt—but there is a kind of grimace in everything she does, a deliberate distortion of life, and we don't cultivate the *macabre* over here. When she was only known to a small circle of Londoners for her occasional rather amateurish performances at a more or less literary nightclub called The Cave of Harmony, I used to write . . . about the queer young girl with wild red hair running a nightclub in London, who would make herself heard beyond literary cliques before long. Well you can hear her now from Hammersmith to Northumberland Avenue.[22]

When she was appearing in both *Riverside Nights* and *Midnight Follies*, Elsa was forced to change her costume in the back of a taxi traveling between the two venues. One evening, the temporarily covered car windows caught the eye of a policeman, who insisted on seeing what was going on, and was treated to an eyeful of exposed Elsa. "I think my frantic expression was too much for him," she would tell a journalist years later. "He just shrugged, raised his eyes and waved us on."[23]

Her time in the *Follies* ended abruptly, after a member of the royal family walked out in protest during one of her songs. While sources disagree on which song was the culprit, the upshot of all of them is the same: the future king of England walked out, and Elsa was fired.

Between matinee and evening performances of *Riverside Nights*, Elsa would spend time with her boyfriend, a Russian who lived near the theater. She had met him at the 1917 Club, and she described the relationship as "uncomfortable" because of her lack of control over her feelings. "The Russian could have been a spy, for all I knew," she would later admit, "but I found him rather attractive—enough to make my singing and dancing and acting more vivid. He gave me that extra

20. Higham, *Charles Laughton*, 12.

21. Curtis, *James Whale*, 44.

22. *Yorkshire Post and Leeds Intelligencer*, October 1, 1926.

23. *The Gazette*, November 7, 1960.

excitement that a creative person needs to excite others."[24] He gave her more than that; during the run of *Riverside Nights* Elsa had an abortion. In her effort to find someone to carry out the then-illegal procedure, she was assisted by Tallulah Bankhead. Fortunately for Elsa, she suffered no ill effects from the operation, and she claimed later that she did not miss a single performance.

Although Elsa does not name the Russian in her writing, referring to him only as "Stanis," Freda Utley revealed his identity in her memoirs:

> One evening at our flat Philip Rabinovitch, chairman of the Russian Trade Delegation in London, "fell for" Elsa after she and Harold had delighted us all by their comic skits. Philip Rabinovitch had been a tailor in New York before the Bolshevik Revolution, had a fine baritone voice and enjoyed singing, fun and good company. . . . That evening long ago in London he and Elsa Lanchester sang a duet.[25]

However emotionally overwhelmed she may have been initially, Elsa still turned down the Russian's proposal of marriage: "by then I was in one of my virtuous virginal periods and Stanis looked like a piece of ectoplasm."[26]

As Elsa's early celebrity blossomed, the distance between her and her family grew—with Elsa actively maintaining the divide. Although she called on Waldo's skills as an electrician when she needed help with the lighting at the Cave of Harmony, there is no evidence that her shy and awkward brother ever attended the club socially.[27] In the late 1920s, Waldo was building his skills as a maker and master of marionette puppets, a field in which he would gain national, lasting recognition. In fact, Elsa's unassuming brother was the first in the family to be the subject of a full-length biography (Steve Cockayne's *Master of the Marionettes*, published in 2018), an achievement that feels like one of those small victories that Shamus occasionally enjoyed over Biddy—another census-night secret, or a dinner of bloaters.

Although Elsa would escape from Biddy's overbearing personality—partly by counterbalancing it with her own, and partly by leaving the country—Waldo never really managed to do so. His biographer sees these two outcomes as causally related: "[Elsa] was trying to maintain some distance between herself and her rather intrusive mother. Biddy, perhaps feeling at something of a loose end, threw herself into organising her son's life." She showed up at his workroom to help out and make tea, and was soon also writing scripts, weaving scenery, and making costumes. Her involvement with his marionette company would continue for another two decades.[28]

---

24. Lanchester, *Elsa Lanchester, Herself*, 75.

25. Utley, *Odyssey of a Liberal*, 53.

26. Lanchester, *Elsa Lanchester, Herself*, 76.

27. Cockayne, *Master of the Marionettes*, 39.

28. Cockayne, 47, 48.

Shamus, already a background figure by this point in Elsa's life, continued fading out in the same quiet way. Elsa told of a family lunch at a hotel, followed by tea at Shamus's sister's flat, and her words evoke the near claustrophobia she felt in their company. Her father's visible pride was, it seems, the only thing keeping her physically in the room: "I could not enjoy the excitement that I seemed to provide by being there. I only enjoyed seeing Shamus looking proud—well, just plain cocky. I really did want to justify Shamus's shining moment, so I behaved very well—never showing that I wanted to get away, hating the strong tea (mostly tannin) and the prospect of going down the narrow stairs with brown embossed wallpaper and out into the streets near smelly Euston."[29]

Such family gatherings became fewer as Elsa's stage career continued on its upward trajectory. She appeared in *Cautious Campbell* at the Q for a week in November 1926, and ended the year by recording two of her *Riverside Nights* numbers—"Please Sell No More Drink to My Father" and "He Didn't Oughter"—for release as a ten-inch record.

Theater critic Alan Dent, a friend of Elsa's, recalled attending a party on Doughty Street in 1926, probably at the house of fellow critic James Agate, who was Dent's boss at the time and who lived across the road from Elsa. Dent wrote about this party in a newspaper article more than twenty years later, remembering that those present—including Elsa and Harold Scott—discussed the casting of a new "London dockside" drama that Harold was to direct and Elsa was to perform in:

> They were at a loss to find an actor to play a tough called Charley. And suddenly, though I was very, very Scottish and still more silent in those days—I heard my own voice suggest "What about Charles Laughton?" And Miss Lanchester turned to me—I defy her to deny it!—and said: "But who's Charles Laughton?" And I told them . . . and they all said it sounded interesting, and then somebody thought of another actor for the part, and I re-entered my state of mute ingloriousness.[30]

The play being discussed was *The Pool*, which opened at the Everyman in February 1927, with Elsa in the lead role. The plot of the play, which was adapted by Anthony Bertram from his own novel, concerned a young lady who falls from grace when intoxicated and has a child out of wedlock, scandalizing her friends and neighbors. The part of Rosie Betts made demands on Elsa's acting abilities that she had never encountered before, and her lack of dramatic training and experience was noticed. "Her performance was throughout too much on the one metallic note and the character did not ring true," was the conclusion in *The Era*, while Harris Deans in the *Illustrated Sporting and Dramatic News* wrote:

---

29. Lanchester, *Elsa Lanchester, Herself*, 79–80.

30. *Illustrated London News*, April 10, 1948. Although Elsa never denied the story, she did refashion it somewhat, and attributed Dent's role to James Agate. See Lanchester, *Elsa Lanchester, Herself*, 81–82.

"In lighter moments, except for a tendency to burlesque, she was fairly good, but when depth of feeling was required she was at sea. If Miss Lanchester wants to be an actress she must realise that there are other things to do with one's arms that fold them across the breast, or keep them akimbo on the hips."[31] However, J. T. Grein saw an honesty in Elsa's performance and promise for the future: "If she remains unspoilt, if a producer of artistic insight could have her under the sway of his moulding hand, he could make a great actress of her. Among the younger players, I know no one who has so fervent and, as yet, so unfathomed a temperament."[32]

In April 1927, perhaps aware of her lack of theatrical training, Elsa embarked on her first touring production: *Double Dan* by Edgar Wallace, a comedy in which she played a Cockney maid. The show was tried in the provinces before coming to London, opening in the seaside town of Blackpool and then playing in Liverpool, Belfast, and Edinburgh. Elsa's reviews were uniformly positive. *The Era* wrote of her Liverpool performance, "some capital comedy comes from the servant Gladys, excellently handled by Miss Elsa Lanchester," while in Belfast she was "superb," and "the audience received her rapturously."[33] However, despite such acclaim, Elsa did not remain in the cast for the play's short London run. On April 23, the *Illustrated Sporting and Dramatic News* used a full-page picture of Elsa in costume and brandishing a gun to promote the show's imminent opening at the Savoy, but when the curtain went up on May 7, Wish Wynne was playing Gladys. No reason is given in the press for this change in casting, and Elsa does not seem to have any work commitments that would have prevented her from appearing.

Elsa does not mention this show in her autobiography. Nor does she mention what followed it, which is a little surprising as it was her first professional screen role. Filmed in July 1927 at Gainsborough Pictures' Islington Studios, *One of the Best* was a silent costume drama that did not live up to its title. Film historian Rachel Low summarized it as "unsophisticated," adding that director T. Hayes Hunter was "melodramatic and old-fashioned." However, Elsa did well in her role as Kitty, yet another servant, as noted by an otherwise damning contemporary review: "the acting—except for a charming study as a maid by Elsa Lanchester—is insignificant."[34]

Later that month, Elsa reprised her role in *Cautious Campbell* when the show opened at the Royalty, receiving mixed reviews. Harris Deans once again criticized her dramatic range, saying that she "seemed to think a few mannerisms sufficient to cover some poor character acting," but Herbert Farjeon disagreed,

---

31. *The Era*, February 9, 1927; *Illustrated Sporting and Dramatic News*, February 19, 1927.

32. *Illustrated London News*, March 5, 1927.

33. *The Era*, April 13, 1927; *Northern Whig*, April 19, 1927.

34. Low, *The History of the British Film*, 169; *The Graphic*, November 26, 1927.

praising her comedic skills with the unusual observation, "she has, of course, the comedy nose."[35]

By this time the Cave of Harmony had outstayed its welcome in quiet, residential Bloomsbury, and was on the move for what would prove to be the final time. Its new home was in the heart of the theater district, in a disused inn in Seven Dials called The Old Grapes. The pub came with its own quirky history—it had been sketched by George Cruikshank and was on the site of an ancient Roman vineyard—and Elsa, Harold Scott, John Armstrong, and others spent September 1927 painting and decorating, a process followed with keen interest by the press.

Opening night was a hit, with *Sketch* columnist Mariegold reporting: "If a crowd be a test of success, there can be no doubt that the opening night of the new Cave of Harmony . . . was a *succès fou*, but some of us thought it was a little *too* packed for comfort."[36] Celebrities listed as attending included artist Colin Gill, singer Ursula Greville, actress Tallulah Bankhead, and writer Arnold Bennett. This last was author of Elsa's next project, the play *Mr. Prohack*, which would be a life-changing experience.

---

35. *Illustrated Sporting and Dramatic News*, August 6, 1927; *The Graphic*, August 6, 1927.

36. *The Sketch*, October 5, 1927 (emphasis in original).

John Armstrong's illustration of Elsa in her *Riverside Nights* costume adorned the cover when the script of the show was published in book form in 1926.

7   A Subconscious Cleansing

In times past, Charles Laughton would need no introduction. Indeed, by the time Elsa first met him in 1927, he was well on his way to becoming a household name after several stage successes and praise from the critics. James Agate called him a genius. However, the wheel of fate continues to turn even after death, it appears, and some of the familiar faces of Hollywood's golden age are completely unknown to Generations X, Y, Z, and beyond, particularly those for whom talent rather than appearance was their calling card. Simon Callow's biography of Laughton was published in 1987, and in an introduction to the 2012 edition he notes: "There have been no subsequent biographies of Laughton. Indeed, I'm sad to say that Laughton—as an actor, at any rate—has increasingly slipped out of public consciousness . . . even within his own profession, he is virtually unknown to anyone under the age of forty."[1]

Charles was an unlikely movie star; overweight and heavy-featured, he had a complex personality and questionable personal hygiene. He was born in 1899 in Scarborough to hotelier parents, but Charles's passion was always for the theater. After the First World War ended (he fought in the trenches in 1918), he joined an amateur theater. Although he worked for several years in hotels owned by his family, he auditioned for RADA at the age of twenty-five and was awarded the prestigious Bancroft Gold Medal by RADA in 1926.

By the time he was cast as the lead in *Mr. Prohack*, Charles Laughton had only been a professional actor for eighteen months. Elsa commented: "He played the lead and I was his secretary, Mimi Winstock, which wasn't a very large part, but I drew the same salary as Charles—such were our relative positions at that time."[2]

It was not love at first sight between Elsa and Charles; indeed, she was to record her first impressions of him at rehearsals as follows: "He looked quite without color—pale plump face, mouse-colored hair—wearing wrinkled clothes, arms hanging rather listlessly at his sides." They made awkward small talk and

---

1. Callow, *Charles Laughton*, vii.
2. Lanchester, *Charles Laughton and I*, 69.

went for lunch together with other members of the cast. Slowly, carefully, they established a comfortable companionship: "We found in each other a friendship that we both needed badly—Charles because he felt lonely and was called ugly, and I because I was too 'bohemian,' with too many odd friends who stayed up half the night. I was probably drinking sherry or maybe port, and dancing the Charleston, and soon progressing to dry martinis and body-close dancing. This was beginning to add up to despair within myself."[3] During the rehearsals of *Mr. Prohack*, these two flamboyant but insecure individuals found a safe space with each other—or at least Elsa found that in Charles, seeing him as someone solid and dependable, perhaps the first person in her life to fill the role of reliable protector. Charles was perhaps not quite so relaxed with Elsa. On a trip to go walking in the countryside, he wore a loud checkered cap at which Elsa "screamed with laughter"; he swiftly put it in his pocket and never wore it again.[4] And, of course, he was keeping his sexual orientation a closely guarded secret.

Mr. Prohack opened at the Court on November 15, 1927, launching an avalanche of praise for Charles, who had played the title role as a caricature of the play's author, Arnold Bennett, much to the press's amusement (and the writer's fury). Elsa's secretary Mimi—shown in photographs clad in short dress, cape, and cloche hat, perched seductively on the edge of a desk—was "a spritely apparition among humans," a description of her that would be used frequently in these years.[5] It was the review in the *Bystander*, however, that would most signal the future press interest in the couple. There, columnist Jingle wrote of the play: "a very able sketch of a confidential secretary is given by Miss Elsa Lanchester. But the interest of the play is centred in Mr. Charles Laughton . . . first, last and all the time."[6]

Toward the end of the run of *Mr. Prohack*, around Christmas 1927, Elsa and Charles's friendship evolved into something more. They had attended a party together, at which Elsa—clad in a silver lamé and mauve taffeta evening dress—danced with several people, and then alone, showing off and adoring the attention. Charles sat sullenly and silently at the buffet table, hardly speaking. Elsa checked in with him occasionally, but he always declined to join her, and she would dash back to the dance floor. At around three in the morning, the pair got a taxi, with Charles intending to get out at Elsa's accommodation and then walk to his own lodgings from there. At the door, Charles shocked Elsa and himself by kissing her, rather clumsily. They broke apart and stared at each other in happy surprise, before Elsa invited Charles inside.

In all their country walks and dinners together as friends, Elsa and Charles had never discussed their respective romantic pasts, and each had their own rea-

3.   Lanchester, *Elsa Lanchester, Herself*, 83.

4.   Lanchester, *Charles Laughton and I*, 70.

5.   *The Sketch*, November 30, 1927.

6.   *The Sketch*, November 30, 1927; *The Bystander*, December 14, 1927.

sons for doing so. Elsa was afraid that Charles would be shocked at her "wild" exploits, and that it would render her unacceptable to him. Charles, as far as can be ascertained, had never had a relationship with a woman before Elsa, and his dalliances with men had by necessity been furtive and purely sexual. Elsa wrote that "our lack of curiosity about each other was, I would think, a sort of subconscious cleansing process. A making of space between the past and the present."[7]

However, it was space for their developing physical relationship that soon became a concern: Elsa's flat was always filled with visitors and assorted housemates, and Charles boarded with a theatrical landlady, Mrs. Forscutt, who was—according to Elsa—"very attached to her 'lodger,' so it was impossible for us to meet there."[8] Both Charles and Elsa thus moved to other accommodations. While Elsa's relocation to a different flat in Bloomsbury seems to have been voluntary, however—perhaps marking another deliberate step away from her "bohemian" lifestyle—Charles may not have had a choice in the matter.

The evidence for this comes from Claude Rains, who had appeared with Elsa in *The Insect Play* in 1923; two years later he was an instructor of Charles's at RADA, and had introduced the young actor to Mrs. Forscutt, having been a lodger of hers himself at one time. One day Rains went to visit his former landlady and was surprised to discover that Charles was no longer living there, but when he asked about the matter, Mrs. Forscutt was evasive. Eventually, she admitted, "He was not alone when I brought him tea in the morning. So I thought he'd better go." According to Rains's biographer, David Skal, "Rains assumed that Laughton had been sneaking his well-known, however improbable, girlfriend, Elsa Lanchester, into his rooms at night." But with Elsa's insistence on the impossibility of such a thing, Skal concludes: "It was perhaps significant that Mrs. Forscutt never told Rains the exact identity of the other party in Laughton's room."[9]

Whomever he had been caught in bed with, Charles moved from Mrs. Forscutt's to Garland's Hotel, and was presumably ever grateful for his former landlady's discretion.

After *Mr. Prohack*, Charles went straight into rehearsals for *A Man with Red Hair*. Opening night found Elsa in attendance, with *Sketch* columnist Mariegold remarking that she was dressed in "black, white, a white shawl, and [was] wearing stockings—rather an unusual addition to her costume for—at all events at her cabaret—she usually does without them." Elsa remembered things differently, recalling that she wore a blue sari that evening, which she had made herself from fabric so fine that it was almost transparent.[10] But whatever she wore on the night in question, her eccentric appearance was becoming a cause for concern for

---

7.   Lanchester, *Elsa Lanchester, Herself*, 84.

8.   Lanchester, 85. Elsa misremembers Charles's landlady's name as Mrs. Forster.

9.   Skal and Rains, *Claude Rains*, 55–56.

10. *The Sketch*, March 7, 1928; Lanchester, *Elsa Lanchester, Herself*, 88.

Charles, who insisted on taking her to a dressmaker and paying for new clothes. Looking back, Elsa seemed divided between being thankful that someone was showing such an interest in taking care of her, and being angry at this threat to her independence and personal style. What she doesn't comment on is the double standard at work here: it was Charles's personal style, far more than Elsa's, that attracted criticism. As Laughton's biographer Simon Callow remarks, "[Journalists] were too polite to mention it, but he was somewhat unusually dressed: not to put too fine a point on it, he was scruffy. And had perhaps had not had a bath recently? Ever?"[11] Indeed, later on, in Hollywood, Tallulah Bankhead would refuse to shake Charles's hand because his fingernails were so dirty.

But despite it all, the relationship progressed to the point that Elsa was introduced to Charles's mother, the "tiny but dominating" Eliza Laughton.[12] A strict Catholic, she had told her three sons that they should avoid actresses and redheads, so she must have been less than thrilled when presented with Elsa, who was both. However, the version of Elsa that Eliza Laughton met in the dining room of Garland's Hotel was a watered-down version of the original. Charles had outfitted her in a conservative black dress and green beads, and afterward he told Elsa that she had spoken "beautiful English and that it pleased him very much."[13] Elsa would tell of her own feeble attempts at self-deprecating humor and her conscious efforts to avoid shocking the conservative older woman. Sadly we have no record of Charles's first meeting with Biddy, so for that we must rely on our imaginations, although we are told that Biddy was very fond of him.

Professionally, things also seemed to be changing, and Elsa's theatrical workload declined dramatically in 1928 compared with the previous year. While Charles followed *A Man with Red Hair* with leading roles in *The Making of an Immortal*, Agatha Christie's *Alibi*, and *The Pickwick Papers*, Elsa does not seem to have set foot on a stage for over a year after finishing in *Mr. Prohack* on January 7, 1928. A few offhand remarks in her writings seem to indicate that this was not a voluntary state of affairs. Looking back on this time a decade later, she wrote: "I did not seem to be making much progress. Charles's career was rocketing ahead, but mine was not." Rather unconvincingly, she added: "I think it was just as well, as I would not have liked it if I had succeeded and Charles had had a bad time."[14]

However, Elsa's name continued to appear in the press. She is reported as attending John Armstrong's first exhibition at the Leicester Galleries; a portrait of her in her *Riverside Nights* costume, painted by R. G. Eves, was displayed at the Royal Society of Portrait Painters show at Grafton Galleries; Mariegold spotted her at the Gargoyle, "the intellectual dance club with the 'highbrow' library and

11. Callow, *Charles Laughton*, 29.

12. Lanchester, *Elsa Lanchester, Herself*, 85.

13. Lanchester, 85.

14. Lanchester, *Charles Laughton and I*, 72.

drawings by Matisse"; and she continued to perform her Victorian music hall numbers at charity events and private parties.[15]

She also made several appearances on film. The first was in a brief but noticeable scene in *The Constant Nymph* (1928), a successful silent movie that starred Ivor Novello and Mabel Poulton. Elsa plays a guest at a private recital, and also performs a song (a curious thing to see in a silent film); she makes the most of her screen time and seems to have rid herself of the ugly snarls that punctuated her performance in *The Scarlet Woman* (1924). This film was followed by (and referenced in) a series of silent comedy shorts directed by Ivor Montagu and written by H. G. Wells. These three 1928 films—*Bluebottles*, *The Tonic*, and *Daydreams*— also featured Charles Laughton in small roles.

Although *Daydreams* seems to be lost, *The Tonic* and *Bluebottles* can be viewed online, where Elsa's skills as a comedienne are still apparent nearly a century later. In *The Tonic*, she plays a hopeless maid whose attempts to take care of an ailing woman get ever more bizarre, but it is in *Bluebottles* that Elsa really shines. In this slapstick comedy about cops and robbers (the latter easily identifiable by their striped jerseys), Elsa plays herself and is frequently referred to by name in the surtitles. We first see her coming out of a cinema, where she has been watching *The Constant Nymph*. She then finds a whistle on the street, which when blown attracts a swarm of policemen, who then raid a house full of criminals. Elsa is swept inside the house and, through a series of pratfalls and wrong turns, manages to accidentally round up all the crooks, for which she receives a reward from the police.

In his essay on the film, Seb Manley remarks that *"Bluebottles* resembles the slapstick films of Chaplin and Keaton on a basic narrative level, where an innocent hero is propelled into a world where he or she does not belong, and comedy arises from the hero's efforts to cope with the new and unfamiliar situation."[16] Slapstick comedy was popular at the time, and Elsa proves herself extremely skilled at it, even being called a "female Chaplin" in the press.[17] Her arms seem a couple of inches too long, and she moves like a marionette, with every movement perfectly controlled for comic effect. It is one of her best screen performances and was recognized as such at the time, with the review in *Bioscope* saying that Elsa "is revealed as a character-comedienne with enormous screen possibilities. . . . She acts not alone with her face and hands, but with every muscle in her body."[18]

During the filming, Elsa and Charles were invited to H. G. Wells's house at Easton Glebe, which was on the property of Daisy Greville, the scandalous

---

15. *Westminster Gazette*, January 16, 1928; *The Sketch*, June 27, 1928; *The Stage*, May 24, 1928; *The Tatler*, June 27, 1928.

16. Manley, "Comedy and Experimentation in British Alternative Film."

17. *Daily News*, September 12, 1929, quoted in Manley. See also *The Sketch*, October 30, 1929.

18. *Bioscope*, September 18, 1929.

Countess of Warwick, by this time in her sixties. While there, they dined with Lady Warwick and Wells, but Elsa remembers that Charles was ill at ease in the company of this "Socialist aristocracy": he was "more or less subservient to people like Wells and his friends. He was impressed and quiet, absorbing and drawing from their words of wisdom, which he later was not above using himself."[19] One of Wells's gems of wisdom that Charles did not repeat was his opinion on talking pictures, which had taken off in the United States, but were a bit slower to arrive in England: "No future in talkies," opined Wells in 1928. "No future in talkies at all!"[20]

Elsa's career might have progressed differently if she'd had time to develop her slapstick comedy skills in the silent era, but time was against her, and the next film that she made was to be the first by the newly established British Talking Pictures Limited, filmed at its studios in Wembley. A commitment to this company to film the short domestic comedy *Mr. Smith Wakes Up* (1929), which was used mainly for demonstration purposes, to show the possibilities of sound films, meant that Elsa had to drop out of a planned radio adaptation of Compton Mackenzie's 1912 novel *Carnival*. The short film did little to advance Elsa's career.

Meanwhile, Charles's ever-increasing fame was putting pressure on the status of their relationship. Elsa and Charles had started by spending weekends at the Dog and Duck (where their activities left Elsa once again in need of an abortionist), before moving together to a flat on Dean Street, and then to a flat on Percy Street, this one a former servants' quarters. But their well-known names meant that the risk of their living situation becoming public knowledge was growing steadily. Marriage had to be considered, as Elsa explained:

> Charles and I were too shy to remain unmarried, if that can explain it. To go on living together was just too embarrassing for us to cope with. Certainly it would have acted as a brake to Charles' growing career and also hurt his northern hotelier family and his Catholic mother. These people would have been made ill rather than shocked. I felt rather blank about the whole thing, having had no moral pressures in my life.[21]

For Charles, as a closeted gay man in a time of intolerance, having a wife would be the ultimate protection, and marriage would provide him with the opportunity of becoming a father, which is something he wanted desperately. It is unclear to what extent he intended to be faithful to Elsa, whether he hoped through matrimony to escape what he viewed at the time as his immoral desires. Arnold Ben-

---

19. Lanchester, *Elsa Lanchester, Herself*, 84.

20. Lanchester, 84.

21. Lanchester, 84, 90.

nett counseled Charles against the marriage, telling him, "She's a pixie. Besides, you need cosseting, and she won't cosset you. But you'll marry her anyway."[22]

Simon Callow writes that "Elsa attributes the marriage to Charles' desire to please his ever-formidable mother . . . [and] implies that the further seal of respectability was not entirely unwelcome to Charles, too."[23] This is undoubtedly correct as far as it goes, but Elsa craved respectability as well, more than she ever admitted. Both Elsa and Charles were outsiders; both were considered different, although that did not mean they were similar. Marriage, they must have individually reasoned, would provide both of them with much-needed security.

It is also easy to imagine that there was a spark of rebellion in the idea on Elsa's part: how better to finally, fully escape from Biddy than to take part in the very institution that her mother had so famously shunned?

A wedding date was set for February 10, 1929.[24]

22. *The Salt Lake Tribune*, February 22, 1960.

23. Callow, *Charles Laughton*, 281.

24. There is some confusion regarding the date. Charles Higham writes that it was February 9, 1929, but also that it was a Sunday (February 9 was a Saturday). Elsa's naturalization papers list the date as February 10, 1929.

Bluebottles was one of three short silent films written by H. G. Wells in which Elsa starred. Her skill at slapstick led to her being labeled a "female Chaplin" in the press.

8   Placed in Parentheses

The wedding did not take place in a church as neither of the participants considered themselves religious. Charles had been steadily rejecting the Catholicism he was raised with for a number of years; this was not Elsa's influence, his cousin recalled that during the war, Charles had refused "religious consolation" from a priest before going into battle.[1] Elsa admitted that "Charles's great pride was that he had the strength to question and give up his Catholic faith," although her own religious views were less extreme. Despite the outspoken atheism of her parents—which had led to her removal from the classroom during prayers in her brief time at a regular school—Elsa preferred to refer to herself as agnostic. "I began to think that if these people were so certain there was no God, it was just as silly as someone who is certain there is a God," she explained.[2] This tolerance was not obvious to everyone. The actress Maureen O'Hara, a fervent Catholic whom Elsa detested, remarked that Elsa possessed "hatred for religion of any kind."[3]

Elsa and Charles paid extra to the registry office to get married on a Sunday in an attempt to avoid attention from the press, but news of their "secret engagement" and imminent plans to wed were reported in the week leading up to the ceremony. An article in a Yorkshire newspaper—which always championed Charles as a local boy done good—was headlined "Charles Laughton to marry actress." In the article, the author (identified only as "Northerner") offered his impression of Elsa: "His fiancée I first met at a bottle party which E.X. Kapp, the caricaturist, once gave. She was a striking figure who was not at a loss for words when she discovered she had been sitting on a squashed orange during the evening."[4]

Unsure of the details, but desperate to report *something*, the *Coventry Evening Telegraph* wrote that Elsa and Charles's "marriage at the end of the

---

1. Letter from Jack Dewsbery to Elsa, quoted in Lanchester, *Elsa Lanchester, Herself*, 295.

2. Lanchester, 294, 23.

3. O'Hara and Nicoletti, *'Tis Herself*, 36.

4. *Yorkshire Post and Leeds Intelligencer*, February 5, 1929.

week, after a secret engagement, is the biggest social event of the theatre this year."[5] In actuality, however, it was one of the smallest. Once Charles and Elsa had avoided the journalists gathered outside their flat by arriving in separate taxis, they were joined by just three people: Elsa's friends John Armstrong and Iris Barry, and Charles's brother Tom. Elsa's relationship with Tom was always stormy, and she doesn't discuss his attendance in any of her writing, but he is mentioned in press reports of the time.

Elsa wore a black coat, a gray hat, and a sprig of grape hyacinths in her buttonhole. The ring used in the ceremony was one she had worn in the previous months when faking her marital status at the Dog and Duck, but once the wedding was over, she rarely wore it again. A small luncheon party followed, which Elsa's parents attended. Despite their own views on marriage, they were "glittering with delight," which Elsa saw as "one of the many paradoxical twists to their life. . . . Their bright expressions shone with illogical satisfaction."[6] It does not seem to occur to Elsa that her parents' delight simply came from seeing her so happy.

After lunch, the new Mr. and Mrs. Laughton set off on their honeymoon. First a boat train, then a Channel steamer, then an overnight train took them from London to Arosa, Switzerland, via Folkestone and Boulogne. Their marriage, destined to be so unconventional, began that way almost at once, when Elsa and Charles were joined on their honeymoon by his mother Eliza and brother Frank. "All my friends found it hilarious," Elsa later commented, although she herself did not see the funny side at the time.[7] The presence of the older Mrs. Laughton made Elsa feel self-conscious and unable to relax, a state of mind aggravated by her inability to ski. Charles had skied previously and was quite skilled, but he lacked the patience to accompany Elsa as she found her feet. Although the odd foursome spent two weeks in Arosa, Elsa opted to remain in her bed for several days.

Things improved when Charles and Elsa—alone at last—moved on to Italy, but the fundamental differences in their personalities were becoming readily apparent. Elsa found a trip up Vesuvius wildly exciting, fitting well with her enjoyment of violent elemental displays such as thunderstorms and rough seas. Charles, however, was much more wary. Elsa, perhaps still angry at the cold way she felt Eliza had treated her in Switzerland, blamed Charles's timidity on his upbringing: "His mother . . . is afraid of thunder. If a child is brought up to see people hide under blankets when a storm is on, he begins to think it is dangerous. I was brought up to stand at the window and watch lightning."[8]

---

5. *Coventry Evening Telegraph*, February 5, 1929.

6. Lanchester, *Elsa Lanchester, Herself*, 80.

7. Lanchester, 91.

8. Lanchester, *Charles Laughton and I*, 73–74.

After visiting Naples and Pompeii, Elsa and Charles went finally to Ravello, a picturesque town on the Amalfi Coast that has a history as a haven for artists and writers. Here was a place that agreed with them both, and they would return many times over the years with friends including John Armstrong and playwright Jeffrey Dell. The author Osbert Sitwell remarked in his autobiography: "[Charles] and his wife—whose character and wit matched his own—used to stay at Ravello every winter for several years running, while I was a mile or so away, downhill, at Amalfi. Certainly Charles Laughton, like myself, found here some attraction that he could not define or resist."[9] Here Charles and Elsa expanded on the countryside walks they had enjoyed in the early days of their courtship, "climbing up the rocks and among the crenelated gray walls like goats and, however tired, triumphing with a worthy ardor over every obstacle."[10] Sitwell also recalled that Elsa's charm was "as unlike that of anyone else as [was] her individual style in clothes and conversation."[11]

In an interview later in life, Elsa remarked, "You know how some people say 'the honeymoon is over' after five or six years? With Charles and me the honeymoon was over on the honeymoon. Not just because of the relatives in attendance; his primary interests were work and keeping up appearances."[12] It certainly was an inauspicious beginning to married life, but despite Charles's obsession with work, Elsa was actually the first back on the stage upon their return to London, her theatrical dry spell at last at an end.

Her first appearance on the stage following her wedding was in *The Outskirts*, which saw Elsa playing an Austrian cocotte who is strangled by her lover. This lover was played by Derrick De Marney, whom Elsa described as "rather awful—all tongue and little acting technique on the stage."[13] Their passionate scenes together stirred Charles up into a lather of jealousy. One afternoon he burst into Elsa's dressing room, where she was resting between matinee and evening performances, and seemed surprised not to have caught her in flagrante with De Marney. Elsa was less than amused, thinking his "dramatic, suspicious entrance was more like cheap melodrama than flattering."[14] The play, at the Gate Theatre, received mostly good reviews, with Elsa often singled out for her "delightful, impudent-lyrical performance."[15]

Charles was less lucky with the critics upon his return to the stage in *Beauty*, "a ludicrous farrago," which he followed with the equally unsuccessful *The Silver*

---

9. Sitwell, *The Scarlet Tree*, 99, quoted in Lanchester, *Elsa Lanchester, Herself*, 92.

10. Sitwell, 99, quoted in Lanchester, 92.

11. Sitwell, quoted in *Los Angeles Times*, October 13, 1946.

12. Hadleigh, *Leading Ladies*, 88.

13. Lanchester, *Elsa Lanchester, Herself*, 99.

14. Lanchester, 99.

15. *Daily Herald*, May 10, 1929.

Tassie, in which he was "seriously miscast as a young Irish footballer, knew it, and looked miserably tormented."[16]

However, despite his bad reviews, one of Charles's projects was proving a success. Elsa's appearance at the opening night of *The Silver Tassie* had caught the attention of fashion journalist Florence Roberts, who related the intricacies of Elsa's outfit—doubtlessly chosen by Charles—in her newspaper column, Fashions from Stage and Screen: "a gold tissue coat lined with velvet, and a charming gown of softly blue taffeta, with a 'waisted' bodice and a full ankle-length skirt, and long scarf ends looped under the little hip-basque on the left side."[17] This was certainly a long way from Elsa's eccentric, handwoven garb.

The publicity value of Elsa and Charles as a celebrity couple was exploited by the Alpha Film Corporation, which cast them alongside each other in the "super revue" film *Comets* (1930).[18] As one of several variety acts, Elsa and Charles sang "Frankie and Johnny," which they had previously performed at the Cave of Harmony during the early days of their relationship. The club had slowly fizzled out since then, with Elsa dating its demise to the end of 1928. She later wrote:

> I don't know why the Cave of Harmony eventually finished. Several people would have liked to go on running it and literally hundreds of people asked us to please re-open it. Perhaps it was because the inventiveness of the group of friends that ran it had come to a standstill. . . . Sometimes we used to fight like tiger cats, and sometimes we were inseparable, but the Cave just ceased to exist and we all went about our various other jobs.[19]

It is difficult not to see significance in the fact that the Cave of Harmony closed just before Elsa's marriage to Charles; as a physical monument to her bohemian past, the club needed to be dismantled before she could move forward into respectability. But as life became ever more focused on Charles, Elsa would crave a return to the music hall burlesque world that she had made her own.

Comets provides a rare occurrence of Elsa and Charles singing together on-screen, and it is a great shame that the film is now lost. Press reports at the time indicate that they had fun together during filming. The lyrics of the song had been changed to please the censor, but Charles accidentally sang the original lyrics. "He wanted a word to describe a certain type of lady and to rhyme with the word 'floor,'" *Bioscope* reported. "Well, out it slipped, and the recording booth . . . rocked perceptibly. After Elsa Lanchester had arrested her bolting orbs the verse was resung with correct, though perhaps less effective verbiage."[20]

---

16. Callow, *Charles Laughton,* 30; Emlyn Williams, quoted in Higham, *Charles Laughton,* 19.

17. *Illustrated Sporting and Dramatic News,* October 19, 1929.

18. *Bioscope,* December 25, 1929.

19. Lanchester, *Charles Laughton and I,* 58.

20. *Bioscope,* January 8, 1930.

Aside from *The Outskirts*, Elsa's only other stage performance in 1929 was in a sketch called "Always Apologise," part of a charity gala. Described as "the merest trifle, light as air," it included Tallulah Bankhead and Eric Cowley in the cast.[21] Elsa ended the year in rehearsals for *Ten Nights in a Bar Room*, which opened at the Gate Theatre in January 1930. Although a new decade had begun, Elsa was still performing the same kind of music hall parodies that she had perfected at the Cave of Harmony. In this "boisterous burlesque of the temperance play," Elsa sang the familiar "Please Sell No More Drink to My Father" in her role as the Drunkard's Child. Reviews were positive, with *The Graphic* calling her "one of the most comic and delightful curiosities on the stage today," while the *Daily Herald*'s reviewer wrote: "She wears a look of startled innocence and a blonde wig, and shatters her angelic appearance by her ripe Cockney accent. A neatly observed and well-polished performance."[22] Perhaps as a result of her success in this show, Elsa would be cast as a child twice more the following year, 1931: in *Little Lord Fauntleroy* in January, and in *Payment Deferred* in April.

While Elsa was onstage at the Gate, Charles was appearing in *French Leave* at the Vaudeville. A visitor to his dressing room after a performance reported that "the actor got rid of other callers as quickly as courtesy permitted, for he was anxious to change and go over to the Gate Theatre for his wife." The same source saw the gifts that Elsa had given to her husband for luck: a pot of white hyacinths and a "crystal lidded box" that would release a brown moth when Charles opened it, although he had not done so.[23]

During the run of *French Leave*, Charles's health deteriorated to such an extent that he missed almost as many performances as he made. For months he had suffered from repeated throat infections and coughs, and these were beginning to affect the quality of his voice. Critics noticed and commented on his weak vocals, which helped convince him to have his tonsils removed. To recuperate after the operation, he traveled to Ravello with Elsa and John Armstrong. Armstrong was welcome company for Elsa on this trip because Charles also brought with him the script for his next play, Edgar Wallace's *On the Spot*, in which Charles would play a Capone-type gangster. Elsa, with no work on the horizon, watched as her husband threw himself into preparations for his role, speaking to as many Italians as he could, learning their mannerisms, and reading everything about Al Capone that he could find. At a time when Method Acting was just beginning to find a foothold in the West, Charles became well known for living his roles and embodying his characters. The press would come to regard this practice as an amusing quirk, as an article from 1943 demonstrates: "For years Charles Laughton has had a strange habit of keeping himself in character during his home hours with

21. *The Stage*, November 20, 1929.

22. *Illustrated Sporting and Dramatic News*, January 25, 1930; *The Graphic*, January 11, 1930; *Daily Herald*, January 2, 1930.

23. *Illustrated Sporting and Dramatic News*, January 18, 1930.

the character he is playing at the studio." Elsa, the article claimed, "has always been patient about it."[24]

Patient she may have been, perhaps even—at this early stage in their marriage—supportive, but such devotion to his craft must have been trying to live with, especially when Elsa was in the middle of one of her increasingly frequent professional dry spells. Charles, however, was not insensitive to Elsa's feelings when she was out of work, and Elsa remarked that whenever she was unemployed, he would buy her something to occupy her time: first it was a box of paints, and on this trip to Italy it was a Leica camera. A later gift would be an eight-millimeter movie camera. She wrote in 1938, "He tries to get me something that will make me bury myself for several days in a new occupation."[25] Whether such purchases were made out of the kindness of his heart or in anticipation of a quiet life is not clear—but having Elsa busy with her camera enabled Charles to devote all his time to his character development.

In the case of *On the Spot*, Charles's preparation paid off handsomely; the show was the biggest hit of 1930 and confirmed the popular opinion that Charles was one of the greatest actors of his generation. However, Elsa was not a witness to his performance on opening night, as Florence Roberts reported in her column:

> [Charles Laughton had] a marvellous spray of orchids from his wife Elsa Lanchester, who—in a green dress and shimmering gold and green coat—had come round to his dressing room after the play, though she had obediently stayed away during its performance. "He was nervous enough already," she explained, "and it would have made it worse for him if he had known that I was there feeling still more nervous."[26]

On the Spot ran for nearly a year, during which time Elsa and Charles began searching for a house in the countryside. Long walks and a shared love of nature had been one of the foundation stones of their courtship, and Charles had been advised by his doctor of the healing power of escaping city air as often as possible. An incident that occurred in August 1930 must also have added to the couple's dissatisfaction with London living.

One weekend, when Elsa and Charles were not at home, thieves broke into their flat on Percy Street; they entered through the basement, forced the apartment door, and pocketed some of Elsa's costume jewelry before helping themselves to whiskey. To have one's home ransacked is violation enough, but to add insult to injury, the article reporting the crime began, "Thieves broke into the flat of Mr. Charles Laughton." When Elsa was eventually mentioned, she was

---

24. *Hull Daily Mail*, May 6, 1943.

25. Lanchester, *Charles Laughton and I*, 103.

26. *Illustrated Sporting and Dramatic News*, April 12, 1930.

placed in parentheses: "The thieves stole two rings and a bracelet belonging to Mr. Laughton's wife (Miss Elsa Lanchester)."[27]

Sidelined as she was in newspaper reports, Elsa did take a lead role in discovering the perfect property for the Laughtons' country retreat. It happened when she attended a dinner party held by the eccentric architect Clough Williams-Ellis and his wife, Amabel, one evening while Charles was performing in *On the Spot*. Elsa was determined to ask Clough for his advice about finding a property that was in the countryside but was still within thirty miles of London, believed to be the maximum distance traversable for showfolk after an evening performance.

The architect gave the question serious consideration. Maps were produced and perused. Eventually Clough turned to Amabel and asked, "Do you think they'll do?" After she replied in the positive, Clough began to tell Elsa about his own cottage in Surrey, which he was reluctantly selling due to spending so much of his time in Wales working on what would become the famous Portmeirion village. Elsa's reaction to hearing the details of this rural retreat was physical: she began shaking, and she ran to call Charles as soon as he came offstage. Elsa spoke "economically like a telegram" in her eagerness to pass on the information: "Come at once Clough's party thatched log cabin 28 miles London 625 feet up heart of wild woods bracken up to front door two miles nearest village no water no light pine trees bluebells."[28] There would be no such brevity of description when Elsa came to discuss the property in *Charles Laughton and I*, where she spends thirteen pages composing what is essentially a love letter to a distinctly unusual home. That a full five of those pages are devoted to the multiple methods she tried in order to rid the place of ants is also distinctly unusual, and an indicator of how bored Elsa got when out of work.

Elsa and Charles would refer to the property as "Stapledown," although Clough's moniker of "The Hut" was more accurate. About thirty feet long and twenty-five feet wide, the building was fashioned from rough wood topped with a thatched roof, and was about a foot from the ground, supported and held in place by the four pine trees growing through it. *The Bystander* sent the photographer Sasha to take pictures of Elsa and Charles's new home, which resulted in a four-page spread in the magazine. The text that accompanies the pictures is similar in tone to the celebrity "at home" features common to today's glossy magazines, but the home being described could not be more different from these mansions:

> Having walked up the steps I entered a large room, at one end of which is a well-equipped kitchen. The other end is portioned off into two bedrooms on the ground floor . . . and there is a third bedroom on a sort of balcony above them. This is reached by means of a ladder cut out of branches of trees. The main portion of the room serves as a dining and living room. . . . Nearly everything about the house made me feel myself transported into a wild adventure story, until I was brought to

---

27. *Lancashire Evening Post*, August 12, 1930.
28. Lanchester, *Charles Laughton and I*, 80; Lanchester, *Elsa Lanchester, Herself*, 95.

Charles and Elsa at Stapledown, their treehouse escape from the city and their growing fame.

earth by the sound of a telephone bell, for, yes! let me admit it, the Laughtons are on the 'phone, and also have a wireless. . . . There is always something to do, and when new parts have to be learned, what peace and quiet is theirs living in the kind of house that some people with fantastic imagination might dream about, but only they possess. Every evening they play their parts on the stage, and then they leave London and theatres and go back to their mystery home in the treetops. What romantic lives the Laughtons lead![29]

Although the home was not quite the "in the treetops," Elsa and Charles could certainly be said to be living in a treehouse, and its quirkiness matched something in the shared oddness of its new owners. Simon Callow wrote that Stapledown was "an idyll, and Elsa and Charles were as happy here as they would ever be in their lives, picking flowers, playing games."[30]

The exact location of the house was a closely guarded secret, and even those in the know required guidance to find it. Indeed, to get there required a half-mile trek across a field where foxgloves grew to well above head height, and once they had arrived, any houseguest had to earn their keep by fetching drinking water or

---

29. *The Bystander*, July 15, 1931.
30. Callow, *Charles Laughton*, 41.

chopping wood. Despite this, there was no shortage of visitors; the photographs taken by Sasha show faces at every window. One regular visitor was Iris Barry, who at this time was involved with the American tap dancer Paul Draper. During this presumably brief affair (her biographer does not mention it, and Iris was still married to Alan Porter), the couple regularly visited Elsa and Charles in London and at Stapledown, despite Charles's dislike of Paul, whom he considered to be brash, overbearing, and no match for Iris, whom Charles liked very much. Fortunately Charles was frequently working and away from home during their visits. When he was there, Elsa claimed he would sit and watch the frivolity but would never participate, acting like a man much older than his thirty years.

Although Elsa's theater roles declined in the early 1930s, she was finding more work in films. Some of these were so-called quota quickies, made to fulfill the requirements of the Cinematograph Films Act of 1927. An attempt to save the country's struggling film industry, this act stipulated that British cinemas (many of which were owned by the big American studios) had to show a certain quota of British-made films, and quota quickies were produced to make up the numbers, usually on a shoestring budget. An example is *The Officers' Mess* (1931), in which Elsa played opposite Richard Cooper and Harold French. In this adaptation of a stage play, the farcical plot concerns the antics of two naval officers on shore leave. Elsa had a strong part as the actress Cora Melville, who was in love with Cooper's character. She also appeared in three other films that were released in 1931: *The Love Habit*, *The Stronger Sex*, and *Potiphar's Wife* (aka *Her Secret Desire*). Not bound by any contract, she worked for Gainsborough and British International Pictures, and she filmed scenes at studios across London—Elstree, Islington, and Nettlefold.

The Love Habit was also based on a stage play. It starred Seymour Hicks (who had written Elsa's earlier film *One of the Best*), on whom most reviewers focused their attention. According to *The Bystander*, "Elsa Lanchester suffers from having a part that gives her no chance, and also, I suspect, a lack of adequate direction."[31]

Topping the bill in *The Stronger Sex* was Colin Clive, with whom Elsa would appear a few years later in *Bride of Frankenstein* (1935). Although he was already battling the alcoholism that would kill him before the decade was out, Clive was well known at the time for his role in the stage version of *Journey's End*, directed by none other than future *Bride* director James Whale. In a 1979 interview with Gregory William Mank, Elsa recalled that "Charles and I stayed in the country in England with Colin Clive and his wife, Jeanne de Casalis, once or twice. . . . Theirs wasn't a very happy marriage. She was very precious, very affected; he was very nice, an English gentleman."[32] Jeanne de Casalis was also an actress, and would appear alongside Elsa and Charles in the play *Payment Deferred* in May 1931. Although *The Stronger Sex* was a drama, Elsa played a comedic role along-

31. *The Bystander*, January 28, 1931.

32. Mank, *Women in Horror Films*, 307.

side Gordon Harker, for which a reviewer called her one of "the best artistes now playing in British pictures."[33]

Laurence Olivier was the star of the last of Elsa's 1931 films, *Potiphar's Wife*. In this Gainsborough picture, Elsa played a small role as a maid; a reviewer wrote that her talents were "deplorably wasted" in the "slow" film.[34]

A bigger role was to be found in her stage outing as the lead in *Little Lord Fauntleroy* at the Gate Theatre. The play was based on the book by Frances Hodgson Burnett, and had first been presented on the stage in 1888. Therefore, this production, which opened in January 1931, was another opportunity for Elsa to pay tribute to the Victorian era of entertainment in which she felt so comfortable. Dressed in "authentic laces and velvet" and sporting another blonde wig, Elsa played the part "in the spirit of mild burlesque," and received good reviews, in which her performance was described as "a riot of fun" and "excellently played."[35] Co-star Alan Napier would later describe her Little Lord as "exquisitely revolting."[36] Even so, one review, while positive, did seem to echo a warning from years earlier regarding the dangers of getting typecast in a certain genre: "It really is extraordinarily funny. . . . Elsa Lanchester confines her rather limited but quite uncanny talents to poking fun at the Past, and here she is in her element."[37]

Elsa's next play, however, would be something very different, and much darker. The play *Payment Deferred*, in which she appeared onstage alongside Charles for the first time since their wedding, was to prove a milestone in their lives and their marriage. For Charles, it would be "the crowning glory of a brilliant succession of triumphs," and the play that would take him to Broadway.[38] But with dizzying highs often come shattering lows, and the firm ground on which Elsa felt they had built their marriage was about to be split wide open.

33. *West Midland Gazette*, August 22, 1931.

34. *Daily Herald*, March 30, 1931.

35. *Illustrated London News*, February 7, 1931; *Daily Herald*, January 8, 1931; *Illustrated London News*, February 7, 1931.

36. Napier and Bigwood, *Not Just Batman's Butler*, 110.

37. *Illustrated Sporting and Dramatic News*, February 7, 1931.

38. Callow, *Charles Laughton*, 38.

9 Get Rid of the Sofa

In *Payment Deferred* (1931), Charles played the part of tormented murderer William Marble, while Elsa was cast as his twelve-year-old daughter, Winnie.[1] It was adapted from the C. S. Forester novel by Jeffrey Dell, who quickly became a friend and another frequent guest at Stapledown, along with his girlfriend, Eileen Weatherstone. Sometimes Elsa and Charles would spend time in Brighton, where Jeffrey and Eileen lived, and the two couples enjoyed each other's company during long walks on the beach.

One evening in or around March 1931, Elsa was at the flat on Percy Street, in bed, unaware of the drama that was beginning on the street outside. A young man had been seen loitering around the building, and a police constable had arrived to see what was going on. While they were talking, Charles and Jeffrey Dell arrived back from a night out, and the policeman explained to them that the young man was claiming that Charles had "picked him up in a park the previous day and had taken him home, promising him money, which he had not given him."[2] The youth was now demanding payment. Indignantly, Charles denied the story, and the policeman took the young man into custody.

Badly shaken, Charles went upstairs and roused Elsa. While Dell sat in the kitchen, Charles haltingly stammered out words that Elsa would remember forever: "Something awful has happened. I have something to confess."[3] In a disjointed, anguished narrative, Charles told Elsa that he was "partly" gay and had engaged in brief, furtive sexual encounters with men such as the one he had picked up at the park. He cried and begged forgiveness.

Elsa did not cry. Although she claims that this was the first time she had any inclination of the truth of her husband's proclivities, and therefore the lie of their union, she did not rage at him or break down. Instead, she retreated, instantly and forevermore, back into the self-protecting shell she had been living in before her marriage. "It's perfectly alright," she told Charles. "It doesn't matter. I understand

---

1. Some sources say that she was twelve; others say that she was fifteen.

2. Higham, *Charles Laughton*, 24.

3. Higham, 24; Lanchester, *Elsa Lanchester, Herself*, 97.

it. Don't worry about it."[4] Upon hearing these words, Charles cried even more. Dell joined them in the living room, and they all drank in silence.

The case came to court, but a judge who was, as Simon Callow puts it, "either very naïve, very worldly-wise—or gay," dismissed the case with a warning to Charles about his "misguided generosity."[5] The case was reported briefly in the local newspaper, but Charles's name was not mentioned. The closest hint to his involvement published in his lifetime was in a strange little article from 1939:

> Charles Laughton . . . had still only three loves in his life—his wife, his work, and the "under dog." Only he and his wife, Elsa Lanchester, know exactly to what extent his hand is moved to his pocket by his heart in efforts to lighten the load of men struggling for existence, but at least one London magistrate felt justified in rebuking him for his promiscuous charity. I think Charles and Elsa must be one of the happiest couples in the theatrical world.[6]

Perhaps it is only with hindsight that this paragraph seems to be almost bursting at the seams with innuendo, but it provides an insight into the constant fear Charles must have felt that someone would discover his secret. Now that Elsa knew, they were bound together much as her parents had been all those years earlier, in an unhealthy dependence lined with resentment that would only increase as the years passed. At the time, they only discussed the matter on one further occasion. Charles confessed that he had had sex with a man on the couch in their flat, to which Elsa's response was, "Fine, okay, but get rid of the sofa."[7]

Much later, Elsa would wonder whether her muted reaction, her lack of hysteria and anger, had actually made things worse. She wrote, "Perhaps my overtolerance in the beginning did Charles—and me—more harm than good. If only I had known all this before we were married it might have been very different, one way or another. But the deception is what hurt so deeply."[8]

Immediately following Charles's revelation, Jeffrey Dell suggested that they all take a two-week trip to Salzburg together, to pick up the pieces and to prepare mentally for the upcoming rehearsals of *Payment Deferred*. Elsa refused to go, saying she couldn't stomach the hypocrisy, so Dell, Eileen Weatherstone, and Charles went without her. While he was away, Charles wrote a letter to Elsa that shows his agonized state of mind:

---

4. Lanchester, *Elsa Lanchester, Herself*, 97.
5. Callow, *Charles Laughton*, 39.
6. *Liverpool Daily Post*, January 28, 1939.
7. Lanchester, *Elsa Lanchester, Herself*, 98. See also Callow, *Charles Laughton*, 39; Higham, *Charles Laughton*, 25; Mank, *Women in Horror Films*, 302.
8. Lanchester, *Elsa Lanchester, Herself*, 98.

Through these last two days when we have arrived at our hotel in the evening, in the mornings, and in fact at all times when I have been alone, the refrain has been going through my head: "She's married a bugger, she's married to a bugger, she's married to a bugger," and then you saying to me, "and to think this has happened to me," as you did once. And I know Elsa what matters most in life to me is to face it with you. I don't care and I know now I never will care so much as I did about doing but only about being . . . our parting at Victoria was a very sad one this time darling, wasn't it? We seemed to be reaching out to each other all the time inside. Ever since I left you the side that belongs to you has been sad and listless.[9]

The guilt and anguish that Charles felt served him well in *Payment Deferred*, which opened at St. James's Theatre on May 4, 1931, and was described as "one long nervous nightmare."[10] Critic A. E. Wilson wrote with innocent insight about Charles's performance: "There was a moment when, thinking his wife has discovered his secret, he collapses in hysteria. Here was an utter abandonment to funk and terror, no detail was spared. The sight of the quivering, blubbering wretch aroused mingled feelings of disgust and pity."[11]

Elsa's reviews were good. *The Stage* celebrated the fact that she was "at last seen in a straightforward part," and *The Sphere* wrote that she had "shed her quaint little tricks and successfully struck out a new line as the daughter."[12] But despite the long-awaited critical acclaim for a serious role, Elsa could not enjoy the play. Looking back on it, she said that "it seemed to be raining every day during the production. It was such a dreary time because it was such a dreary play."[13]

During performances, when Charles was onstage, Elsa would have long talks with Jeffrey Dell, who became the only person to whom she could express her true feelings at this time. Elsa later claimed, "We had actually a sort of quietly passionate time—not actually an affair. It was partly because there was no opportunity. . . . If it had been convenient, there might have been."[14] It is not clear what constitutes a "quietly passionate time," but this would not be the last time that Elsa would come close to having an affair, only to steer just clear. Perhaps the attention made her feel desirable, and that was enough.

Although it received good reviews, *Payment Deferred* was too dark for most audiences, and so after three months producer Gilbert Miller decided to close the

9. Quoted in Callow, *Charles Laughton*, 283–84.
10. *Daily Herald*, May 5, 1931.
11. *The Star*, quoted in Lanchester, *Elsa Lanchester, Herself*, 98.
12. *The Stage*, May 7, 1931; *The Sphere*, May 16, 1931.
13. Lanchester, *Charles Laughton and I*, 91.
14. Lanchester, *Elsa Lanchester, Herself*, 98.

show in London and move it to Broadway. Elsa and Charles would both remain in the cast.

In the time between closing in London and opening in New York, Elsa and Charles went on a month-long holiday with Jeffrey Dell and Eileen Weatherstone. They then returned to London, where they kept themselves busy attending a private screening of *The Flying Fool* (1929) and arranging to give up the Percy Street flat. The reason for this, according to Elsa, was that an Indian restaurant had opened on the ground floor and the smell of spices had become overwhelming. However, the decision to live elsewhere was surely prompted by the desire to rid themselves of a place that would be forever tainted by what had occurred there. Composer Constant Lambert, who had just been appointed conductor and musical director of the Vic-Wells Ballet, took over the lease, and Elsa and Charles prepared to leave for New York.

They traveled from Southampton on September 2, 1931, on the RMS *Olympic*, a White Star Line vessel whose sister ship had been the *Titanic*. With their producer Gilbert Miller paying for their first-class passage and without the worry of line learning and character preparation, Elsa and Charles were free to enjoy the luxury on offer. They enjoyed themselves in other ways as well; Elsa recalled that they brought with them a pornographic book to read together, claiming with a hint of innuendo, "We were getting along fine in those days, despite the sofa incident."[15] It seems that Elsa was not willing to give up on the physical side of her marriage, and this was an attempt to move things forward in that department. How successful this effort was in the short term we will never know, but as the ship got closer to its destination, Elsa and Charles started to worry that the book would be discovered among their possessions at customs, and so they decided to rid themselves of it by tearing out the pages and throwing them overboard. However, the wind was against them, and the boat docked in New York with the pages sticking to its sides.

Despite some trepidation about the infamous Ellis Island, Elsa and Charles were greeted warmly by reporters and photographers before being taken in a taxi to the Hotel Chatham, where Iris Barry awaited them, bearing bathtub gin and words of wisdom. While Charles was reading through a stack of telephone messages, Iris told Elsa, "Now you're in America, Towser, don't trust anyone—even your own mother. And don't forget, the only thing that counts is the dollar."[16] Unhappy in her failing marriage, Iris found solace in drinking despite Prohibition, and she was soon unconscious in Elsa and Charles's hotel room. "She smelled like a polecat," Elsa observed. "The gin was coming out of her skin."[17]

Payment Deferred opened out of town on September 21, 1931, at the Playhouse in Wilmington, Delaware, and its planned move to Broadway's Lyceum

---

15. Lanchester, 100.

16. Quoted in Lanchester, 101.

17. Lanchester, 101.

Theatre was postponed from September 24 to September 30 due to an unseasonable heat wave. When the critics finally got to see the play, they liked what they saw. The lion's share of the praise went to Charles, as it had in London, with little attention paid to the rest of the cast, although J. Brooks Atkinson of *The New York Times* did remark on Elsa's "nervous gayety."[18] Despite the superlative-laden reviews, the play proved too heavy going for Depression-era audiences, and it closed on November 1, after seventy performances. Charles's critical acclaim had not gone unnoticed, though, and offers began to flood in from all the major Hollywood studios. Elsa and Charles were determined that he should maintain creative control over the parts he played, which was not something the studios (Warner Brothers, Universal, and Metro-Goldwyn-Mayer [MGM]) were offering. Elsa wrote in a letter to Jeffrey Dell:

> The big film companies are all trying to buy Charles's body as if it's a bit of steak—they haven't even seen him act in most cases. C. is in a strong position with them as the stage will always come first and he *will not* be bought by the films for any money in the world. He came back yesterday a sweating wreck after being rude to the head of Metro Goldwyn Mayer!! I don't know what will happen—for my part I shall not stay here long. I'm very white, covered in spots, feel faint, and my feet hurt!!! So there![19]

But Elsa was not heading home just yet; *Payment Deferred* was to have a three-week run in Chicago beginning on November 30. Although Charles's research into Al Capone for *On the Spot* caused them some initial apprehension about the city, the Laughtons loved Chicago. The winter weather was in full force, so that ropes were strung between the lampposts to hold on to while walking along the street, and Elsa and Charles spent much of their time in a hotel suite with a kitchen, which enabled Elsa to prepare food to their liking. Charles Higham mentions in his biography of Laughton that while in Chicago, the couple was "forced to attend a horrible party in which pornographic and gynecological films were shown," but this appears to be the only low point of their stay.[20]

Back in New York, Charles and Elsa went backstage to meet the actress Ruth Gordon, and a close and lasting friendship followed. She was at the time living with theatrical wunderkind Jed Harris (with whom she had a child, although they would never marry), and Elsa recalls pleasant evenings spent with the couple in their brownstone. During these evenings, Charles was persuaded by Harris to appear again as Hercule Poirot in a Broadway version of Agatha Christie's *Alibi*,

18. *The New York Times*, October 1, 1931.
19. Letter from Elsa Lanchester to Jeffrey Dell, undated but written on Hotel Chatham notepaper so can be dated to October 1931. Used with permission from Simon Dell. Emphasis in the original.
20. Higham, *Charles Laughton*, 30.

to be retitled *Fatal Alibi*. Jed Harris was equally admired and despised in New York, and Charles would quickly join the ranks of those who loathed working with the bullying, abrasive director. Depressed by the way he was being treated at work, Charles began to take his frustrations out on Elsa.

In a letter to Jeffrey Dell, Charles made the cryptic remark, "Elsa has, thank god, found a young man to accompany her songs (so probably her acute depression will vanish)."[21] This may have been a reference to Elsa's friendship with Joseph Losey, the stage manager on *Payment Deferred*, who would later become a noted director and screenwriter. During the rehearsals for *Fatal Alibi*, Losey would take Elsa's side after her clashes with Charles, and he and his friend John Hammond introduced her to the seamier side of New York nightlife, taking her to see jazz musicians in tiny, smoke-filled clubs. Although Elsa claimed that Charles only accompanied them once, staying away because "Harlem frightened him," and Callow writes that Charles "preferred to stay home, brooding and angry," John Hammond remembered it differently, writing in his autobiography: "Night after night Charles and his wife, Elsa Lanchester, went to Harlem to listen to Billie [Holiday]. Billie's appeal to theatrical people, the gay crowd, and others outside the social norm was tremendous."[22]

As Charles's behavior toward Elsa hardened, she took refuge in her friendship with Joe Losey. Again, like her relationship with Jeffrey Dell, this is one of Elsa's near affairs. This time, things were prevented from progressing further by Losey's coming down with the mumps; although they continued to write to each other and speak on the phone, Elsa was to return to England before his recovery. She later said that "if Joe hadn't got the mumps, we might have become involved—two lost angry people floating around, overshadowed by Charles."[23]

Fatal Alibi opened at the Booth Theatre in New York on February 1, 1932, and although Elsa was there for the opening, she returned to England during its run; sailing alone on the *Majestic*, she landed back in Southampton on February 25. Before they left for New York, Elsa and Charles had seen plans drawn up by Clough Williams-Ellis for a country cottage to be built next to Stapledown, with the intention of having somewhere for the help to live, and Elsa returned to see the cottage finished and the couple they had hired prior to their departure living there. Elsa was delighted to be home, and even more so when she heard the news that *Fatal Alibi* was to close in New York on March 1 and that Charles would soon be heading back to England. However, when he docked at Southampton on March 22, he already suspected that his time on home soil would be brief.

---

21. Letter from Charles Laughton to Jeffrey Dell, undated but written on Hotel Chatham notepaper so can be dated to October 1931. Used with permission from Simon Dell.

22. Lanchester, *Elsa Lanchester, Herself*, 102; Callow, *Charles Laughton*, 44; Hammond, *John Hammond on Record*, 119.

23. Lanchester, *Elsa Lanchester, Herself*, 102.

As his ship, the *Europa*, had pulled away from New York, Charles had received a telegram from Jesse Lasky at Paramount, offering him what he'd been waiting for: a three-year contract for two films a year, with Charles being able to choose his parts. As soon as he was on dry land, Charles was on the phone, sending telegraphs and trying to decide what to do. His frenzy of activity was chronicled in the press:

> Mr. Laughton only arrived in London on the Tuesday . . . , spent a couple of days with his wife in the quaint house they have built for themselves in the tree-tops, came back to London, decided at 11 o'clock on Friday night to accept the film of-fer, and [they] were off to America on Saturday by the boat which had brought Mr. Laughton over. . . . I am told that Mr. Charles Laughton and his wife, Miss Elsa Lanchester, went off to Hollywood at such short notice that they and their friends literally had to sit up all night packing their belongings in order to catch their boat.[24]

The neatly typed passenger list for the *Europa* bears witness to the last-minute nature of their journey, with their names added in pencil at the bottom. Years later, Elsa would write about that journey in late March 1932: "at the back of both our minds was the thought that we might get home to see the last of the bluebells around the hut and the cottage in May. We left with light hearts and no knowledge of the film business."[25]

24. *Belfast News-Letter*, March 31, 1932.
25. Lanchester, *Charles Laughton and I*, 98.

10   Less Than Dust

When the curtain fell on the Chicago production of *Payment Deferred* in December 1931, little did Elsa know that she would not appear on the stage again for nearly two years, and would not work at all for eighteen months. For six months, from April to September 1932, she would be an out-of-work actress in Hollywood, watching from the wings as Charles was feted and fussed over, shooting film after film. It was an experience that nearly broke her.

Elsa and Charles traveled from New York to California by train, with a stop to visit the Grand Canyon on the way. After a couple of nights at the Beverly Wilshire hotel, they were taken to the house that Paramount had found for them in the Hollywood Hills, the very last house on La Brea Terrace, with a back garden that led out onto a wild hillside. The publicity men came to take photographs of Charles, and Elsa was included in some, although she was surprised when they asked her not to smoke in the pictures for fear of alienating Charles's future fans, who might feel such behavior to be inappropriate for a woman.

Despite the hurry to get him to Hollywood, Charles's first movie for Paramount, *Devil and the Deep* (1932), was delayed, so he was loaned out to Universal to appear in a horror movie directed by James Whale and co-starring Boris Karloff and Ernest Thesiger, just as would happen for Elsa a few years later. Charles's film was called *The Old Dark House* (1932), and after filming was finished for the day, several of the British cast and crew would come over to Elsa and Charles's house to enjoy a meal prepared by their houseman Rogers, who also performed the roles of cook and chauffer. Although Elsa enjoyed having people to talk to, Charles's dislike for his director and co-stars presumably made these gatherings somewhat awkward affairs. Charles felt that Whale was vulgar and showy, and he inexplicably never got on with Karloff; another co-star, Lilian Bond, "came over to La Brea Terrace in her pretentious automobile, with a mother the Laughtons never really warmed to."[1] Although Charles found Thesiger "aggravatingly mannered,"[2] Elsa described him as "a delightful laugh for anyone who saw him

---

1.   Higham, *Charles Laughton*, 32.
2.   Higham, 32.

or talked to him—a weird, strange character! Very acid-tongued—not a nasty person at all, just *acid!*"[3] She remembered Thesiger presenting her with forbidden fruit when he turned up on their doorstep brandishing two full-size yuccas after picking them and carrying them down Hollywood Boulevard. The picking of yuccas from the hills was strictly prohibited, and Elsa recalls Thesiger's joy at having gotten away with his "crime."

Although Elsa would later reside in Hollywood by choice, it was certainly not love at first sight, and—as is often the case—her insecurity manifested as a kind of cultural snobbery. She mocked the architecture by calling it "Late Marzipan" or simply "horrifying," and claimed the workmanship on her locally made clothes was "pathetic."[4] American food, she declared, was "odd," and there was too much choice—California's climate meant seasonal fruits were available year-round, which rendered food uninteresting. "I tried Coca-Cola and chewing gum," she concluded, "but in those early days in Hollywood I never lowered my Union Jack."[5]

It is very likely that much of this newfound nationalism stemmed largely from the fact that Hollywood was showing no interest whatsoever in Charles Laughton's wife. At first, this may have been what she intended: there is no evidence that she was looking for work when she arrived, and when she boarded the *Europa* in Southampton, she told a journalist that she was traveling "strictly as Mrs. Laughton. . . . No film work for me."[6] But as Charles worked twelve-hour days on the set, Elsa's loneliness and boredom threatened to overwhelm her. She recognized these dark feelings later, writing, "I found myself cut off from the world for months, which became a sort of illness, mentally. I was so unhappy, so lonely. A new country. An isolated house." In interviews, she would later refer to being treated by Hollywood as "less than dust."[7]

Occasional trips to visit Charles on the set provided variety and opportunities for socializing, but also emphasized the ever-widening gulf in their respective careers. As Simon Callow astutely observed, "Nothing is more distressing for an out-of-work actor than to visit a place of others' work. Elsa's bright, acerbic self would not take well to sympathetic enquiries. They may not even have known that she *was* an actress."[8]

Charles followed *The Old Dark House* (1932) with *Devil and the Deep* (1932), co-starring Tallulah Bankhead and Gary Cooper, and then was directed by Cecil

3.   Mank, *Women in Horror Films,* 307.

4.   Lanchester, *Charles Laughton and I,* 99; *Elsa Lanchester, Herself,* 104.

5.   Lanchester, *Elsa Lanchester, Herself,* 105; Lanchester, *Charles Laughton and I,* 106.

6.   *The People,* March 27, 1932.

7.   Lanchester, *Elsa Lanchester, Herself,* 105; *Star Tribune,* June 10, 1934.

8.   Callow, *Charles Laughton,* 54 (emphasis in original).

B. DeMille in *The Sign of the Cross* (1932). In this last, Charles played Nero as a "flaunting extravagant queen," showing shocking audacity given the prejudice of the era and his own secret sexuality.[9] He attempted to get Elsa cast as the naked young catamite who sits by Nero's side in every scene, but DeMille felt the part should be played by a man.

Charles was beginning to worry about Elsa's state of mind, and it was a relief for everyone when Iris Barry came to stay, moving into the studio apartment adjoining the Laughtons' house. Iris was seeking writing work in Hollywood, but was having as much success in capturing the town's attention as Elsa was. The two women enjoyed each other's company, going for walks along Hollywood Boulevard or being driven to see wildflowers in the desert; it seemed that things were beginning to look up.

It was thus a tremendous blow when Elsa found out that she would not be cast in MGM's film version of *Payment Deferred* (1932), even though Charles had been asked to reprise his performance as William Marble. Her anguish at being replaced by Maureen O'Sullivan is palpable in her autobiography, where she writes, "Charles joined me in my despair. I was said to be so extraordinarily good in the part—why? how could this happen? Iris said, 'That's life, Towser.' I nearly became blind with crying and wanting to scream for England and our bluebell woods."[10] It was the last straw, and Elsa made up her mind to return home. Before she did, she went to visit Irving Thalberg at MGM, to tell him that he had made a mistake. When the film came out, British reviewers agreed with her, with *The Bystander* writing, "one sadly misses Miss Elsa Lanchester," and *The Tatler* concurring that Maureen O'Sullivan was "not a patch upon" Elsa.[11]

Elsa arrived back in England on September 20, 1932, having been away for less than six months. She took a room above an Italian restaurant in London, the ceiling of which was painted with cherubs, clouds, and pink roses, and here she licked her wounds and took stock of her life.

The black mood that had settled on her in California did not lift immediately, and Elsa was consumed with feelings of failure and what she labeled "cowardice."[12] She visited Stapledown, where the familiar charms of the English woodland were a balm to her pride, and sought out the company of friends, especially John Armstrong. John was dating Benita Jaeger, whom he would later marry, and they helped Elsa pick out a London flat on Gordon Square, Bloomsbury, for when Charles returned to England.

During this period of reflection and restoration, Elsa also spent a great deal of time with her parents, especially her mother. Although she disliked it when

---

9. Review of *The Sign of the Cross* by James Agate, quoted in Callow, 53.

10. Lanchester, *Elsa Lanchester, Herself*, 107.

11. *The Bystander*, November 16, 1932; *The Tatler*, November 16, 1932.

12. Lanchester, *Elsa Lanchester, Herself*, 108.

Biddy gathered the neighbors to gawk at her, mother and daughter were the closest that they had been in years. They even took a trip to Brighton together, calling on Aunt Mary on the way, who was as eccentric as ever.

But although Elsa found comfort in the familiar faces and places of home, she still craved the security, attention, and independence that she got from working. Charles was going from hit to hit in Hollywood, following *Payment Deferred* with *Island of Lost Souls* (1932) and *If I Had a Million* (1932), and he was beginning to use his growing star power to fight for Elsa. A newspaper article published after Elsa left America read:

> Since he went to Hollywood, Laughton has been handed from one company to another, as each producer firmly believes that no production can be really successful unless it features this brilliant, podgy little man.
>
> So far so good. But Laughton is accompanied by his wife, Elsa Lanchester, an actress with talents peculiarly her own, who is tired of idling in Hollywood. So the ultimatum has gone forth. Unless work of some kind is found for his wife Charles Laughton will return to his own country, where Miss Lanchester enjoys a considerable stage reputation.[13]

It is unclear how Elsa felt about such attempts by Charles to assist in her career. Was she grateful? Embarrassed? Resentful? Simon Callow argues that "It is not quite clear to what extent Laughton tried to promote her, but the very fact that she would need 'promotion' must have been unbearable to her."[14] Although Elsa never made her feelings on the matter clear, one thing that certainly did make her angry was the people she termed the "Laughton-grabbers."[15] These were men, predominantly producers, who would cozy up to Elsa and feign an interest in furthering her career, with the sole intention of using her to snare Charles for their project. The first and greatest of these was Alexander Korda.

Born Sándor László Kellner in Hungary, Korda began his directing career in his home country before political reasons forced him to flee. By 1932, after spending time in Austria, Germany, and America, Korda was in London, where he had directed two films, the unremarkable *Service for Ladies* (1932) and *Wedding Rehearsal* (1932). But he was an ambitious man, and had set up his own production company, London Films. He made contact with Elsa in late 1932, and she went to visit him in his Grosvenor Street office, excited at the thought of finally getting back to work. Korda was witty and delightful, and Elsa was charmed by the attention and by the script he described called *A Gust of Wind*.

---

13. *Dundee Courier*, October 5, 1932.

14. Callow, *Charles Laughton*, 279.

15. Lanchester, *Elsa Lanchester, Herself*, 145.

She dutifully wrote to Charles about the script, but did not hear back. Within the week, Korda called her back into the office with an even bigger, even better proposal: he would film the story of Henry VIII's fourth wife, the German Anne of Cleves. Charles would play Henry VIII, and Elsa would play Anne, both of them title roles of sorts as the film would be called *The Fourth Wife of Henry VIII*. Delighted and excited for the first time in months, Elsa wrote to Charles again, singing Korda's praises. Once again, no reply came. Charles, Elsa knew, did not regard the British film industry as having any merit—London was where the theater work was, Hollywood was for the movies.

Charles Laughton made his triumphant return to England on December 13, 1932, and photographs of him being greeted by his wife and mother featured heavily in the press. Trips to the family home in Scarborough and to the British premiere of *The Sign of the Cross* were all detailed in the newspapers, as Charles told journalists his plan was to find work in the theater. He repeated this intention when he had a meeting with Korda, but the wily Hungarian was able to change his mind with the offer of the role of Henry VIII, "the first film role that really excited his imagination."[16]

Once Korda had Charles's signature on the contract, his attitude toward Elsa changed completely, as did the size of her role in the picture. Although *The Fourth Wife of Henry VIII* remained the film's working title during filming, another wife was introduced to the script, and then another, and the title was changed briefly to *Royal Husband* before ultimately changing to *The Private Life of Henry VIII* (1933).[17] Five of Henry's six wives feature in the picture, played by Merle Oberon (as Anne Boleyn), Wendy Barrie (Jane Seymour), Binnie Barnes (Catherine Howard), Everley Gregg (Catherine Parr), and, of course, Elsa in the comedy role as Anne of Cleves. Elsa was hurt by Korda's dismissive treatment of her. Although he was angry on her behalf, Charles got on well with the director and would have it written into his Paramount contract that he could be loaned out to make movies for London Films—something that would later cost him a lot, literally, as he would be taxed on his film star salary on both sides of the Atlantic.

Filming for *Henry VIII* began at Elstree Studios in May 1933, with Elsa and Charles's bedroom scene the first to be shot. Prior to filming, Charles had done his usual research through books, visits to art galleries, and trips to Hampton Court, and this time Elsa had been able to join in, gathering all the information she could about Anne of Cleves, learning a German accent, and practicing the

16. Higham, *Charles Laughton*, 42.

17. For mentions of the working title, see, for example, *Yorkshire Post and Leeds Intelligencer*, March 8, 1933; *Leeds Mercury*, April 13, 1933; *Pittsburgh Press*, April 3, 1933.

accent with Benita Jaeger, who had been born in Germany. John Armstrong designed the costumes for the movie.

Although Anne of Cleves is traditionally thought of as Henry's ugliest wife, the decision was made that in the film she only makes faces and pretends to be ugly to avoid intimacy with a man she is not attracted to. Indeed, wearing a blonde braided wig and exceptionally low-cut dresses, Elsa is attractive in the film. The bedroom scene where she and Charles play card games is delightful to watch—it is said they had a marvelous time filming it—and many rate this as one of her greatest performances, including Simon Callow:

> Although Elsa Lanchester is essentially of the James Whale school of acting—extraordinariness for extraordinariness' sake, of which her exceptional performance in *The Bride of Frankenstein* is the apotheosis—when working with Laughton, she often transcends her quirkiness. As Anne of Cleves she is at her very best, direct and sparkling and unexpected.[18]

Before filming was over, Charles was called back to America, where he had been cast in *White Woman* (1933) with Carole Lombard, so the schedule was adjusted to film all his scenes first, with the rest being completed after he left. Although Elsa was once again alone, this time in a temporary flat on Jermyn Street while their Gordon Square residence was being renovated, there was no melancholy mood; she was working again, and she had more work lined up: before Charles had left for California, he had made arrangements to appear in several plays at the Old Vic for the 1933/34 winter season, and Elsa was to join the company as well. Indeed, she began rehearsals for their first play of the season, *The Cherry Orchard*, while Charles was still overseas. He was sailing on the *Île de France* back to England when he received a telegram telling him to continue his journey on from Plymouth in England to Cherbourg in France. Elsa joined him at Plymouth, and together they traveled via Cherbourg to Paris to attend the premiere of *The Private Life of Henry VIII*. They arrived at the Prince de Galles Hotel at seven o'clock, with just enough time to wash, dress, and grab a sandwich before arriving at the theater by eight o'clock. Elsa had never previously attended a premiere of a film she appeared in, and she was in a state of nervous excitement, hyperaware of every sound. She later remembered, "I think my own heart beating made more noise to me than anything else."[19]

She had nothing to fear. Although the reviews were centered on Charles, Elsa was labeled "a big success" by James Agate, and praised as "the best" of the wives. The American press called the film "easily the best product ever to

---

18. Callow, *Charles Laughton*, 60.

19. Lanchester, *Charles Laughton and I*, 127; *Elsa Lanchester, Herself*, 113.

come from the English studios," and it was the first British-made movie to be a hit in the United States.[20] It must have been particularly satisfying for Elsa to read in the *Los Angeles Times*: "Next to Mr. Laughton's performance the most arresting is that contributed by Elsa Lanchester, who, as everyone in Hollywood knows, is Mrs. Laughton, but no one there apparently knew she is a scintillating comedienne."[21]

20. *The Tatler*, July 26, 1933; *Coventry Evening Telegraph*, November 2, 1933; *Los Angeles Times*, October 22, 1933.

21. *Los Angeles Times*, October 22, 1933.

Of Elsa's 1934 turn in *The Tempest*, critic James Agate wrote, "May I be forgiven for saying that until Miss Elsa Lanchester, the part of Ariel has never been acted?"

11 Learning Greek Backward

The 1933/34 season at the Old Vic was the first time either Elsa or Charles had performed in repertory theater, where a company of actors presents a series of shows, performing one in the evenings while rehearsing the next during the day. The plays chosen for the season were demanding—including several by Shakespeare—and many people at the theater felt that Charles would be out of his depth. Prominent among these was the manager of the Old Vic, Lilian Baylis, who referred to Charles as "that rich film star," and seemed to delight in his missteps.[1] Baylis seemed to feel that Charles had been foisted on her by the season's director, Tyrone Guthrie, and that because his famous name had helped the theater secure much-needed funding, she could not turn him away. If this was the attitude toward Charles, who had trained at RADA and more than proved himself in the West End and on Broadway, then we can only imagine the disdain reserved for Elsa, whose place in the company was entirely due to her being Charles's wife. If ever she needed to prove herself, now was the time.

Neither Elsa nor Charles was in the first play of the season, *Twelfth Night*, which opened in September 1933; Charles was still filming *White Woman* in Hollywood, and although no reason is given for Elsa's absence, it might be assumed that she held no value at the Vic without Charles. The company included several well-known and respected actors, including Flora Robson, Roger Livesey, Ursula Jeans, and Marius Goring, as well as a young unknown called James Mason, who certainly had a bright future ahead of him but for now was, as Elsa said with her usual self-deprecation, "in my bracket, on the second payroll."[2]

The first play in which Elsa and Charles appeared was Chekhov's masterpiece *The Cherry Orchard*, which opened in October 1933 and was considered "one of the Vic's peak successes."[3] Charles had only attended a few rehearsals, and critical comments suggested that he did not seem entirely at ease. Elsa, cast as the eccentric Charlotta, fared better. Her performance was said to give "a haunting

---

1. Quoted in Lanchester, *Elsa Lanchester, Herself*, 116.

2. Lanchester, 121.

3. Williams, *Old Vic Saga*, 128–29.

impression of loveliness," but overall she received little press attention.⁴ During
the run of *The Cherry Orchard*, the London premiere of *The Private Life of Henry
VIII* was held at the Leicester Square Theatre. It took place on a Monday so that
the Laughtons could attend, as there were no Monday performances at the Old
Vic. However, they were a little embarrassed when they discovered that it had
been arranged for Charles to watch the film in the front row of the dress circle,
surrounded by the five actresses who had played his wives. Elsa wrote of the
event, "I don't think this polygamous evening was very pleasant for Charles, and
I certainly didn't care for an enforced night in a harem any more than Henry's
other wives did."⁵ But however awkward they may have felt, the cast members
were all delighted to take a bow on the stage after the film was finished, enjoying
the audience's enthusiastic reaction.

The next two plays at the Old Vic were both works by Shakespeare, and
Elsa's role in each was small. In *Henry VIII*—in which Charles, of course, played
Henry—she was a lady in waiting and sang Linley's "Orpheus with his Lute"
with "a delicate sweetness," while in *Measure for Measure* she sang "Take, O take
those lips away" as a page boy and also played the small role of Juliet.⁶

Although she was not making much of an impression in such parts, Elsa was
enjoying herself immensely. The snobbish attitudes of the management toward
her and Charles had not filtered through to the other actors in the company, and
Elsa delighted in the hard work and camaraderie of repertory theater. After rehearsing the next production from half past ten in the morning until four or five
in the afternoon, Elsa and Charles would dash back to their Jermyn Street flat
for dinner, before returning to the theater for curtain up at eight o'clock. After the
show, with the whole cast exhilarated and wide awake, everyone would pile into
the Laughtons' small rooms, where they would "sit shoulder to shoulder, drinking
beer and eating cold tongue and salad and talk[ing] about the theatre until two
in the morning" before dispersing.⁷ Then they would wake at half past nine and
begin again.

With their American houseman Rogers to drive and prepare the Laughtons'
meals, and Sundays and Mondays spent at Stapledown, Elsa would view this as
one of the happiest times of her life. Things were about to get even better.

Elsa's star turn in the Old Vic season, which would be remembered fondly by
theater critics for decades afterward, was as Ariel in *The Tempest*. Ariel is an "airy
spirit" who serves the magician Prospero, played in this production by Charles.
If playing in Shakespeare was difficult for Charles with his drama school background, then it must have been a terrifying challenge for Elsa, who was not only

4.   Guthrie, *A Life in the Theatre*, 113.

5.   Lanchester, *Elsa Lanchester, Herself*, 114; see also Lanchester, *Charles Laughton and I*,
      128.

6.   *The Tatler*, November 22, 1933.

7.   Lanchester, *Charles Laughton and I*, 136.

lacking in theatrical training, but had barely any formal education at all. Regarding her difficulty with the script, she said: "I sat with [director Tyrone Guthrie] for hours, trying to interpret one great long speech that was very confusing. It was a little like learning ten alphabets in Greek backward. . . . I've read and reread that speech, and to this day I still cannot understand most of it."[8]

It did not hold her back. Dressed in a short silver tunic, Elsa as Ariel outshone everyone on the stage, including her husband. James Agate wrote, "May I be forgiven for saying that until Miss Elsa Lanchester, the part of Ariel has never been acted?" A myriad of superlatives followed, before he concluded, "in short, it is a lovely performance of exquisite invention."[9] Charles Morgan in *The Times* declared Elsa's Ariel to be "a rare creature with extreme swiftness, lightness, vitality, grace, such a translation of airy imagination to bodily form as the stage is seldom blessed with." Other critics agreed, with her performance described as "a marked success," "entirely delightful," "exquisite," and "quite perfect."[10] The credit was all hers: Guthrie would later claim that his own "feeble and confused" direction resulted in "the worst production of *The Tempest* ever achieved," with the exception of Elsa's "weird and lyrical" Ariel, "which was at odds with everything else in the production and which better direction would never have permitted."[11]

But despite the near-universal praise she received, the management at the Old Vic was not about to relax its stance of condescending disapproval. Looking back on the season, company director Harcourt Williams wrote, "Elsa Lanchester gave a highly stylized interpretation of Ariel. The pitfall awaiting those who indulge in that particular form of art is that the spectator too often is set thinking about the style instead of the character and its relation to the play."[12] Thankfully, holders of such views were in the minority, with most instead feeling, as one reviewer put it, that "Miss Lanchester's future prognosticates itself in glamour and promise." Elsa herself would sum up her experience by saying, "In *The Tempest* I began to learn to act rather than perform."[13]

The Russian dancer and producer Nicholas Sergeyev saw Elsa in *The Tempest* and was inspired to cast her in the show he was putting on at the Vic-Wells Ballet (predecessor to the English National Ballet), the first production of *The Nutcracker* ever staged in the West. This production was also notable for the professional debut of Margot Fonteyn, who played a snowflake. Elsa performed the "Danse Arabe," and the reviewer for *The Times* declared that she "scored another

---

8. Lanchester, *Elsa Lanchester, Herself*, 199.

9. Quoted in Lanchester, 120.

10. *The Times,* January 11, 1934; *The Stage,* January 11, 1934; *The Tatler,* January 17, 1934; *The Sketch,* January 17, 1934; *The Sphere,* January 13, 1934.

11. Guthrie, *A Life in the Theatre*, 114.

12. Williams, *Old Vic Saga*, 132.

13. *The Sketch,* January 24, 1934; Lanchester, *Elsa Lanchester, Herself,* 118.

success" in the role.[14] Photographs of her in costume show her at perhaps her most beautiful; wearing a midriff-exposing top and translucent skirt, she strikes a graceful pose with utmost confidence, despite admitting that the entire experience was extremely nerve-wracking. From performing Shakespeare alongside trained actors, and outshining them, to dancing alongside prima ballerinas, Elsa was more than making up for her years in the professional wilderness.

However, as the cliché tells us, pride comes before a fall, and Elsa's next appearance in the Old Vic season was roundly condemned as one of her all-time worst performances. Doubtlessly miscast as the governess Miss Prism in *The Importance of Being Earnest*, Elsa was likely also simply overwhelmed by the volume of work: she was appearing in *The Tempest* at night while rehearsing *The Importance of Being Earnest* and her part in *The Nutcracker* during the day, and she was also cast in Alexander Korda's next film, *The Private Life of Don Juan* (1934), around this time. When the curtain opened on *The Importance of Being Earnest*, Elsa was not ready. She admitted later that she forgot her lines frequently "and used to appeal to the prompter, not caring a hoot what the audience thought of me. I just stood and said 'What' and got practically my whole part from him in a sort of despairing condition."[15] Such unprofessional behavior was unlike Elsa, and seems more likely to have stemmed from exhaustion than from indifference. Some critics were forgiving, with *The Stage* reporting that although she had "been seen to greater advantage," Elsa "made some capital out of the oddities of the blameless spinster, Miss Prism."[16] James Agate, however, was relentless, writing, "This young actress was recently said by me to have given one of the most beautiful performances I had ever seen; and now she gives very nearly, and I really think quite, the worst!"[17]

Elsa's state of mind during this production was not helped by the practical jokes that were played on her during the run, a common-enough occurrence in repertory theater, but not something that Elsa enjoyed or had the quick-thinking improvisational skills to deal with. Fellow performer Roger Livesey was the chief culprit. One night he placed stage weights into a bag that Elsa had to pick up; although Livesey carried the bag onto the stage as if it weighed nothing, Elsa was quite unable to lift it and had to finish the scene from a kneeling position on the floor. After that, she said, "I had a fear that every prop I touched would jump into my face or be glued fast to the stage."[18]

This production was enough to undo the confidence Elsa had gained from *The Tempest*. "On the last night I think I had a good cry when I got to bed," she would later say. "Nothing is quite so lowering as being a miscast character actress,

14. *The Times*, February 1, 1934.

15. Lanchester, *Charles Laughton and I*, 136.

16. *The Stage*, February 8, 1934.

17. Callow, *Charles Laughton*, 73.

18. Lanchester, *Elsa Lanchester, Herself*, 118.

especially when you have just begun to gain sufficient confidence to feel that you can portray anything."[19]

Thankfully, the next play of the season was William Congreve's Restoration comedy *Love for Love*, which was of the sort of bawdy humor that had once been Elsa's bread and butter. She was cast as the young Miss Prue, who is seduced by the fop Mr. Tattle, played by Charles. Elsa relished being able to sink her teeth into this role. The scenes in which Mr. Tattle and Miss Prue appeared together were so laden with innuendo and double entendres that previous productions had been obliged to censor them dramatically. However, because Elsa and Charles were married in real life, such naughtiness was seemingly more permissible, and the production was an enormous success. The reviewer for *The Era* wrote: "The scene between [Charles Laughton] and Elsa Lanchester, during which, as the affected and licentious Mr. Tattle, he instructs her, as the crude country girl, in the art of subtle love-making, is probably the most amusing scene on the stage in London at the moment," while *The Observer* called Elsa's Miss Prue "deliciously absurd."[20] Although the theater's management largely disapproved of the tone of the piece, Tyrone Guthrie recalled that "the uproarious enjoyment of packed houses buttressed Miss Baylis against the disapproval of some of her governors, who made strong objections to what they considered a licentious play."[21]

Love for Love would be Elsa's final play of the season, so despite her ups and downs, she had the satisfaction of ending on a high note. The same could not be said for Charles, whose performance in the title role of *Macbeth* was not well received, being described by Harcourt Williams as "more of the Sassenach tradesman than the Highland laird."[22] On the last night of *Macbeth*, which closed out the season, Charles was heckled from the gallery, with one person shouting, "Why don't you bring your wife up?" Charles replied, "Many people have tried to do that, my friend, but none have succeeded."[23]

It is not clear how well Charles and Elsa got along during their Old Vic season. Although they both enjoyed their individual moments of acclaim, Elsa's habit of what she viewed as constructive criticism cannot always have been welcomed. An example can be found in her appraisal of Charles's Macbeth:

> For an actor like John Gielgud, who has a talent for speaking verse, I imagine a sense of achievement is possible; but for Charles, whose talents do not lie in that direction, there can only be a feeling of disappointment. . . . In *Macbeth*, I think Charles got the murderer and I think he got the husband, but I do not think he got the soldier and he certainly could not speak the verse; the sense was thrust far

---

19. Lanchester, *Charles Laughton and I*, 139.

20. *The Era*, March 28, 1934; *The Observer*, March 11, 1934.

21. Guthrie, *A Life in the Theatre*, 114.

22. Williams, *Old Vic Saga*, 133.

23. Higham, *Charles Laughton*, 51; Callow, *Charles Laughton*, 80.

in advance of the rhythm . . . he would give his right arm to be able to speak verse with the grace and ease and power of John Gielgud.[24]

If Elsa was willing to publish this opinion in 1938, when Charles was truly a global celebrity, then we can assume she was not shy about making her views known during the season, all the while claiming that she was trying to be helpful. Charles recognized that Elsa's barbed remarks were "salutary and invariably thought out for my own good—like castor oil in childhood," but that does not mean he enjoyed taking the medicine.[25]

Another example of Elsa's curiously heavy-handed approach to Charles's feelings came on that final night of *Macbeth*. It was a tradition for the last-night audiences at the Old Vic to show their appreciation for their favorite actors by placing small gifts on the stage for them at curtain call. Elsa was concerned that due to the tensions between the Vic old guard and the man they viewed as a Hollywood interloper, Charles would not receive anything, so she bought three presents—flowers, fruit, and a book—and wrapped them in different ways, so that they would appear to have come from three individual admirers. Her fears were confirmed, and those three presents were the only ones Charles received. Elsa remembered being "very glad that I had done this as he would have felt exceedingly lonely with nothing to hold when he took his bow."[26] But such kindly sensitivity went out the window when Charles came off the stage and Elsa immediately informed him of the true source of his gifts. His reaction to the news was allegedly a muttered, "Well, I'll be damned"; he had genuinely thought that people cared for him. As Simon Callow pertinently remarked, for someone to buy the gifts as she did "suggests a wifely devotion of the most touching variety. For her to then *tell* him suggests the opposite."[27] I would add that to then publish her account of the event four years later seems to indicate that Elsa did not think there was anything unusual or hurtful about her actions. This odd combination of kindness and cruelty, devotion and disregard would continue throughout the marriage.

---

24. Lanchester, *Charles Laughton and I*, 140–41.

25. Laughton, introduction to Lanchester, 7.

26. Lanchester, 142.

27. Callow, *Charles Laughton*, 81 (emphasis in original).

12 Nothing to Lose

Throughout their Old Vic season, the flat that Elsa and Charles had bought at Thirty-Four Gordon Square was being renovated. This work was a family affair of sorts: the architect Wells Coates, who had designed the sets at the Vic, was tasked with modernizing the oppressive Victorian rooms into something more airy and open, and John Armstrong, who had been in charge of costumes at the theater, helped with decoration. Elsa was very proud of the spacious flat, calling it "the most perfect home that I have ever seen," but no sooner was it finished, than the couple was on the move again, back to Hollywood.[1]

The Laughtons' journey was another rushed affair, with Elsa lamenting that they always had to leave in such a hurry that she was forced to pack dirty clothes. To speed things up, it was decided that the couple would take an airplane from New York to Hollywood, which in 1934 meant a twenty-three-hour journey and six changes of aircraft. Charles had previously flown from Hollywood to New York and was able to convince a reluctant Elsa of the ease and comfort of such a mode of transport, only to be proved immediately wrong by a series of flights plagued by turbulence and bad weather. Convinced that the end was nigh, Elsa and Charles sat silently, clasping each other's hands as the plane dove and rocked. The experience put Elsa's usually steely nerves on edge for several days afterward, and she declared that "unless somebody were dying at the other end I would not travel by 'plane again."[2] They were met at the airport on one of their stops by playwright Thornton Wilder.

The work they were rushing toward was, of course, Charles's. During the run of *The Tempest* at the Old Vic, someone had pinned a telegram to the notice board that informed Charles that he had been awarded the Academy Award for Best Actor for his role in *The Private Life of Henry VIII*. Although neither Charles nor Elsa understood the award's significance, as it had only been established a few years earlier, Hollywood knew what it meant. Charles was big box office, and he was swiftly signed up for two films, *The Barretts of Wimpole Street* (1934) and *David Copperfield* (1935), at the greatest studio of them all, MGM.

---

1. Lanchester, *Charles Laughton and I*, 190.

2. Lanchester, 147.

Presenting a united front: Charles and Elsa on arrival in
New York, 1934.   *Everett Collection Inc. / Alamy Stock Photo*

Although Elsa had enjoyed critical praise for her role in *Henry*, this did not immediately lead to offers of work, something she put down to the fact that she had made herself look as ugly as possible in the film. "I had done my best to look like hell," she remarked, adding that "the cameraman lit my nose so that it would look like a potato—knobbier than usual at the tip. And I spoke with an accent of the most guttural kind, and wore a straight blonde wig."[3] Although she had been far from unappealing in the film, Elsa's looks were certainly never going to make her a glamorous leading lady, as one writer remarked:

> Taking after her father, her face was so full of characteristic features there hardly seemed to be room for them all: the large, dark, googly eyes, the oddly blunted nose, the uneven teeth, the dimpled chin, not to mention what Arnold Bennett described in 1924 as a "wonderful shock of copper hair." In her youth, the total effect was not unpleasing, for all its lack of classic lines and conventional beauty.[4]

Unfortunately for Elsa, it was conventional beauty that filmmakers wanted. Elsa's more glamorous co-stars from *The Private Life of Henry VIII*, Merle Oberon and Binnie Barnes, also graced the screen in Alexander Korda's next film in the "Private Lives" series, *The Private Life of Don Juan* (1934). This movie starred the aging silent movie idol Douglas Fairbanks Senior in what would be his last picture. Elsa's involvement in this film is unclear; she was certainly cast in the role of a maid, and several staged publicity photographs show her alongside Fairbanks and assorted actresses as part of a harem that would put Henry VIII's to shame.[5] She also featured in a BBC radio broadcast made at Elstree Studios during the filming, where she was interviewed alongside other members of the cast. However, she is not credited in the film itself, and it is impossible to glimpse her in it. The role of the maid, which is the kind of comedy role that Elsa might have been cast in, is played by Binnie Barnes. Was Elsa replaced? Or did she play a smaller role that ended up on the cutting room floor?

Strangely, two other members of the Old Vic company were also involved in the movie but do not appear in the final cut; Flora Robson had her scenes deleted, and James Mason—who was to make his film debut in the picture—did not last long on the set and was recast.[6] Whatever the story behind Elsa's removal from the film, it was unlikely to improve her opinion of Korda, whom she already disliked for his previous dismissive attitude toward her.

With such disappointment in British films, Elsa turned her attention to raising her status in American movies instead. Things seemed to be looking up in

---

3.   Lanchester, *Elsa Lanchester, Herself*, 115.

4.   Nissen, *Actresses of a Certain Character*, 92.

5.   See, for example, *The Era*, February 7, 1934; *Miami Herald*, March 16, 1934; *Lancaster New Era*, April 17, 1934.

6.   Morely, *Odd Man Out*, 30.

May 1934 when influential gossip columnist Louella Parsons wrote: "Leave it to Irving Thalberg to grab Elsa Lanchester (Mrs. Charles Laughton) when two or three other producers were trying to make up their minds to sign her. Irving works like that. Miss Lanchester will make her screen debut with Norma Shearer in 'Marie Antoinette.' She will play the Countess Gabrielle de Polignac, the close friend of the ill-fated queen."[7] This was typical Hollywood hokum; Elsa was not the focus of any kind of bidding war among producers. She was given a "courtesy contract" with MGM of $150 weekly, which she later dismissed as "a little nothing of a contract. Just to keep me busy, since Charles was here," but through her husband she was beginning to make some influential acquaintances.[8] Chief among these was legendary MGM producer Irving Thalberg and his movie star wife, Norma Shearer, who was starring alongside Charles in *The Barretts of Wimpole Street*. Elsa would visit Thalberg in his office, where he would take time out of his busy schedule to offer her advice and to help her. Although he, like other producers, was primarily concerned with keeping Charles Laughton happy and working, Thalberg did not make Elsa feel unwanted or incidental. As well as instructing her on what parts she could play and what was involved in taking a screen test, Thalberg also gave Elsa valuable advice about her appearance:

> Often I used to walk into Thalberg's office after being out on the beach, with my hair all cockled up from the ocean, wearing ragamuffin-length coveralls. Once, when I had an interview with another producer, Thalberg said to me, "I must tell you, Elsa, that you cannot go and see other producers like this. Do something with your hair and wear a skirt." So I smoothed down my hair and wore a suit, realizing that Thalberg had given me some very good practical advice.[9]

Although the promised work did not begin immediately—the planned *Marie Antoinette* was delayed, and was finally completed after Thalberg's untimely death in 1936, without Elsa in the cast—Elsa and Charles were beginning to make more of an effort to fit in with their Hollywood contemporaries. Rather than remaining in their isolated bungalow on La Brea Terrace, they took up residence at the infamous Garden of Allah Hotel, which Elsa described as being "peopled with the famous and hangers-on, the hopeful and a few forlorn locus eaters," and they began attending industry parties.[10] They enjoyed the mixture of English, American, and Chinese cuisines provided by director Harry Lachman and his wife, Jue Quon Tai; and they rubbed shoulders with stars including Jean Harlow and Maurice Chevalier at a party given by Jeanette MacDonald, at which Elsa was described as "a combination Hepburn and Dietrich in a white-trousered

7.   *San Francisco Examiner*, May 23, 1934.

8.   Mank, *Women in Horror Films*, 304.

9.   Lanchester, *Elsa Lanchester, Herself*, 126.

10. Lanchester, 128.

suit."[11] An evening at the home of Kay Francis was less of a success, with the actress acting in a manner that was "boringly, absurdly hostessy," constantly correcting her guests and demanding silence when she was speaking.[12] Elsa's favorite parties by far were those held at Thalberg and Shearer's Santa Monica beach house, which she claimed were the only parties at which she felt comfortable. Sometimes these would be dinner parties, and at other times a movie would be premiered exclusively for guests. At one party Elsa noticed that the grunions were spawning, an event exclusive to South California, at which silvery fish come up onto the beach to breed by the hundreds after the full moon. Elsa dashed out onto the beach, hiking up her evening gown, and wandered happily among the squirming fish. Charles joined her, as did the actress Jeanette MacDonald, whom Elsa would remember fondly as "an unaffected, gay, and natural person who seemed to enjoy being successful and famous."[13]

The Laughtons were starting to see their names in print regularly (perhaps in no small measure due to the MGM publicity team assigned to them). Elsa was often presented in the press as a comic and a caution; she interrupted one interview of Charles's to remark, "I say, Charles, why don't you tell him about that time in Yorkshire when you hit three ducks with your bicycle and we had a dinner party."[14] Their relationship was promoted as a devoted and loving one, with one newspaper reporting that Elsa arrived on *The Barretts of Wimpole Street* set daily in order to have lunch with her husband. That this was completely untrue did not seem to matter in a town where appearances were everything.

Eventually Elsa was signed to a film project at MGM. Her American debut was to be as the maid Clickett, playing opposite Charles as Mr. Micawber, in the blockbuster retelling of the Dickens novel *David Copperfield* (1935). However, after just a few days of filming, Charles dropped out of the film, to be replaced by W. C. Fields, for reasons that were never made entirely clear. Cameraman Hal Kern claimed that Charles was replaced because he played the part in a threatening manner and "looked as if he was going to molest the child," while Elsa reported that Charles "lost his confidence completely" and managed to convince the powers that be to recast the part.[15] *David Copperfield* director George Cukor, who ought to know, backed up Elsa's story, but he also felt that Elsa herself played a part in Charles's state of mind. "Laughton's confidence and self-esteem were never very high," Cukor said. "Least of all when he began a picture. I'm surprised he didn't walk off more sets. . . . A lot depended on his relationship with

11. *Dayton Herald*, June 20, 1934.
12. Higham, *Charles Laughton*, 54.
13. Lanchester, *Elsa Lanchester, Herself*, 127; see also Lanchester, *Charles Laughton and I*, 157.
14. *Dayton Herald*, September 12, 1934.
15. Mank, *Women in Horror Films*, 304; Lanchester, *Elsa Lanchester, Herself*, 125.

Elsa, at home, and her opinion of his latest role. He allowed her to have great emotional sway over him."[16]

Elsa stayed on the picture despite Charles's departure, and she caused some headaches for the hair and makeup department, whose attempts to straighten her corkscrew curls were doomed to failure. Wigs were tried and rejected, before they gave in and piled her hair atop her head, containing it with bobby pins as much as possible. Cukor reported that Elsa was not nervous on the set, despite this being her first Hollywood film. He said that she "displayed little or no stage fright. She always seemed to have the feeling, about a new project or role, that she had nothing to lose. Elsa knew that what she did, she did very well. Within her own range, she was marvelous. But she was very easy to stereotype."[17] Indeed, Clickett was to be at least the eighth maid character Elsa had played since her appearance in *The Way of the World* in 1924, and there would be plenty more to come.

When *David Copperfield* was released, one reviewer wrote that Elsa "makes quite a decided impression of quaint humor which makes one want to see more of her," while another remarked that "some of the smaller parts are beautifully cast and played, notably Elsa Lanchester as Clickett."[18] It is lucky that neither of these critics blinked at the wrong moment, else they might have missed Elsa's American film debut entirely; indeed, several of their colleagues commented on the severity of the cuts, which left Elsa with a bit part of just two lines. She is onscreen for less than ninety seconds, and she spends a large percentage of that time with her back to the camera or with her face at least partly obscured, either by a hat or by the infant in her arms. Elsa would sum up the experience by saying that "the part was not entirely cut out, but there was not much of it left. In fact, it was just a little unnecessary appendage as far as story value was concerned, and I did not care much for either the part or the film. Sour grapes, I suppose."[19] Her bitterness on this occasion is entirely understandable.

After filming for *David Copperfield* was finished, Elsa found herself with time on her hands in which to enjoy the delights of her new American hometown. However, Charles was in the hospital after an operation for a rectal fistula—which he had at first, in a furor of hysterical guilt, thought was a venereal disease—and so was in no state to accompany her. Undeterred, Elsa saw the sights on the arm of British playwright Arthur Macrae, who was in town to work on Charles's next movie, *Ruggles of Red Gap* (1935), and was also staying at the Garden of Allah. They had a wonderful time, taking in roller coasters and fortune-tellers on Ocean Park pier, attending numerous wrestling matches, and seeing the famous evangelist preacher Aimee Semple McPherson at the Angelus Temple. Elsa would describe McPherson's preaching style as "almost sensual"

16. Hadleigh, *Leading Ladies*, 90.

17. Hadleigh, 90.

18. *Ithaca Journal*, February 16, 1935; *The Bystander*, March 20, 1935.

19. Lanchester, *Charles Laughton and I*, 167.

and her appeal as "definitely sexy." During one sermon, the congregation was instructed to hold hands, about which Elsa recalled: "This was an order from On High—and Arthur and I had to do it so as not to offend anyone. We found it very embarrassing. (Except, I didn't mind holding Arthur's hand, as I was very fond of him.)"[20] There is nothing further to suggest that Elsa enjoyed anything more than friendship with Macrae, but his company certainly brought her out of her shell and gave her a few weeks of laughter and enjoyment, which her permanently overworked and overthinking husband did not often provide.

Meanwhile, Irving Thalberg's advice to Elsa to dress nicely when meeting with a producer had borne fruit. She had met with Hunt Stromberg, and he had taken a liking to her, perhaps a little too much. In an era in which movie producers behaved as if all actresses were theirs for the taking, Elsa's marriage to an important MGM property doubtlessly protected her from their more overt advances. As it was, she tolerated Stromberg's habit of putting his hands around her waist "a little too often and a little too high" and was rewarded with a good role in his production *Naughty Marietta* (1935).[21]

Naughty Marietta, which would be nominated for a Best Picture Oscar (losing to *Mutiny on the Bounty*, 1935), earned its placed in motion picture history for providing the first onscreen pairing of Jeanette MacDonald and Nelson Eddy. It was also the latter's very first picture. Although, according to authors Sharon Rich and Jane Ellen Wayne, MacDonald and Eddy would end up having a lasting secret love affair, the atmosphere of this first movie together was decidedly icy, with Eddy inexperienced and awkward, and MacDonald sarcastic and impatient.[22] For Elsa this added to an already tense working environment; the set was, as she described it, "already dark with the shadow of Louis B. Mayer."[23] Mayer—the married head of the studio—had an interest in MacDonald that went far beyond the professional, and any movie she starred in was subject to intense scrutiny from this powerful presence.[24]

Although *Naughty Marietta* was a musical, Elsa was not called on to make use of her singing or dancing abilities; rather, she provided comic support alongside the future Wizard of Oz, Frank Morgan. Their humorous pairing was such that filming scenes with them often proved too much for Eddy, who would struggle to keep his composure on camera.[25] In a plot that concerns a French princess escaping an unwanted marriage by stowing away on a boat to America, Morgan played the stammering, lecherous governor of New Orleans, and Elsa

20. Lanchester, *Elsa Lanchester, Herself*, 129.

21. Lanchester, 126.

22. Rich, *Sweethearts*; Wayne, *The Golden Girls of MGM*, 9–11.

23. Hadleigh, *Leading Ladies*, 91.

24. Rich, *Sweethearts*; Wayne, *The Golden Girls of MGM*, 9–11.

25. Rich, "Live Blogging *Naughty Marietta* (1935)."

his shrewish, social-climbing wife. It is not her best performance, and she makes some peculiar faces—perhaps because of the uncomfortable dental caps she was forced to wear—and seems slightly on edge, with one review saying that her "decidedly acid disposition has a rather grotesque makeup that destroys what is supposed to be a comic portrayal."[26] However, *Naughty Marietta* was a definite step in the right direction after *David Copperfield*, and it allowed Elsa to partake fully in the spectacle of a big-budget MGM musical. She is costumed in a series of ever-more extravagant gowns, some of which were—according to the publicity department—seven feet wide, and her picture appeared on some of the lobby cards used to promote the film. *Naughty Marietta* was well received by the critics, although they reserved their praise for the lead actors and the scene-stealing antics of Frank Morgan.

The movie was shot very fast, something that director W. S. "One-Take Woody" Van Dyke was famous for, and when it wrapped Van Dyke threw a huge party on Christmas Eve to celebrate. Although Elsa does not record whether Charles attended, she does note that she began to feel much more at ease and happy with Hollywood at this party, thanks in large part to her discovery of "a popular American drink called an Old Fashioned."[27] Tipsy and flush with success, Elsa began to relax and let go of her insecurities. "I became very gay," she remembered, "and a homesick expression that was always stuck on my face was wiped off. People looked *at* me, instead of *past* me."[28] The next day, slightly worse for wear, Elsa and Charles spent Christmas Day with Nelson Eddy and his mother at the Eddy family home, where they enjoyed traditional joys of the season such as turkey, plum pudding, crackers, and a Christmas tree, and spent much of the day making records of their own voices on a recording machine that Eddy owned.

Elsa ended 1934 in a good place: she had a contract with a major studio, had played in a lavish MGM musical, and was beginning to feel wanted and appreciated in Hollywood. She had also recently signed up to do a film for Universal in the new year, which paid $1,250 a week for two weeks' work, compared to her contracted $150 a week at MGM.

The picture's working title was *The Return of Frankenstein*.

---

26. *Austin American-Statesman*, May 26, 1935.

27. Lanchester, *Elsa Lanchester, Herself*, 128; Lanchester, *Charles Laughton and I*, 158–59.

28. Lanchester, *Elsa Lanchester, Herself*, 128 (emphasis in original).

13 Feverish Material

After his success with *Frankenstein* (1931), director James Whale was originally reluctant to make a sequel. The powers that be at Universal managed to convince him to do so by agreeing to let him have complete creative control over all aspects of the film, including the casting. Reprising their roles from the original were Boris Karloff as the Monster and Colin Clive as Dr. Henry Frankenstein, while old favorites Ernest Thesiger and Una O'Connor—who had appeared in Whale's films *The Old Dark House* (1932) and *The Invisible Man* (1933), respectively— were added to the cast.

The horror sequel was soon retitled *Bride of Frankenstein*, and featured romantic partners for both the scientist and his monstrous creation, with seventeen-year-old contract player Valerie Hobson signed to play Elizabeth, the new bride of Dr. Frankenstein. In a 1989 interview Hobson discussed Elsa, saying, "Elsa was a brilliant and strange actress and she married a brilliant and strange man. . . . She would have had to have been extraordinary to stay married to such a strange man, I think . . . a strange marriage, between two very strange people."[1] Hobson was certainly familiar with strange marriages: in the 1960s she would find herself involved in a scandal that shook the British government when it was discovered that her politician husband, John Profumo, had an affair with Christine Keeler during the same period that the young lady was sexually involved with a Russian spy. Throughout the sordid newspaper headlines, court cases, and national condemnation, Hobson stood by her husband. They remained married until her death in 1998.

Late in 1934, rumors swirled concerning who would play the Monster's Mate, with the publicity department claiming that actresses Brigitte Helm and Phyllis Brooks were being considered. It was claimed that "a dozen European and American screen players were tried out for this part of the mechanical bride."[2] In his biography of James Whale, author James Curtis writes that Elsa was in London when she received the offer to play the double role of the Bride and

---

1. Mank, *Women in Horror Films*, 325.
2. *Brooklyn Times Union*, April 30, 1935.

Always the Bride: Elsa with co-stars Colin Clive and Ernest Thesiger in *The Bride of Frankenstein* (1935). *ARCHIVIO GBB / Alamy Stock Photo*

Mary Shelley, and that this occurred after filming had already begun, in January 1935.[3] His confusion is understandable, and his source for this information is almost certainly Elsa's own mixed-up timeline of events as presented in *Elsa Lanchester, Herself*. Here Elsa describes in detail a voyage back to England that actually took place *after* the filming of *Bride of Frankenstein*; she certainly did not return to England between finishing work on *Naughty Marietta* on December 24, 1934, and reporting to the Universal lot for *Bride* in early January 1935. Also, her casting had been announced in the American press on December 20, 1934 (perhaps negating the publicity department's attempts at secrecy and speculation).[4] According to author Gregory William Mank, James Whale had known from the outset who he wanted to play the dual role of Mary Shelley and the Bride: his

---

3.   Curtis, *James Whale*, 243.

4.   *Miami Herald*, December 20, 1934.

former tango partner from the Cave of Harmony.[5] Perhaps he remembered those reviews from the 1920s that praised Elsa's work using terms like "grotesque" and "macabre." Elsa, for her part, was flattered to be asked and happy to be working for someone who remembered her as more than the wife of Charles Laughton.

Elsa would work on the picture for nearly two weeks, for which she was paid $2,500.[6] She filmed the prologue first as Mary Shelley, which took two or three days, and then spent the rest of her time as the Bride.

Whale fought to keep the prologue in the film, despite pressure from colleagues, such as editor Ted Kent, who said, "As far as I was concerned, it was a horror picture and I wanted to get on to the Monster. The Shelley sequence was unnecessary."[7] This stylistic scene features Elsa's Mary Shelley alongside Percy Bysshe Shelley and Lord Byron (Douglas Walton and Gavin Gordon, respectively) inside a cavernous room complete with blazing fire, while a thunderstorm rolls and screams outside. This is a different Elsa Lanchester than we have seen before. She is scared of the storm, and giggles girlishly at her husband; she is prim, but never stridently so. Elsa would remark in old age that when she played Mary Shelley, "[I] looked the best I ever had on screen."[8] She is certainly eye-catching in the prologue, and her confidence adds to this; she seems much more sure of herself than she did in *Naughty Marietta*, filmed just weeks before. Her arresting appearance is helped in large part (as had also been the case in *Naughty Marietta*) by her spectacularly low-cut costume, which displayed so much of her charms that the censor felt compelled to order the removal of some of the footage. The dress itself was remarkable: dainty and light as air, it was covered in sequined butterflies, stars, and moons, swathed in net, and accompanied by a lengthy train. Intentionally bridal, the dress became part of the film's publicity, touring the country and being displayed in movie theater foyers. Elsa claimed that it had taken seventeen Mexican ladies twelve weeks to create the dress entirely by hand.[9]

Reading Elsa's account of the making of *Bride of Frankenstein* in *Elsa Lanchester, Herself*, it is clear that she was proud of her portrayal of Mary Shelley, and also fascinated with Whale's idea of using the dual role to highlight the darkness within. In an interview later in life, she explained, "James' feeling was that very pretty, sweet people, both men and women, had very wicked insides . . .

5. Mank, *Women in Horror Films*, 301.

6. Mank, 301.

7. Curtis, *James Whale*, 238.

8. Hadleigh, *Leading Ladies*, 86.

9. Lanchester, *Elsa Lanchester, Herself*, 134; Mank, *Women in Horror Films*, 305.

evil thoughts. . . . So James wanted the same actress for both parts to show that the Bride of Frankenstein did, after all, come out of sweet Mary Shelley's soul."[10]

However proud of it she was, few today remember Elsa's performance in the prologue. Rather, it is her monstrous creation that has captured the public imagination: a figure with towering hair, twisted glamour makeup, and flowing gown. Elsa's first appearance as the Bride, however, features her lying on a slab, wrapped from head to toe in bandages. These were applied by the studio nurse, and they made it impossible for Elsa to walk or visit the bathroom without assistance. Although there is a charming set of publicity photographs showing the largely British cast taking afternoon tea while in costume, Elsa was forced to limit her liquid intake on the days she spent wrapped in bandages.

That was not the only discomfort she endured on the set. Although she was spared the five hours that Boris Karloff had to spend daily in makeup to become the Monster, Elsa still had to be awake before dawn on the days when she was to shoot her scenes in the film's dramatic climax. The makeup for both the Monster and his Mate was the work of Jack P. Pierce, who insisted on applying the makeup for each himself, so when both actors were required for a take, filming could not begin until the afternoon. Elsa—like many on the Universal lot—did not care for Pierce's arrogance and temper, and compared him directly to Dr. Frankenstein: "Jack Pierce did really feel that he *made* these people—that he was a *god* who created human beings."[11] Elsa carried on this theme in her autobiography, where she wrote the following account of the makeup process:

> He had his own *sanctum sanctorum*, and . . . *he* said good morning first. If I spoke first, he glared and slightly showed his upper teeth. He would be dressed in a full hospital doctor's operating outfit. At five in the morning, this made me dislike him intensely. Then, for three or four hours, the Lord would do his creative work, with never a word spoken as he built up the scars with spirit gum, pink putty, red paint, and so on. . . . Jack Pierce fancied himself The Maker of Monsters—meting out wrath and intolerance by the bucketload.[12]

After the scars had been painstakingly painted (Elsa joked that he could just as easily have bought them from a gag store), it was time for the crowning glory. Director James Whale was personally responsible for the now-iconic, Nefertiti-inspired hairstyle of the Bride of Frankenstein. Valerie Hobson claimed that Whale wanted a visual contrast between her character, Elizabeth Frankenstein, and the Bride, and so Elizabeth's hair "hung down in sad tresses,"[13] while the Bride's stood shocked upright, as unnatural as the creature herself.

10. Mank, *Women in Horror Films*, 305.

11. Mank, 306 (emphasis in original).

12. Lanchester, *Elsa Lanchester, Herself*, 135.

13. Valerie Hobson, quoted in Curtis, *James Whale*, 243.

Elsa's own hair was used, meaning that the Bride of Frankenstein was a redhead, rather than the raven-haired gothic queen she is often portrayed as today. Elsa was frequently asked about how the effect was achieved, and she described the process as follows: "from the top of my head they made four tiny, tight braids. On these was anchored a wired horsehair cage about five inches high. Then my own hair was brushed over this structure, and two white hair pieces—one from the right temple and one from the left—were brushed onto the top."[14]

The effect was nearly complete; all that remained was the final costume. While Elsa's hands and arms remained bandaged, the rest of her was clad in a high-fashion version of a shroud, complete with squared shoulder pads. The gown was appropriately bridal and also long enough to cover the stacked shoes needed to raise Elsa's five-foot-four frame to the Bride's full height. Several sources claim that she was elevated to seven feet tall, but seeing her standing next to other actors proves this not to be so. She was likely closer to the six-foot mark.

Perhaps more interesting than what the Bride wore was what she did *not* wear; according to a source close to James Whale, Elsa was completely nude beneath her costume, and wasn't shy about flashing the crew between takes.[15] Although the truth of this is now impossible to determine, several previous incidents suggest that Elsa was not shy when it came to nudity. She had gone skinny-dipping in the river with the cast of *Riverside Nights* (1926)—which had included James Whale—and she once removed all her clothes during afternoon tea when she was living in Mary Butts's house in London. On this latter occasion the lawyer E. S. P. Haynes was visiting, and paying Elsa a little too much attention: "He then said he would like to see me in the nude, so I stripped immediately, sat down again, and went on sipping my tea from one of Mary Butts' dainty china cups. Everybody in the room seemed to enjoy the gesture, which oddly enough was quite decent. E. S. P. Haynes looked like a stuck pig."[16] Although these incidents had taken place during Elsa's wild youth, perhaps working with Whale reminded her of that time and sparked a little of that old rebellious spirit.

Although the Bride of Frankenstein never speaks, she does emit a series of strangled screams upon seeing her intended. Elsa's inspiration for these curious sounds was the hissing of swans in Regent's Park. She screamed so much and for so long during filming that she completely lost her voice, and when she finished shooting and returned with Charles to England, the press reported that she was "still hoarse from her terrific scenes in the finale" of the picture.[17]

Cast members largely reported that they enjoyed filming *Bride of Frankenstein*, but there were some tensions on the set. Colin Clive's by now rampant alcoholism meant the director had to tread carefully; Whale's friend Jack Latham

---

14. Lanchester, *Elsa Lanchester, Herself,* 135.

15. Curtis Harrington, quoted in Mank, *Women in Horror Films,* 308.

16. Lanchester, *Elsa Lanchester, Herself,* 67, and see p. 78 for the skinny-dipping story.

17. *Tampa Times,* March 16, 1935.

recalled that the actor was "very excitable. Whale had to be careful so that Colin wouldn't shoot his mouth off."[18] Clive would die of alcoholism and consumption two years after filming *Bride of Frankenstein*, at the age of thirty-seven.

James Whale's own behavior was also a cause for concern, when he made disturbing demands of his actresses. He reportedly told seventeen-year-old Valerie Hobson that she must not wear underwear beneath her bridal gown, and he forced Ann Darling, who played the shepherdess, to change her panties in front of the cast and crew, replacing the white ones she was wearing with black lace ones, even though they would not show beneath her costume.[19] As Whale was not sexually interested in women, this was all presumably some kind of cruel joke or power play for him. Elsa admits that Whale, although brilliant, was very bitter, something she put down to his heart having been broken by Doris Zinkeisen in the 1920s. When his career and health faded in the late 1950s, Whale committed suicide by drowning himself in his swimming pool. A movie was later made about Whale's final days, *Gods and Monsters* (1998), for which Ian McKellen was nominated for an Oscar for his portrayal of the director. Rosalind Ayres plays Elsa in several flashback sequences.

Although *Bride of Frankenstein* received largely positive reviews upon its release, it was not immediately hailed as the masterpiece it is viewed as today. There was less respect for the genre in the 1930s—a snobbery that still continues in some quarters—and most critics praised it as being very good for a film "of its kind." "The story cannot, of course, be taken at all seriously," one reviewer rather condescendingly wrote, before warning readers, "it is quite unsuitable for children."[20] Charles Laughton, it is said, was not impressed with the picture; his only comment after watching it concerned the beauty of his wife's "shell-like ears."[21]

Others were more lavish with their praise for Elsa's performance, with one reviewer writing that she "injects sex into already feverish material with strangely disturbing results," and others saying that her "remarkable performance" was "one of the high spots of the picture."[22] One of the most frequently remarked-on elements of the film today is how little screen time the Bride of Frankenstein has in the movie that bears her name. Contemporary critics noticed this as well, with a typical review reading, "It is Elsa Lanchester as the mate who is the real success

18. Curtis, *James Whale*, 240.
19. Mank, Women in Horror Films, 305–306.
20. *Coventry Evening Telegraph*, July 4, 1935.
21. Curtis, *James Whale*, 251.
22. *Philadelphia Inquirer*, May 10, 1935; *Baltimore Sun*, May 3, 1935; *Salt Lake Telegram*, May 4, 1935.

of the picture. She gives a very clever performance and it is a great pity that she does not have more to do."[23]

Elsa had gone into *Bride of Frankenstein* with high hopes, saying, "I thought—and Whale practically convinced me—that *Bride* could make me famous in my own right. That I could write my own ticket professionally."[24] While certainly ensuring her iconic immortality for decades to come, the film did not have the immediate effect that Elsa had hoped for. In fact, it would be six years before she would make another movie in America.

23. *Coventry Evening Telegraph*, July 4, 1935.
24. Hadleigh, *Leading Ladies*, 86.

14 Rosy Promises

While Elsa had been on the set of *Bride of Frankenstein* at Universal, Charles had been hard at work on *Les Misérables* (1935) for Twentieth Century Pictures. By uncanny coincidence they both finished on the same day, and—exhausted and homesick—they immediately began the journey back to England. They were in demand; cables had been arriving for them regularly in California, suggesting work back home for both Charles and Elsa. "Whether I was just a sort of worm that they put on the end of the line, I do not know," Elsa recalled. "I think I must have been. Certainly there were at that time terrific efforts to get us to return to England."[1] She was right to be cynical, as the driving force behind most film offers was Alexander Korda, and his eyes were firmly fixed on the prize of Charles, whom he aimed to secure by any means necessary.

Elsa was taking codeine for her throat, and Charles was shattered after filming back-to-back pictures, but if the couple had looked forward to a restful time aboard ship then they were destined to be disappointed. Their ocean crossing on the French liner *Champlain* was plagued by bad weather from the beginning, with wild seas causing the journey to take longer than expected. Always a lover of thunderstorms and volcanoes, Elsa seems to have thoroughly enjoyed the experience, although in her memoirs, in typical fashion, she mixes this trip up with an equally wild solo crossing she would make in 1939, remarking, "Thank goodness Charles was not on the *Champlain*."[2] He was, of course, and he certainly did not enjoy himself, telling the British press upon their arrival in Plymouth in March 1935, "I have never seen such high seas. They swept over us. We could not stand on deck and could only sleep on the first night. We are absolutely exhausted."[3] He would not have much time to recover; he was only in England for two weeks, during which time he was to meet with Korda to finalize plans for filming in the summer, before returning to America to film the naval drama *Mutiny on the Bounty* (1935). For a man not particularly fond of boats, it was a rough few weeks.

---

1. Lanchester, *Charles Laughton and I*, 180.

2. Lanchester, *Elsa Lanchester, Herself*, 132.

3. *Hull Daily Mail*, March 2, 1935.

Charles's arrival in England raised eyebrows and press comments due to the change in his appearance. Always insecure about his looks, Charles had found the experience of being surrounded by Hollywood's beautiful people torturous, and so he had embarked on a diet and exercise regime. Elsa was at this point still svelte, and she was perhaps neither as supportive as Charles might have hoped nor shy about letting people know. When asked about exercise, Charles told a reporter in America that he had taken to swimming daily in the hotel pool; "Like a whale," remarked Elsa.[4] She told the British press that her husband now reminded her too much of his brother, especially from the back.[5]

When Charles returned to America to film *Mutiny on the Bounty*, Elsa remained in England, later claiming that she was "persuaded into staying away from Charles by rosy promises of film parts under my English contract with London Film Productions."[6] Perhaps unsurprisingly, such promises did not amount to any immediate action, and Elsa's only time in front of a camera was in the home movies she made with John Armstrong and Benita Jaeger.

Elsa's brother, Waldo, got married in London on July 6, 1935, to Muriel Bell, who would join him in his marionette business. There is no evidence as to whether Elsa was present at the registry office ceremony. She would claim in *Elsa Lanchester, Herself* that she never attended a wedding except for her own, but in *Charles Laughton and I*, she writes about attending the "smart wedding" of E. D. O'Brien and Sylvia Denny in Chelsea, so—as is common with Elsa—it's hard to know what to believe.[7] Regarding her relationship with her brother, Elsa would say that "acute undemonstrativeness" was a Lanchester family trait.[8] Waldo's biographer concurs that "Waldo was not a demonstrative man," but his creation of clown puppets named Baldo and Belsa in the mid-1930s suggests that he missed his sister. A friend of his would remark that "those two clowns were always special to Waldo."[9]

Although Elsa may not have been at the family wedding, she did visit her parents around this time. They were still living on Leathwaite Road, no longer moving from house to house, but otherwise Elsa found that little had changed. Her parents' extended period at this address was probably due to the fact that Elsa and Charles were now providing them with an allowance, a practice that would continue for the rest of Biddy and Shamus's lives.

Charles's Hollywood salary had also enabled Elsa to employ staff for the Gordon Square flat, including cook and housekeeper Nellie Boxall, who had

---

4. *Los Angeles Times*, June 27, 1934.

5. *Yorkshire Post and Leeds Intelligencer*, March 13, 1935.

6. Lanchester, *Charles Laughton and I*, 186.

7. Lanchester, *Elsa Lanchester, Herself*, 315; Lanchester, *Charles Laughton and I*, 255.

8. Lanchester, *Elsa Lanchester, Herself*, 315.

9. Cockayne, *Master of the Marionettes*, 116.

previously worked for Virginia Woolf. Nellie was unsure initially whether she wanted to work for show-business folk, but she was apparently convinced to do so upon discovering that they owned the same salt and pepper grinders as the members of the Bloomsbury Group. Although Charles and Elsa's irregular hours when working would often test Nellie's patience, it seems to have been a happy household for the most part, completed by a communist housemaid, who referred to her employers as the "idle rich." Keeping in the spirit of things, Elsa referred to the maid as a "serf."[10]

In August 1935 there was a sudden flurry of activity from Alexander Korda and London Films, no doubt prompted by Charles's imminent return to England. It was announced in the press that Elsa would be appearing with Robert Donat in *The Ghost Goes West* and alongside her husband in *International Quartet*; Charles was also slated as appearing in *Cyrano de Bergerac* with Vivien Leigh. In the end, only one of these projects reached completion, and for Elsa it was the same old story. Discussing *The Ghost Goes West* (1935) many years later, Elsa said: "Korda produced. Charles was supposed to star, and at the last minute couldn't, owing to some technical Hollywood hitch. So Korda got Robert Donat to play the ghost and his descendant, and also got stuck with me—*I* didn't have a hitch! Naturally he gave me the smallest possible role. Once again."[11] This is not an exaggeration. Although she was billed fourth, her character—the glamorous Miss Shepperton—does not appear until over an hour has passed, and even then has remarkably little to say. Elsa's former neighbor James Agate would write in his *Tatler* review, "Miss Elsa Lanchester, with exactly two and a half minutes to do it in, wipes everybody and everything off the screen."[12] A modern viewer might find this description overgenerous, both in its praise and in its estimation of Elsa's time on the screen. Although she looks spectacular in a backless evening gown and heavy makeup, and her haughty party guest is well played and has plenty of comic potential, in the final cut she is cruelly underused once again.

This humiliation was followed by another raising and dashing of hopes when Korda cast Elsa in the title role in *Miss Bracegirdle Does Her Duty* (1936), based on the short story by Stacy Aumonier, concerning a young woman who stays in a Paris hotel and finds a corpse beneath her bed. Elsa suspected that this project was arranged "more to keep me quiet than anything," and she may have been right. Despite some considerable work going into the filming, *Miss Bracegirdle* was deemed to be "not up to standard" and was never released.[13]

So far, Elsa's track record with Korda and London Films included being cut entirely from one picture, receiving one high-billed bit part, and being named the lead in a film that went unreleased. Only her role in *The Private Life of Henry VIII*

---

10. Lanchester, *Charles Laughton and I*, 198.

11. Hadleigh, *Leading Ladies*, 91 (emphasis in original).

12. *The Tatler*, January 1, 1936.

13. Lanchester, *Charles Laughton and I*, 187.

The mutual dislike and distrust between Elsa and producer Alexander Korda is clearly evident in this photograph from the mid-1930s.   *Everett Collection Inc / Alamy Stock Photo*

provided something for her to be proud of, and that part had been dramatically reduced from the one she had originally agreed to. When Charles told Korda that he wanted to work alongside his wife, the producer was extremely reluctant to allow this, and was openly critical of Elsa's abilities. It is no wonder that Elsa felt that she was losing ground professionally. "After my rather glamorous *Riverside Nights* years," she said, "I looked in the mirror and felt time was passing me by."[14] Korda also stood in the way of Elsa's career progression outside of films. She and Charles had been approached by the Daniel Mayer Company to appear on-stage together over the 1935 Christmas period in *Peter Pan*—with Elsa as Peter and Charles as Captain Hook—but Korda refused to release either of them from their contracts, and they were forced to turn the offer down.

---

14. Lanchester, *Charles Laughton and I*, 202; Lanchester, *Elsa Lanchester, Herself*, 145.

Despite Korda's dismissive attitude toward Elsa, she was still required to interact with him socially, and even to have him attend parties in her own home. While in England the Laughtons threw several parties at their flat, including one for visiting American performers Fredric March, Florence Eldridge, Helen Hayes, and Ruth Gordon.[15] There was a Christmas party in 1935 at which it was decided that guests would be provided with wigs to wear, which led to some amusing sights later in the evening, with people engaged in serious conversation while seemingly oblivious to their extraordinary appearance. One of these was Alexander Korda, whom Elsa delighted in remembering as wearing a blonde wig with long pigtails, finished with pink bows. Further merriment was provided by their replacing the mottos in the Christmas crackers with bawdy rhymes by John Armstrong: "Christmas comes but once a year; Not like you and me I fear."[16] New Year's was spent at Charles's family's hotel in Scarborough.

After the failure of both *International Quartet* and *Cyrano de Bergerac* to develop, Charles had nearly a year away from work between mid-1935 and mid-1936, during which time he was anxious to get back in front of the cameras. He did undertake one live performance in French at the Comédie-Française in Paris—to which Elsa accompanied him and tried unsuccessfully to calm his nerves—but he wanted to work in films. Elsa just wanted to work. The announcement that they were to appear together in the London Films production *Rembrandt* (1936), the first to be shot at the company's new Denham Studios, was thus met with elation from both performers. Charles, of course, would play the artist himself, with Elsa in a smaller role as Hendrickje Stoffels, the painter's longtime partner.

Both Charles and Elsa had an interest in art, and they owned an eclectic range, including works by Horace Pippin, Henri Rousseau, and Maurice Utrillo, as well as a portrait of Elsa as her character from *Love for Love* (1934), painted by Ethel Walker. The centerpiece of their collection was Pierre-Auguste Renoir's *Judgment of Paris* (1908), for which Charles had paid $36,000 in 1935.[17] When his casting in *Rembrandt* was confirmed, Charles set forth once again on his intensive research procedure, visiting museums, reading biographies, and taking trips to France and the Netherlands. While he was away, Elsa decided to accompany John and Benita Armstrong—who had married earlier in the year—to Scarborough, where John was commissioned to do some painting work at the hotel run by Charles's mother and brothers. Intending for the journey to be a comfortable and leisurely one, they hired a chauffeur, enabling John to doze while Elsa and Benita played chess to pass the time. Seven miles outside of York, their car was hit by a vehicle traveling in the opposite direction. Elsa was thrown from

---

15. *The Era*, September 25, 1935; Lanchester, *Charles Laughton and I*, 203; Lanchester, *Elsa Lanchester, Herself*, 143.

16. Lanchester, *Elsa Lanchester, Herself*, 143.

17. Callow, *Charles Laughton*, 107.

the back seat into the front, striking her head in the process and opening up a large cut over her left eye that bled heavily. The chauffeur and the other passengers were unhurt, while the driver of the other car, Charles Mein, suffered from cuts and a concussion. He would eventually be fined £5 for driving a car without due care and attention.[18]

A farmer in his jalopy drove by the scene and gave them a lift to York Hospital, but Elsa refused to let the doctors stitch her wound, fearful that they would leave her with extensive scarring. She insisted that she was friends with one of England's most prominent facial surgeons, and would permit only him to carry out any necessary work. Although furious, the York doctors acquiesced and limited themselves to cleaning her up and putting a strap on the cut. Meanwhile Benita had been frantically telephoning around to locate both the surgeon and Elsa's husband. The surgeon was eventually located playing golf on the Isle of Wight, while Charles was found in France, where he was doing research with Alexander Korda. All agreed to meet in London, and so Elsa got the slow milk train back with John and Benita, drinking straight brandy for the shock and occasionally lapsing into frantic crying bouts.

Although the scar would end up being so small as to be unnoticeable, Elsa suffered what she described as "real mental torture" for a few weeks while she was healing, anxious that her appearance would be so damaged that Korda would remove her from yet another picture.[19] Once again, when the news of her accident was reported, Elsa was placed in parentheses: "Mrs. Charles Laughton (Miss Elsa Lanchester, the stage and film star), wife of Charles Laughton, the film actor, was involved in a motor accident at Askham," read an article beneath the headline, "Film actress in crash: Wife of Mr. Charles Laughton slightly hurt."[20]

But luck was on Elsa's side, and by the time *Rembrandt* starting shooting in June 1936, her injury was fully healed. This did not, however, mean that Elsa was able to enjoy the experience of making the picture; she was aware that people were saying she had only been cast because she was Charles's wife. "This was not a very happy position," she would recall, "because I felt I was acting with a pistol at my head."[21] Due to the chatty behavior of co-star Gertrude Lawrence and others on the set, Charles requested that screens be put up during filming, so that the actors would not be distracted by goings-on behind the camera. In her memoirs, Elsa mentions shooting a scene in this manner, a close-up during an important love scene, and hearing giggling coming from behind the screens. Not only did

18. *Leeds Mercury*, March 30, 1936.

19. Lanchester, *Charles Laughton and I*, 211.

20. *Leeds Mercury*, March 2, 1936.

21. Lanchester, *Charles Laughton and I*, 221.

this noise disturb and distract her, but Elsa's anxiety was such that she felt that she was being mocked and laughed at.[22]

Another curious incident during filming concerned the little song that Hendrickje Stoffels sings, which Elsa wrote herself when a suitable folk song could not be found. Although it was only a simple refrain, it was registered to her, and she was still drawing a small royalty from it decades later. Charles told her, however, that she should not make it public knowledge that she had written the song: she was playing a simple character, and if the public knew she was clever then it might detract from her performance. Elsa remarked that this "hurt me very much—I love to be thought bright," and indeed there seems no obvious reason for Charles to have acted in this manner. As Charles's biographer Simon Callow would observe, it would appear that "the processes of mutual destruction which increasingly characterized their relationship" were already well under way.[23]

Although *Rembrandt* was not destined to be a commercial success, it is widely seen as one of Elsa's best screen performances. Authors have described it as "the best dramatic performance of her career" and "her finest dramatic showcase," with Callow opining simply, "She never did anything better; they never did anything better."[24] Contemporary reviewers agreed, with one writing that hers was "a rarified performance of remarkable spirituality," while another ironically commented that "[Korda's] flair for casting . . . is never more evident than in his choice of Elsa Lanchester as the tender third wife; few would credit her with such depth of understanding."[25] Perhaps due to the pressure she felt to prove herself or perhaps because she was well aware that Korda did not like her style of acting, Elsa is, in *Rembrandt*, as far from her own personality as we ever see her onscreen; here is the gentleness she gave to Mary Shelley, but even more so. She is delicate and frail and radiant, demonstrating what might have been had directors and producers been able to look past her dominant, strident personality and cast her against what they perceived as her "type." She was also praised for her looks more in this film than in any other, perhaps showing that feminine timidity was more attractive to 1930s audiences than outspoken confidence. Journalist Jean Burnup wrote, "Elsa Lanchester has curly red hair, a provocative little face, lovely legs and a whole lot of talent. But I don't suppose she's ever thought of herself as beautiful. In 'Rembrandt,' however, they tucked up her hair into a severe Dutch white cap,

---

22. Lanchester, *Elsa Lanchester, Herself*, 146–147; Lanchester, *Charles Laughton and I*, 220–221.

23. Lanchester, *Charles Laughton and I*, 226; Callow, *Charles Laughton*, 110.

24. Nissen, *Actresses of a Certain Character*, 93; Mank, *Women in Horror Films*, 310; Callow, *Charles Laughton*, 109.

25. *The Tatler*, November 18, 1936; *Exeter and Plymouth Gazette*, May 28, 1937.

and there she is on the screen, giving a flawless performance, and looking as near beautiful as matters."[26]

The premiere of the film was held in the Netherlands, an event that Elsa describes in detail in her 1938 book. She discusses the floral arrangements, the spotlights, the press photographers, the crowds, and the applause for an entire chapter before concluding that she does not like attending premieres, and would much rather be at home peeling potatoes.[27]

Perhaps weary with doing battle with the Laughtons, Alexander Korda finally agreed to loan them out to the Daniel Mayer Company to take part in *Peter Pan* at the London Palladium over the 1936 Christmas season. However, another obstacle now presented itself: the author J. M. Barrie wrote to the actors to tell them that he did not believe they were suitable for the parts of Captain Hook and Peter Pan and that he did not want them to appear in the play. During a face-to-face interview between the author and the Laughtons, it was revealed that he had never seen Elsa perform, and that his main concern was that Charles's Captain Hook would scare the children, presumably based on the nasty characters he had portrayed onscreen. Barrie was eventually persuaded otherwise by a timely phone call from actress Elisabeth Bergner, who praised the Laughtons unconditionally. The knowledge that Elsa and Charles would donate their entire salaries to Barrie's beloved Great Ormond Street Hospital for Children may also have helped change his mind.

This was not the only disagreement that J. M. Barrie would have with the actors. Once rehearsals began, the author and Elsa would argue heatedly about her costume, with her wanting to be dressed less like a fairy and more like the other boys: "Having been a dancer and called 'elfin' until I am sick of the word, I knew from past experience that I have quite enough of that quality about me naturally," she argued. "What I needed was to add to the boyishness of the character. Barrie would not have it. . . . But he appeared to enjoy the argument."[28] Elsa also had very strong opinions about how she wanted to play Peter, by emphasizing his bossiness and his liking for power, while Charles toned down his portrayal of Hook so as to appease Barrie.

The results and reception of these interpretations were mixed, with Elsa generally faring better than Charles, whose performance was described as "the biggest disappointment of the season" by a first-night attendee, who went on to remark that Elsa's Peter "was better, if not good enough."[29] Tyrone Guthrie, in his book about the theater, wrote that "Hook, a heavyweight Don Quixote, became

---

26. *Britannia and Eve,* January 1, 1937.

27. Lanchester, *Charles Laughton and I,* 227–35; "peeling potatoes" appears on p. 230, and is repeated in Lanchester, *Elsa Lanchester, Herself,* 150.

28. Lanchester, *Charles Laughton and I,* 241–42.

29. *The Era,* December 31, 1936.

the hero of the evening. It was when Peter Pan came on that little children hid their faces in their mothers' skirts and strong men shook with fear."[30] Although some reviewers recognized what Elsa was trying to do, most seemed to suggest that they preferred their Peter as the jolly boy he was usually portrayed as, rather than this darker, more dictatorial character, "frowning, intense, and even a little haggard."[31]

Once the Palladium run was finished, Charles went back to London Films to work on *I, Claudius*, yet another movie that would never be finished. Elsa stayed with the Daniel Mayer Company and toured in *Peter Pan*, performing six nights and four afternoons a week in towns across England and Scotland, including Liverpool, Blackpool, Leeds, Glasgow, and Birmingham. During the tour Elsa was involved in another car accident when her taxi met a violent collision with another vehicle, that one driven by a man named John Travis Ingle. Although Elsa escaped unhurt, the incident would have been traumatic; both cars were damaged, and Ingle's car overturned completely. When the case came in front of the magistrate, Ingle admitted to having misjudged a right corner, and was fined £5.[32]

Elsa did not escape injury in the theater, however, and was forced to miss some performances after cracking two ribs when her flying equipment malfunctioned. Other than these mishaps, she enjoyed her time on tour. When she wasn't onstage, Elsa went to watch football matches with the stage manager, and she enjoyed meals with the famous harmonica player Larry Adler, who was playing in vaudeville houses along the same touring route. Elsa and Adler's friendship continued after their respective shows had closed, although Charles would sometimes find Adler's strong political views hard to deal with, having no personal interest in politics. Despite this, the Laughtons would come to Adler's aid when he was courting a model named Eileen Walser. Having endured an appalling first date, Walser told Adler in no uncertain terms that she had no interest in seeing him again. Frantic not to let her get away, Adler reminded her that they had discussed visiting Elsa and Charles at Stapledown; "I told her the Laughtons were expecting her, that I would hurt their feelings if I didn't come down and I certainly wouldn't go there without her." Wasler reluctantly agreed and Adler rang Elsa and pleaded with her and Charles to make a fuss over Wasler, which they agreed to do. "They were good friends and did everything they could to help," Adler recalled. "Eileen had a good time and agreed to see me again."[33] Eileen Wasler and Larry Adler were married soon after.

---

30. Guthrie, *A Life in the Theatre*, 6.

31. *Birmingham Daily Gazette*, April 7, 1937.

32. *Lancashire Evening Post*, April 2, 1937.

33. Adler, *It Ain't Necessarily So*, 92.

Elsa's strong opinions about how she wanted to play Peter Pan brought her into conflict with the play's author, J. M. Barrie, in 1936.

15   This Ought to Be Good

Frustrated at the failure of another London Films production, Charles Laughton decided that he needed to be more involved in the production side of movie making, in order to be able to control some of the processes that he had battled with elsewhere. In response, he set up Mayflower Pictures with director Erich Pommer and John Maxwell of Associated British Pictures. Pommer, in England after fleeing Hitler's Germany, was experienced and respected, having previously directed such films as *The Cabinet of Dr. Caligari* (1920), *Metropolis* (1927), and *The Blue Angel* (1930), and he and Charles sparked off each other creatively. The company's name reflected its aim of taking British movies to American audiences, and it was announced that the first three Mayflower films would be Somerset Maugham's *The Beachcomber* (*Vessel of Wrath* in the United Kingdom, 1938), *Sidewalks of London* (UK title, *St. Martin's Lane*, 1938), and Daphne du Maurier's *Jamaica Inn* (1939).

Elsa was delighted with the situation, believing that the new company would remove many of the obstacles that had seen her confined to bit parts, and this seemed to be confirmed almost instantly when she was cast in the lead female role of Martha Jones in *The Beachcomber*. Charles would play opposite her as Ginger Ted, and Bartlett Cormack was chosen to direct, although the undertaking would prove too much for him and Erich Pommer would end up taking over. Set in the South Seas, it was filmed at Elstree Studios and on location in the South of France. On a location scouting trip along the French coast before filming started, while Charles and Pommer were hard at work, Elsa and Benita Armstrong sunbathed on the balcony, swam, window-shopped, and relaxed on the beach. They occasionally roused themselves to look at the script, at which point Elsa would feel panic beginning to stir within her: "It was the biggest chance in films that I had ever had," she would say later. "The usual terror got hold of me: it was Mayflower's first picture, and I am Charles's wife, *I had to be good*. I would feel that anyway without these outside circumstances, but in this case I got into rather a blue funk."[1] The pressure was not only coming from within; many newspaper re-

---

1.   Lanchester, *Charles Laughton and I*, 262 (emphasis in original).

porters had commented in the past that they would like to see Elsa playing larger parts, and they were eagerly anticipating the results of her attaining one. A typical article read, "I am one of those who strongly believes that Elsa Lanchester . . . has by no means had the screen opportunities which her original talent and style deserve. So I look forward hopefully to 'Vessel of Wrath,' in which she is a starchy school-marm who falls in love with a ne'er-do-well. . . . This ought to be good."[2] Also in the cast was Tyrone Guthrie, who had directed Elsa and Charles's season at the Old Vic; he was chosen, despite a lack of experience in front of the camera, because Charles thought he looked enough like Elsa to play her brother.[3]

Filming near Saint-Tropez in the relentless heat of mid-August was physically tiring, especially for Elsa, whose modest costume prevented her from taking refuge in the sea between takes as the others did. She did manage an unexpected dip when Charles slipped while filming a scene in which he carried her to shore. Her costume was laid out on a rock to dry, and Elsa relished the attention she attracted while clad in just her silk chemise. In another scene she had to fall on a live octopus, a feat she had to repeat eight times for various shots. "As the octopus, which had been caught locally, gave a good performance, it was allowed to swim out to sea again instead of being killed and eaten," she remembered. "My reward was . . . eight lovely dips in the water."[4]

Elsa's performance is strong, proof for those who needed it that she was more than capable of leading a picture. While a few critics dismissed her portrayal of Miss Jones as "a burlesque of a spinster," others praised it as "her finest work yet" and "a remarkably good performance."[5] Elsa remained fond of the film all her life, and proud of the character development that the part enabled her to demonstrate—a skill she had rarely had the chance to showcase. However, despite the critical praise, the film was not a commercial success on either side of the Atlantic. Elsa blamed the censors for making a "non-sensationalistic" picture into a dull one by removing "any scenes with sexual connotations," while Simon Callow surmised that Charles's unusually laid-back approach to character development made his Ginger Ted—and therefore the film—less memorable than his previous powerhouse performances.[6]

Whatever the reason for the film's lack of success, it could not be attributed to a lack of publicity. Elsa and Charles embarked on a grueling personal appearance tour of England and Scotland in August 1938 to promote the film. Starting in Scarborough—Charles's hometown—they would go on to visit Hastings, Birmingham, Nottingham, Brighton, Liverpool, Newcastle, Black-

2. *Star Green*, October 23, 1937.

3. *Nottingham Journal*, October 19, 1937.

4. Lanchester, *Charles Laughton and I*, 268.

5. *Nottingham Journal*, March 5, 1938; *Daily Herald*, March 4, 1938; *Hull Daily Mail*, March 3, 1938.

6. Hadleigh, *Leading Ladies*, 92; Callow, *Charles Laughton*, 125.

pool, Hull, Plymouth, Portsmouth, Eastbourne, Glasgow, Dundee, and Edinburgh. Elsa and Charles stuck to the same punishing routine at every stop. After arriving by car or train they would visit a place of local interest before dining with local dignitaries. Then they would check in to their hotel for a quick change of clothes before heading to the cinema for a screening of the film, after which Charles would give a speech and Elsa would be brought up on the stage. Then it was back to the hotel to try and grab some sleep before beginning the whole thing again the following day. They visited J. M. Barrie's birthplace and the Mayflower Stone, accompanied Nottingham's police chief to his "crime museum," and made awkward small talk with the mayor of Brighton; "I made a few corny jokes about the big brass chain . . . around his neck—'I see you're weighed down by your office!'" Elsa recalled. "I don't remember whether he laughed or not."[7]

They were mobbed by fans almost everywhere they went; in Portsmouth crowds broke through the cordon, and in Blackpool, on the hottest day of the year, a police escort was required to get them back to their hotel safely.

Elsa's appearance was scrutinized like never before, and her wardrobe was described in detail, sending columnists such as Miss Humber and Femina into raptures. "Slim and slight," read a typical article, "she wore a plain frock of fine black wool marocain, fluted taffeta in scarlet and emerald making the vivid tartan collar and matching sash, and a swinging hip length cape introducing flat pleats to match those which edged the skirt hem." On another occasion, "over a dress of white net, the lower half of the skirt patterned in a bold flower design of gold galon, and tied with a sash of red velvet, she wore a floor-length cloak of wine colour."[8]

Charles's post-film speech seems to have varied little between towns. After doing bits from *Mutiny on the Bounty* and Mayflower Pictures' next film, *Sidewalks of London*, for about fifteen minutes, he introduced the audience to Elsa: "She's not the nagging spinster she appears in this picture," he would quip, "and she's insisted on coming along to prove it to you." As the audience dutifully roared with laughter and welcomed Elsa to the stage with "a thunderous outburst of applause," Charles would often add as an aside, "She doesn't hit me—often."[9] The seeming spontaneity of his remarks was proven false when they were repeated in one regional newspaper after another, but they had the effect of cementing a public image of their marriage that both Elsa and Charles were happy to promote. He was the put-upon, henpecked husband; she was the little woman who wore the trousers. Although containing some grains of truth, it was a gross simplification of a complicated and caustic pairing.

7.　Lanchester, *Elsa Lanchester, Herself*, 156.

8.　*Hull Daily Mail*, August 5, 1938; *Liverpool Echo*, August 5, 1938.

9.　*Nottingham Journal*, August 3, 1938; *Hastings and St. Leonard's Observer*, August 6, 1938.

The Laughtons finished their tour in Scotland, where they were invited to afternoon tea at Glamis Castle by Lady Rose Leveson-Gower, the older sister of England's Queen Elizabeth. While Elsa and Charles affected to be unimpressed by high society, they were pleasantly surprised by the lack of pretention on display at Glamis. The very day of their visit, September 27, 1938, the Queen had made a speech at the launch of the luxury liner that bore her name, during which she asked the British people to "be of good cheer" despite the "dark clouds gathering." Speaking on behalf of her husband, King George VI, she expressed the hope that "by man's patience and goodwill, order may yet be brought out of confusion and peace out of turmoil." Listening to this speech on the radio on the way to Glamis Castle, Elsa was deeply affected; it seems to be the moment when the possibility of war really hit home for her. She recalled, "I have never heard a voice, let alone a royal voice, ring out in such a bell-like, truth-searching fashion. It was a moment to weep—for many reasons."[10] Elsa would later find out that Lady Rose, who had been so poised during their visit, had also wept upon hearing the speech, but had collected herself before their arrival.

However, war was still a year away. Neville Chamberlain's signing of the Munich Agreement on September 30, 1938, seemed to put people's minds at rest, and Elsa and Charles were soon back at work. But not together.

When Elsa read Winifred Ashton's script for *Sidewalks of London*, she felt an instant affinity with the character of Libby, and Charles and Erich Pommer agreed that the part seemed to have been written for her.[11] The film told the story of a troupe of street entertainers who invite a Cockney pickpocket to join their act. The pickpocket's talent for singing and dancing combined with her ruthless ambition leads to stardom, but she rejects and forgets the men who first helped her. Elsa was born and raised in the environments the film depicts, could speak the accent perfectly, and had extensive singing and dancing experience. There were other elements in the character that were perhaps less flattering but still familiar: Libby was direct and cruel, and especially hurtful in her treatment of Charles's character, who is in love with her. Charles would play one of the buskers, and Tyrone Guthrie another, while Elsa's harmonica-playing friend Larry Adler was also in the cast. This was a role in which Elsa felt she could excel, and she looked forward to working with familiar faces and friends.

However, Elsa had reckoned without her old enemy Alexander Korda, who, despite having no artistic involvement in *Sidewalks of London* whatsoever, still managed to break Elsa's heart. He approached Charles and offered to finance the picture, on the condition that Vivien Leigh played the Cockney pickpocket Libby, rather than Elsa. And just like that, according to Leigh's biographer, "with characteristic selfishness, [Charles] expelled his own wife Elsa Lanchester from

10. Lanchester, *Elsa Lanchester, Herself*, 157.

11. Ashton wrote this under her pen name, Clemence Dane.

the cast."[12] Charles Higham would write that this "was the worst blow for Elsa since her rejection for the part of the daughter in *Payment Deferred*, and she recalls that when Charles told her the news, she went pale and actually felt faint."[13] Her sense of betrayal must have been immense.

To add insult to injury, Vivien Leigh had no desire to be in the film; she disliked Charles and was repulsed by him physically, and she also felt absolutely no affinity with the part. She was also preoccupied with developments in her personal life, as Larry Adler recalled: "Laurence Olivier was courting Vivien Leigh. He would visit the set, they would go to her dressing room and that was the end of shooting."[14] Her lack of interest showed in her performance, which Simon Callow describes as "inept beyond words."[15] Although Leigh was undoubtedly a wonderful actress when she wanted to be, her attempt at the accent and characterization in *Sidewalks of London* is half-hearted at best, and her stunning beauty is the only part of her performance that stands out. Contemporary reviewers agreed, with James Agate writing that Leigh was "miscast" in the part. He added: "The only actress in the wide world who could imaginably have made a credible character out of Libby is Miss Elsa Lanchester. That cute and knowing smile of hers would have knocked the whole thing into a sensible gear."[16] The reviews were a small vindication, perhaps, but it was too little too late, and the damage was done.

The London premiere of *Sidewalks of London* was televised, and Elsa appeared alongside BBC reporter John Snagge, interviewing the celebrities as they arrived. According to the *Daily Mirror*, the "conversational exchanges were hardly electrifying," and they were presumably conducted through Elsa's gritted teeth.[17]

A particularly hurtful irony was that just when she was reeling from Charles's professional betrayal, Elsa was actively publicizing their happy marriage in her book *Charles Laughton and I*, which was published in October 1938, having previously been serialized in the *Daily Express*. "All things considered," she writes in the book's prefatory note, "I think that Charles and I are weathering the storm of art and marriage as well as anybody else—of course *we* think much better."[18] Nothing could have been further from the truth.

Charles began working on the third (and, it would transpire, final) Mayflower picture, *Jamaica Inn*, in late 1938. Directed by Alfred Hitchcock and, of

12. Walker, *Vivien*, 146.

13. Higham, *Charles Laughton*, 88.

14. Adler, *It Ain't Necessarily So*, 96.

15. Callow, *Charles Laughton*, 128.

16. *The Tatler*, November 2, 1938.

17. *Daily Mirror*, October 21, 1938.

18. Lanchester, *Charles Laughton and I*, 17 (emphasis in original).

course, starring Charles, the movie once again had no part for Elsa. In December 1938 she boarded a boat to New York to take part in promotional work for *The Beachcomber* and *Charles Laughton and I*, leaving Charles behind in England. The couple would spend Christmas and New Year's apart.

Elsa's old friend Iris Barry, now married to the Museum of Modern Art (MoMA) treasurer John Abbott, was there to greet Elsa in New York and provided her with a place to stay during her visit. As *The Beachcomber* was being distributed by Paramount in the United States and Canada, the studio assigned Elsa a publicist, George Fraser, who kept her busy with a series of interviews and appearances. On Christmas Eve she attended the American premiere of her movie at the Rialto on Times Square, although union difficulties prevented her from appearing on the stage and making a speech; instead, she waved from the box. Her appearance in Toronto in January was canceled for similar reasons.[19] She was interviewed for newspapers and on the radio. In Hartford, Connecticut, she was asked whether she felt her talent had been submerged by the "greater glory" of Charles. Her answer was a public relations triumph, concealing all Elsa's recent pain behind a good-wifely façade: "We can't both be terribly ambitious and if he is working long and hard at some thing or other I do not distract him with plans for myself. After all, our marriage is most important . . . and just so [long as] I am laboring at some sort of artistic endeavor I am happy."[20]

Despite the distance between them—both physically and metaphorically— Elsa and Charles did manage to perform together in a sketch from *The Beachcomber* that was broadcast on the *Magic Key* radio show on New Year's Day 1939. The press made much of the event, with the *Daily News* writing, "For the first time in the history of radio, two continents were used as the stage for a dramatic sketch."[21] Before the broadcast started, Charles, in London, attempted small talk with Elsa, in New York. "In the midst of a rough rehearsal the boom of that tremendous voice alarmed early comers to the Magic Key studio audience," *The Gazette* reported. "Miss Lanchester had to remonstrate with her husband and tell him to 'keep to the script.'"[22] His conversation, according to other reports, concerned what she was wearing, specifically her hat. The broadcast was a success, "and was so well-timed and came through so perfectly that it was impossible to believe that the two players were thousands of miles apart."[23]

During her time in the United States, Elsa also met with accountants and tax inspectors in order to sort out a financial tangle that Charles was snared in, a result of his working in, and paying tax in, two countries. Although Elsa was successful in resolving the problem, this particular financial concern would prove

19. *The Gazette*, January 12, 1939.

20. *Hartford Courant*, December 31, 1938.

21. *Daily News*, January 2, 1939.

22. *The Gazette*, January 14, 1939.

23. *Sheffield Evening Telegraph*, January 12, 1939.

a costly one, and would play a large part in Elsa and Charles's decision-making in the years to come.

Elsa's journey back to England on the French liner *Paris* was another turbulent crossing. When the vessel arrived in Plymouth, its portholes were smashed, its furniture was damaged, and some passengers had suffered from minor injuries. At the height of the storm, the waves broke over the bridge of the ship. In her autobiography, Elsa claimed, "You have hardly lived if you haven't seen waves so fierce and vast that the sky disappears until the ship rises from the trough, and then down you go again."[24] Speaking to the journalists who greeted the *Paris*, she said, "Most people remained in their cabins, but even then were not safe. Dressing tables, wardrobes and beds broke away and careered [*sic*] about the room."[25] The subsequent reports, while focusing on the storm, also mentioned that Charles was not at Plymouth to greet his wife but was instead busy working on *Jamaica Inn*. Elsa told the press that she had heard from her husband during the voyage and said that she expected him to meet her at Paddington.[26] However, although pictures appeared in the press of Elsa waving as the boat train pulled into the station, no mention was made of Charles being there to greet her.

Back in London, Elsa was introduced to Charles's *Jamaica Inn* co-star Maureen O'Hara, then aged just nineteen. Despite describing her as "really beautiful" and "a remarkably good actress,"[27] Elsa disliked O'Hara intensely from the start. The younger woman was aware of this, writing in her own autobiography—the title of which, *'Tis Herself*, is very similar to Elsa's *Elsa Lanchester, Herself*—"I never felt she really liked me. I think she was jealous of my friendship with Laughton, but I'm not sure. Perhaps she was jealous of my career."[28] She wasn't completely wrong. Although there were many other factors, jealousy certainly played a part in Elsa's hostility; through 1939 and 1940, Elsa would be out of work, while O'Hara's career took off rapidly. Charles was responsible for much of O'Hara's success, giving her a part in *Jamaica Inn* and then taking her to America and convincing RKO to cast her opposite him in *The Hunchback of Notre Dame* (1939).

Personality-wise, the two women were complete opposites: where O'Hara was sweet, Elsa was acid; where Elsa was double entendres and a knowing wink, O'Hara was wide-eyed innocence. O'Hara was a devout Catholic and prided herself on being a good girl; the agnostic Elsa regarded O'Hara as unbearably smug and delighted in taking her down a peg or two whenever the opportunity presented itself. For her part, O'Hara saw Elsa as cold and spiteful, saying that

24. Lanchester, *Elsa Lanchester, Herself*, 132.

25. *Birmingham Mail*, January 21, 1939.

26. *Western Morning News*, January 23, 1939.

27. Lanchester, *Elsa Lanchester, Herself*, 160.

28. O'Hara with Nicoletti, *'Tis Herself*, 36.

she "had a special talent for being really mean when she wanted to be."[29] Charles could have played peacemaker, but it seems that at this rocky point in his marriage he went out of his way to make things worse, by appointing O'Hara—who openly adored him—as his protégée, and complaining about his wife to her. Elsa said, "Charles would tell Maureen that he'd always wanted to have children, particularly a daughter. At one point he asked her, 'Do you think your mother and father would let me adopt you?'"[30] According to O'Hara, Charles then confided in her that the reason they had never had children was because a botched abortion Elsa had during her days in burlesque had left her unable to conceive. "Laughton told me many times that not being a father was his greatest disappointment in life," claimed O'Hara.[31]

Although Elsa later admitted to having had two abortions in her twenties—one was Charles's baby—she never mentioned any subsequent complications regarding conception. Another reason sometimes given for their childlessness was that Elsa did not want to have children with Charles because she didn't want the father to be a gay man. Elsa addressed this claim directly in a 1979 interview with Marian Zailian, saying that this was another fiction created by Charles: "I don't know that [his sexual orientation] put me off particularly," she said. "He had accused me when he was angry, saying we didn't have one because he was homosexual. He once said that I was frightened of having one, which I wasn't. It never occurred to me to be *frightened*."[32]

It is quite clear that Elsa was never keen on the idea of being a mother. Besides showing an early disgust at the process of conception and birth, she and her parents frequently discussed Thomas Malthus's theory of the dangers of a growing population, and Elsa admitted to being "very snobbish about people who had big families."[33] She confessed to having no maternal instincts or desires, and suggested that her upbringing may be the cause: "I never saw Biddy or Shamus hold a baby," Elsa claimed, "and I have never held a baby. No, that is wrong. Once I did hold a baby for a busy mother and I nearly dropped it. I remember that it felt like a live snake in a sack."[34]

It wasn't just babies that Elsa disliked. Her time running the Children's Theatre also led her to dislike of "little Alberts and Ethels" with their "smug self-satisfied" expressions, and she once said in an interview, "I don't want to take children on my knee and muzzle them or nuzzle them, whatever you're supposed

29. O'Hara with Nicoletti, 36.
30. Lanchester, *Elsa Lanchester, Herself,* 161.
31. O'Hara with Nicoletti, *'Tis Herself,* 26.
32. *San Francisco Examiner,* September 9, 1979 (emphasis in original).
33. Lanchester, *Elsa Lanchester, Herself,* 34.
34. Lanchester, 315.

to do. There really is nothing wrong with children. But if they like you, they like you too much. They crowd in and choke you to death."[35]

Having discussed the matter with Elsa, Charles Higham concluded that the reason the Laughtons did not become parents was because Elsa "didn't feel fond of children herself."[36] Other factors may also have been at play; in that era, having a child could have meant the end of Elsa's career and relegated her to playing even more of a background role in her own life than she already did. It was also an aspect of her life over which she had complete control and did not have to compromise.

Whatever the reason, her firm stance added to the disappointments and frictions that were eating away at her marriage. Simon Callow wrote that "Elsa failing Charles as a mother, and Charles failing Elsa as a lover contributed a layer to the opaque texture of their life together."[37] Certainly it gave Charles and Maureen O'Hara plenty to whisper about behind Elsa's back.

In early 1939 it was reported that the next Mayflower Pictures film would be *The Admirable Crichton*, based on the play by J. M. Barrie, with Charles in the lead role, and Elsa and Maureen O'Hara heading the supporting cast.[38] First, however, Charles and O'Hara were to travel to America to promote *Jamaica Inn* and film *The Hunchback of Notre Dame*. O'Hara remembered that they expected this to take about three months, after which they would head straight to Paris for *The Admirable Crichton*, and Elsa would meet them there.[39] However, the outbreak of war would cancel those plans, and this, coupled with *Jamaica Inn*'s lack of success, spelled the end for Mayflower Pictures.

35. Lanchester, *Charles Laughton and I*, 103–4; *Independent Press Telegram*, December 26, 1965.

36. Higham, *Charles Laughton*, 27.

37. Callow, *Charles Laughton*, 283.

38. *Belfast Telegraph*, March 8, 1939.

39. O'Hara and Nicoletti, *'Tis Herself*, 31.

16 Remarkably Complex

Considering her feelings about both Charles and Maureen O'Hara, Elsa was not sorry to stay in England when the other two sailed to America in June 1939. However, she was most unhappy about the insinuations the press started making upon their arrival in New York, and when a reporter called her to ask about the nature of the relationship between Charles and O'Hara, Elsa decided that O'Hara was to blame. "I don't know what Miss O'Hara or any others have been saying," she responded, "but she's an actress who is going to appear with Charles in his next picture. He found her, discovered her, and so on—and there's just nothing to it."[1] Of course there was nothing to it: Elsa knew very well that Charles was not romantically interested in Maureen, but she did not care for the humiliation of appearing to be cuckolded, and if her marriage was to offer Charles protection in public then Elsa felt she deserved the same.

What nobody knew until their boat had departed was that O'Hara had secretly married production assistant George Brown while in London. Charles was furious when O'Hara's mother, who was traveling with her as chaperone, told him about the nuptials.[2] Here was another red-headed actress whose behavior he could not control. When he told Elsa over the phone, she laughed "like a lunatic," and she did not hesitate to bring it up in conversation later on, much to the annoyance of O'Hara, who had instantly regretted her impulsive marriage and later had it quietly annulled.[3]

Alone in England, Elsa was enjoying herself. She attended several parties and went on a boating holiday with Allen Lane—the founder of Penguin Books—and his brother Richard. The Lane brothers were old friends; author Ethel Mannin describes weekends in the country with Elsa and Charles, Allen and Richard Lane, and other assorted figures from the publishing world, such as Ralph Straus, Michael Joseph, and Christina Foyle. They would all convene in Mannin's country cottage and consume copious amounts of gin. Mannin recalled, "we led each

---

1. Lanchester, *Elsa Lanchester, Herself*, 161; O'Hara and Nicoletti, *'Tis Herself*, 35.

2. O'Hara and Nicoletti, *'Tis Herself*, 34–35.

3. Lanchester, *Elsa Lanchester, Herself*, 161.

other on, and there was a certain amount of nonsense, but no one rode a horse up the stairs, and no one threw anyone in the lily pond, and around 1 a.m. there would be a great deal of slamming of doors and starting up of engines."[4] Elsa's vacation aboard Allen Lane's boat, the *Penguin*, seems to have been rather more sedate. Plans were discussed to bring out *Charles Laughton and I* as a Penguin paperback, but nothing would come of this as war would intervene.

Concerns were growing in England once again regarding the imminence of war, and in America, Charles was becoming worried. It was reported in the press that although many in Hollywood thought little of the rumors, Charles was "worried enough to send for his wife."[5] When Elsa arrived at Stapledown with the Lane brothers, she found a telegram waiting for her. It was cryptic but clear in its demands: "Leave immediately for Hollywood. Cannot call now. Will explain later."[6] Hoping that the summons was in regard to a job but suspecting the truth, Elsa booked passage on the first ship she could, the *Normandie*. As she departed, Elsa shed a few tears for "poor little England," knowing that tough times were ahead and wondering when she would see home again.[7]

There was quite a lot of press excitement in New York when the ship arrived on July 10, 1939, for there were several movie stars on board, including Mary Pickford, Buddy Rogers, and Myrna Loy. When asked by reporters about her arrival, Elsa said that she was planning a quiet summer in Hollywood while Charles made *Hunchback*, and then they would travel home together in October to make *The Admirable Crichton*. However, within a fortnight of Elsa's arrival in Hollywood, influential columnist Louella Parsons reported that she was to appear in *Vigil in the Night* (1940) with Carole Lombard at RKO, in a part that "will give Mrs. Laughton a good chance to shine." Parsons added, "One thing I admire about the gal is that she makes no bones about being ambitious in her own career and refuses to shine in Charlie's reflected glory."[8] As on many occasions in Elsa's life, this part would end up going to someone else, Ethel Griffies, but the reasons given for this are varied. One columnist, Edwin Schallert, wrote that Griffies was "reckoned more suitable for the part," and then changed his tune three days later to say that Elsa turned down the role because "it was not of sufficient moment."[9] This latter explanation was expanded on by Harrison Carroll, in a gossipy snippet that has a ring of truth to it:

> It happened in a Hollywood late spot. Elsa Lanchester was explaining why she turned down a Hollywood film offer. "I didn't think the part was heavy enough,"

---

4.   Lewis, *Penguin Special*.

5.   *Daily Clintonian*, July 15, 1939.

6.   Lanchester, *Elsa Lanchester, Herself*, 162.

7.   Lanchester, 162.

8.   *San Francisco Examiner*, August 1, 1939.

9.   *Los Angeles Times*, September 16, 1939; *Los Angeles Times*, September 19, 1939.

> she explained, "especially after I starred in 'The Beachcomber.'" Husband Charles Laughton looked up. "Featured in 'The Beachcomber,' my dear," he said. "I was starred in it."[10]

Yet another columnist weighed in with a different reason; Erskine Johnson told his readers that the reason Elsa "does not accept any roles in Hollywood pictures is because of English and American taxes. If both Laughton and Miss Lanchester were working, she would receive only six cents of every $5 paid her."[11]

Stuck at the Garden of Allah Hotel during a horrifically hot summer while Charles filmed *The Hunchback of Notre Dame* with Maureen O'Hara, Elsa was close to the despair she had felt on her first visit to Hollywood. A reporter dispatched to interview her about her husband noticed her loneliness. "Getting her to talk, however, is not difficult," he wrote. "She has conversation bottled up in her, and the first question pops the cork . . . you can see how she appreciates a listener." Elsa told him that due to Charles's long hours on the set, they had "no callers . . . we see nobody."[12]

This was an exaggeration. Larry Adler—the harmonica player Elsa had met while touring in *Peter Pan*—discusses in his autobiography his friendship with the Laughtons, which continued when Adler moved to California in 1939. Adler recalls one anecdote that demonstrates the superficiality of life in Hollywood. "I only knew Charles and Elsa Laughton living at the Garden of Allah, a sprawling collection of flats and villas on Sunset Boulevard. They gave a party at which a man said to me: 'I don't know many people here; are you important?' 'Mummy thinks so,' I answered." Later, when Adler's wife Eileen was expecting their first child, Adler looked to his friends for support. "The night before the birth I was in a panic," he recalled. "The Laughtons coped with me and Charles fed me brandy."[13]

By the time *Hunchback* had finished filming, war had been declared in Europe, and it was clear that Mayflower Pictures was not going to make any more movies. The British press reported: "it looks as if most, if not all, of the British players now in Hollywood are going to stay there. . . . [The Laughtons] are stopping over there even though the film 'Hunchback of Notre Dame' is finished."[14] The suggestion that British film stars were somehow betraying their country by staying in America was amplified in British news reports as the conflict continued, and was very painful for both Elsa and Charles to read. But despite their love for England, the Laughtons were already planning to become American citizens, for tax purposes if for no other reason. Although Charles told the press in July

10. *Daily Times*, October 9, 1939.
11. *Wilkes-Barre Record*, November 23, 1939.
12. *Charlotte Observer*, September 24, 1939.
13. Adler, It Ain't Necessarily So, 99, 102.
14. *Liverpool Evening Express*, October 7, 1939.

1940, "I am a citizen of England and England is at war," the couple would file their declarations of intention before the war was over.[15]

Elsa's questionable luck with modes of transport continued. After previously enduring (and occasionally enjoying) turbulent voyages by ship and plane, as well as a couple of car accidents, she would experience a train derailing and yet another automobile accident in late 1939. Elsa and Charles were traveling on the Santa Fe train from Los Angeles to Chicago in November 1939 when a wrenching motion sent Elsa sliding down the corridor, ruining her shoes by stubbing the toes flat; Charles was in the dining room, where the jolt was such that sugar spilled over the table. Although the locomotive had completely overturned, no one was seriously hurt, and Elsa and Charles found themselves stuck just outside of Raton, New Mexico, for several hours while replacement transportation was arranged. Charles's celebrity meant that they were treated well by the townspeople, and once again Elsa enjoyed herself thoroughly, even taking a souvenir, a heavy nine-inch piece of the broken rail. "Charles was furious that I would carry this piece of rail with us," Elsa would recall, "but I wanted that piece of the accident. The rail. To remember everything that happened that day."[16]

The car accident was not such a good memory. Barely a month after the train derailment, on December 23, 1939, Charles's chauffeur, Floyd Siane, was driving the station wagon when he collided with Mr. and Mrs. Walter W. Hale, who then sued Elsa and Charles for $90,000 in damages. The case went as far as jury selection but was eventually settled out of court.[17]

Although Elsa would not appear in another film until 1941, she did have some work to occupy her on the radio. A meeting with producer and writer Norman Corwin in New York led to Elsa and Charles appearing on his show *The Pursuit of Happiness* in late 1939, reading the poem "John Brown's Body." "In those days it was still possible for actors of the stature of the Laughtons to speak words by writers of the stature of Thomas Wolfe and Stephen Vincent Benét on a commercial network," Corwin recalled. "The experience was new for them and they apparently enjoyed it."[18] Elsa would enjoy success in many more radio dramas, both with and without Charles, throughout 1940; the play "Fanny Kemble" was written for her by Joseph Liss and Louis Lantz, as was "The Women Stay at Home" by Arch Oboler.[19] She was also interviewed regularly, and she appeared on talk shows and quiz shows. In what must have been a bittersweet experience, Elsa appeared alongside Charles in a scene from *Sidewalks of London* in February 1940, to promote the film even though she was not in the cast. Vivien Leigh had

---

15. *Philadelphia Inquirer*, July 13, 1940.

16. Lanchester, *Elsa Lanchester, Herself*, 139.

17. *San Bernardino County Sun*, April 12, 1941.

18. Quoted in Lanchester, *Elsa Lanchester, Herself*, 167.

19. "Fanny Kemble," *Columbia Workshop*, January 18, 1940; "The Women Stay at Home," *Arch Oboler's Plays*, February 24, 1940.

been seen as Scarlett O'Hara before the American release of *Sidewalks*, and was therefore far too busy to promote a film she disliked.

But however much she enjoyed radio, Elsa was still hoping for a career in the movies. Speculation swirled in the press over a picture initially called *Half a Rogue* and renamed *Mr. Pinkie*, which would star Elsa and Charles, along with Lucille Ball and Ann Miller. Despite extensive press coverage, the project was ultimately shelved by RKO. There were hints published that Charles was in conflict with the studio because of its attitude toward Elsa: "Laughton wishes to co-star with wife, Elsa Lanchester," read one gossip column. "The studio considers Miss Lanchester non-box office."[20]

The war in Europe was becoming more serious, after an initially uneventful start for English residents. Allen Lane wrote to Elsa in the early days of the conflict, "There really is an astonishing lack of interest in the whole affair, and except for the fact that there are more people in uniform, and that there are occasional slight hitches in getting through supplies, there is very little to denote that there is really a war on."[21] Elsa was worried about her parents and offered to bring them to America, but "a combination of fatalism, old age, and bravado made them, like so many others, absolutely immoveable."[22]

One who was not so stubborn was an old friend of Charles's, Renee Ruben, whom Elsa had become friendly with in London. Ruben was Jewish and feared what would happen should the Nazis invade England. She wrote of her concerns to Elsa and Charles, and they agreed to bring her out to America, where she would be employed as Charles's secretary and live with the couple in their new house in North Rockingham. Elsa describes Ruben as a curious woman, who referred to herself in the third person and agreed to take on tasks such as driving the car but "made it seem such a terrible chore."[23] She was also possessive over Charles. Ruben would remain in their house for several years, working as a personal assistant and housekeeper.

Despite their efforts to help people such as Ruben, reports in the British press suggested that Elsa and Charles were somehow shirking their duty by playing make-believe in the sunshine while their countrymen and women suffered the effects of war. Charles was especially affected by the criticism, being prone to self-doubt at the best of times, and would defend himself frequently to Elsa by recalling his experiences in the First World War trenches, "bayoneting men, and getting gassed," concluding that "I think once in a lifetime is enough."[24]

In September 1940, the Laughtons heard that their Gordon Square flat had been destroyed in the Blitz. It had been struck not by a bomb, but by a downed

20. *Burlington Daily News*, January 28, 1941.
21. Lewis, *Penguin Special*.
22. Lanchester, *Elsa Lanchester, Herself*, 166.
23. Lanchester, 169.
24. Lanchester, 181.

Junkers Ju 88 dive bomber. Charles put a brave face on the matter, telling *The New York Times*, "I should be glad to sacrifice twenty houses if German dive bombers would smash themselves to bits on them. To hell with the cash if they can bring down the Junkers. It was a glorious end for the house."[25] For Elsa, though, it must have been a painful loss, one that represented the cutting of another tie, leaving her more adrift than ever.

Throughout the war, Elsa and Charles did what they could. They treated evacuees to once-in-a-lifetime experiences and donated thousands of dollars to War Fund charities, Charles read to wounded soldiers and led War Bond drives, and Elsa volunteered at the Hollywood Canteen. In August 1941, they threw a party for the Royal Air Force (RAF) trainees who were in America for desert training. Accounts vary as to whether fifty or 150 men attended, but those that did were treated to an unforgettable experience on the grounds of the Pacific Palisades house overlooking the ocean. Elsa's time running a nightclub and Charles's background in hotels had left them with the organizational skills needed to entertain on an epic scale, and Renee Ruben was always on hand to help.

A large, diaphanous tent covered the lawn, lit and warmed by charcoal braziers, and traditional British food, such as roast beef and trifle, was served. A "gipsy orchestra" and a dance floor were also provided—and so were the starlets. Deanna Durbin, Ida Lupino, and Patricia Morison were among the young beauties who attended, with older actresses such as Gladys Cooper and Flora Robson acting as "den mothers" and ensuring respectability. In her autobiography, Elsa was at pains to point out that while she did not consider herself one of the starlets, at thirty-eight she was really too young to belong to the older set: "I was in between generations, you might say."[26]

Flora Robson wrote a letter to her brother that describes the party and the heightened emotions of the British actors in America: "we all went determined to entertain the RAF, but in the end they entertained us. They pulled the piano out and sang songs, and Deanna led them in 'There'll Always be an England.' That and 'Loch Lomond' got me down and I cried." One young man dancing with Deanna Durbin declared that the war was wonderful because "I'm in Hollywood, dancing with you." Robson concluded that "Charles and Elsa have never given a more perfect party," and Elsa agreed, saying, "It was just a magical night."[27]

The war years would provide Elsa with a roller coaster of emotional highs and lows. Her career, after a slow start, would pick up, and she would find job satisfaction and fulfillment, but her personal life would be less happy, and her relationship with Charles would fracture further. Although there was not one singular reason for this marital disharmony, it has been suggested by Charles's biographer

---

25. *The New York Times*, September 19, 1940.

26. Lanchester, *Elsa Lanchester, Herself*, 181.

27. *Coventry Evening Telegraph*, August 25, 1941; Lanchester, *Elsa Lanchester, Herself*, 182.

Simon Callow that Charles went through a "change of life" in his forties. Having previously only enjoyed fleeting sexual encounters with men, Charles now "began to discover the sexual possibilities of his chauffeurs and masseurs and batmen, and then it would appear . . . he became insatiable, a phenomenon which often overcomes men who feel cheated of their sexual youth."[28]

As indicated by Callow, many of Charles's lovers were employed by him in and around their house, and Elsa found herself having to transition to a situation that she had never agreed to. She had accepted her husband's occasional dalliances with young men as something that was out of sight and never discussed, but now Elsa would find it impossible to ignore what was going on, and Charles made little attempt to hide it from her. Elsa had long ago accepted that she would not be Charles's sexual partner, but she had believed herself to be his partner in every other way. Now, more and more, her role was being eroded, even within her own home.

The constant presence of Renee Ruben also contributed to Elsa's unease. Although Ruben had agreed to work for the Laughtons in a secretarial capacity, she followed instructions with bad grace, especially when they were given by Elsa. More worryingly, she was not above creating trouble between Elsa and Charles, dripping venom in their ears and gossiping behind their backs, setting them against each other.

With such a viper in the nest, Elsa had never needed to work so much, to have something outside of her poisonous home environment to think about. This distraction finally came in the form of a leading role in a Broadway play.

Rehearsals for *They Walk Alone* began in February 1941. It was a curious play, "half comedy, half thriller," and entirely ridiculous, with Elsa playing a sweet and innocent maidservant whose personality is strangely affected by organ music, to the extent that she becomes a "homicidal sex maniac," who then systematically slaughters the young men of the neighborhood.[29] It was a role that called for camp melodrama and dark humor, James Whale–style, which suited Elsa down to the ground. She was understandably dismissive when the director, Berthold Viertel, suggested in an early rehearsal that she should consult her husband on how to play the role. "Indeed not," she responded. "I sent [Charles] a script of the play and told him he could write me one letter of suggestions—just one. Then I'll do as I like."[30]

After premiering in New Haven, Connecticut, the play moved to the John Golden Theatre on Broadway, opening on March 12, 1941. Those who enjoyed Elsa's Bridal histrionics would not leave the theater disappointed, and the consensus in the press was that the play was terrible, but Elsa was a phenomenon. A typical opinion went as follows: "Miss Lanchester is in fact superb in a role

---

28. Callow, *Charles Laughton*, 284.

29. *Hartford Courant*, March 7, 1941; *Brooklyn Daily Eagle*, March 3, 1941.

30. *Pittsburgh Press*, February 14, 1941.

that must have looked impossible on paper. By the sheer magic of her skill she brings to life a complex paranoiac . . . in a performance of such power that the ineptitudes of the play itself are almost forgotten."[31] Brooks Atkinson opined in *The New York Times* that Elsa's character "is like a remarkably complex portrait pinned on the wall. It is something to be admired for its brilliant workmanship. . . . Nothing in the drama is as adroit, imaginative and vivid as her acting."[32]

The reviewer for the *Chicago Tribune* accused her of overacting, but this reviewer surely missed the point: there was no better way to rise above such material, and even this critic acknowledged that Elsa had the audience in the palm of her hand.[33] All the reviews confirmed the spell she cast over the audience. Sadly, Elsa's powerhouse acting could not save the show, which closed after just twenty-one performances. Even so, Elsa made the most of her time in New York, where she was guest of honor at a Theatre Assembly luncheon and was recognized by the Theatre Forum, as well as being interviewed on the radio and in the press. She was emerging from her husband's shadow, but there were inevitably still some questions about Charles. When asked why he had not attended her opening night, Elsa replied, "Charles is afraid of mystery plays."[34]

Even before the end of her theatrical run, Elsa's next project, the film *Ladies in Retirement* (1941), was announced by Columbia Pictures, and this time there would be no disappointments or recasting. The movie was a Grand Guignol–style, slow-paced crime drama starring Ida Lupino as Ellen Creed. Elsa and Edith Barrett played Ellen's disturbingly eccentric sisters, and once again Elsa was able to incorporate a dark humor into her work. This time she underplayed her character's madness, using a flat vocal tone and unflinching gaze effectively, which contrasted well with Barrett's more nervy, chattering, and childish portrayal.

The film would be nominated for an Academy Award for Best Art Direction—Interior Set Design, but the exterior set dressing was another matter. To create a marsh, the props department had created puddles filled with mud and stagnant water, but the constant dampness resulted in some of the actors claiming that they were suffering from coughs, colds, and sinus infections. "I don't mind a sniffle," Elsa was reported to have said, "but that water is a mosquito paradise."[35] Although her period costume's long skirt and sleeves offered her some protection, she had rolled down her black cotton stockings to keep cool, and once the mosquitoes discovered this, her legs were covered with bites.

---

31. *Brooklyn Citizen*, March 13, 1941.

32. *The New York Times*, March 13, 1941.

33. *Chicago Tribune*, March 23, 1941.

34. *San Francisco Examiner*, March 19, 1941.

35. *Arizona Republic*, July 20, 1941.

17   Turnabout

Elsa was enjoying some small success on the screen and stage, but it was becoming clear that this was not enough to satisfy her creatively. Back in October 1940—with things in Hollywood looking bleak and before her starring role on Broadway—Elsa had been in New York, searching for work of a different kind. Newspapers reporting on Charles's promotional tour for his film *They Knew What They Wanted* (1940) wrote that "his most important business on his eastern trip is to talk his wife, Elsa Lanchester, out of her yen to return to her old profession as a cabaret entertainer."[1] Quite why he should want to talk her out of it is not explained, but Elsa was clearly searching for a job as a singer-comedienne in a nightclub, in order to demonstrate to Americans where her talents truly lay. After a few weeks, however, Elsa was back in Hollywood with Charles, apparently having decided to put such ambitions on hold.

But the desire to return to an area in which she excelled did not leave her, and she confided this to her friend Helen Deutsch, a screenwriter. Over lunch one day in 1941, Deutsch would introduce Elsa to an idea that would shape her career for the next decade and beyond. She told Elsa that she knew three "crazy guys" who were opening up a small theater on La Cienega Boulevard, which would feature a revue. Intrigued, Elsa agreed to find out more, and after lunch the two women headed to the unfinished Turnabout Theatre.

The concept of the Turnabout was certainly novel. The auditorium featured two stages, one at either end, with seating in between. The seating was reversible, using old streetcar stock, and the gimmick was that a marionette show would be performed at one end, after which the audience would "turnabout" at the interval, then watch a revue at the other. It was created by a trio called the Yale Puppeteers, who were looking for a more permanent gig after years on tour. The three men—Forman Brown, Harry Burnett, and Roddy Brandon—were joined in the endeavor by actress Dorothy Neumann. They enthusiastically accepted Elsa's offer to appear in the revue.

In his book about the Turnabout, Forman Brown recalled his first meeting with Elsa. "Having only seen her on screen in character parts, we were not

---

1.   *Windsor Star*, October 12, 1940.

Elsa in costume for her "When a Lady Has a Piazza" number at the Turnabout Theatre in Hollywood in the 1940s.
Everett Collection Inc. / Alamy Stock Photo

prepared for the vibrancy of this woman with the tangle of flaming red hair," he wrote. "Elsa would come in, we were told, for two weeks on a trial basis. Her name alone, we knew, would probably fill the house and give us publicity a new venture like ours would need so badly."[2]

Elsa's first night at the Turnabout, July 15, 1941, came five days after the theater's opening. The reason given by Brown for this delayed start was, at Charles Laughton's suggestion, to give the theater two shots of publicity: one for its opening and another for Elsa's appearance. Elsa would later claim that although this was all true, her own stage fright had also played a part. "I had wanted to do this kind of work again for so long and had not found the opportunity," she said. "Now when the opportunity came, I was too scared to get up and do my songs in front of the Hollywood celebrities who would be coming on opening night."[3]

Once Elsa made it onto that stage, however, there was no looking back. That first night, the songs she sang were like old friends, comforting and familiar in a new and frightening place. They were songs she had practiced and polished at the Cave of Harmony and at those private parties back in the 1920s—"He Didn't Oughter (Come to Bed in Boots)," "Someone Broke Lola's Saucepan," and "The Ratcatcher's Daughter." Brown wrote of her opening night: "So she came, and she conquered. . . . Her magnetism was unfailing, and when she became part of the show suddenly everyone else in the cast seemed, not as sometimes happens, to suffer, but to glow the more brightly."[4] Indeed, Elsa proved so popular in her first fortnight that they extended her engagement for another week, and then another. The weeks turned into months, with the songs in her act changing regularly, as did all the other material, so as to keep the audiences coming back. An October 1941 review of her performance in the *Los Angeles Times* read: "While broadly comical in content, Miss Lanchester's rendition of her three Cockney numbers is suave, subtle, with a rippling undercurrent of fun that is at the same time spontaneous and smooth."[5]

Here was somewhere where Elsa could be happy. The Turnabout bore many similarities to the Cave of Harmony in its quirky artistry and team spirit. The author Ray Bradbury visited the theater over thirty times, and remembered that the Turnabouters "not only acted but appeared in the box office selling tickets on the dozens of occasions when I showed up with my hard-earned cash."[6] But although the friendship and camaraderie between the Turnabouters was reminiscent of the Cave of Harmony, Elsa was no longer the carefree girl she had been in her twenties, and the knocks she had taken were beginning to show in

2.   Brown, *Small Wonder*, 202.

3.   Lanchester and Brown, *A Gamut of Girls*, 16.

4.   Brown, *Small Wonder*, 209.

5.   *Los Angeles Times*, October 9, 1941.

6.   Bradbury, "What Else but Elsa?," 9.

her personality. Forman Brown praised her talent and her way with a song, but admitted that "her wit could be sharp" and that she "did not endure fools lightly."[7]

Due to the Turnabout policy of regularly changing the material, Brown began to write songs especially for Elsa. It was agreed that Elsa would take ownership of these in place of payment, which would work out well for all parties involved. There would eventually be over fifty of these songs, the lyrics for many of which were published in the book *A Gamut of Girls* in 1988. With titles such as "Mrs. Badger-Butts" and "Lackadaisy Maisie," they were lighthearted ditties with upbeat endings, packed with puns and double entendres. Elsa recorded many of them on her albums *Songs for a Smoke-Filled Room* (1957) and *Songs for a Shuttered Parlor* (1958), so they can still be appreciated by audiences today.

Charles would say that Elsa and Forman Brown enjoyed "a true artistic marriage of talents," and their creative partnership was reminiscent of Elsa's earlier alliance with Harold Scott.[8] Unlike her pairing with Scott, however, there would be no romance with Brown, who was in a long-term relationship with fellow Yale Puppeteer and Turnabouter Roddy Brandon.

The contribution that the Turnabout made to Elsa's self-esteem at a difficult time cannot be overstated. She would say that "this American acceptance was of almost earth-shaking pleasure."[9] As far as films were concerned, Charles was helping Elsa out where he could. When they were cast as husband and wife in the star-studded episodic movie *Tales of Manhattan* (1942), Elsa was unwell and nearly found herself replaced. She kept the job only because Charles agreed to work an extra two weeks without pay in order to make up the time lost by her illness. The anthology film told the story of a "cursed" tailcoat that gets passed from one owner to another, and it featured such famous performers as Rita Hayworth, Paul Robeson, Charles Boyer, Edward G. Robinson, and Ginger Rogers. These stars shone so brightly that Elsa barely rated a mention in most reviews, although the *Sunday Post* did call her performance "a grand piece of character acting."[10]

Her film career may have received little press attention around the time *Tales of Manhattan* was released, but the gossip columnists more than made up the shortfall with their speculation about the Laughton marriage. From July 1942 onward, Elsa and Charles would go through a series of separations and reconciliations, with each move detailed carefully by the powerful pens of writers such as Hedda Hopper, Louella Parsons, and Sheilah Graham, whose columns were read across America. At first, Parsons was dismissive of the divorce rumors, claiming that "their separations happen often and never last," but the splits continued,

---

7. Brown, *Small Wonder*, 229.

8. Lanchester and Brown, *A Gamut of Girls*, 18.

9. Lanchester, *Elsa Lanchester, Herself*, 172.

10. *Sunday Post*, April 5, 1943.

with one report concluding that the couple had "just about decided to tell it to a judge."[11]

While gossip columns should never be relied on for the accuracy of their reporting, this time they were correct. When looking back on these events, Elsa would say: "The most difficult thing to recall is a bad time in your life. This was a very evil time."[12] The gossip columns were wrong in one regard, however: they reported that no one else was involved in the matter. In reality, one person in particular was doing her best to come between Elsa and Charles—their secretary and houseguest Renee Ruben.

Despite the kindness shown to her by the Laughtons, Ruben used her privileged position in the household to spread discord and misunderstanding between the couple. In this she was aided and abetted by Charles's "masseur," whom Elsa refers to in *Elsa Lanchester, Herself* using the alias Bobby Benson. She uses the name Sheila Schwartz to refer to Renee Ruben.

The extent to which Elsa's home environment affected her mental health at this time is clear in her autobiography, where she writes: "I would get down low, I'd have angry fits. I would cry—something I had always tried not to do. . . . I felt as if I were living in the house with enemies, as if Bobby Benson and Sheila Schwartz and Charles were all together against me." Matters came to a head when Elsa discovered a letter that Ruben was writing to her sister Madge, which read in part, "That red-headed —— is still here. I don't know if she'll ever go. The snub-nosed —— seems to be a fixture."[13] Elsa took the letter to Charles, and together they confronted Ruben, who left the house immediately, never to be seen by Elsa again. In her book, Elsa claims that Ruben went on to work for two other couples, each of whom separated within a year of employing her. "A true Iago by nature," was Charles's opinion of Ruben, which neatly absolved him of any complicity in the matter by allowing him to retreat into the role of Othello, the deceived innocent.[14] However, as had been seen with Maureen O'Hara, Charles was not above bad-mouthing Elsa to those that adored him. His onetime business manager Paul Gregory would later say of Charles: "He was cruel. . . . There was a cruelty there that was frightening. Whatever the situation, he'd pit somebody against somebody then make turmoil, he couldn't help it. He just had to do this."[15]

Another contributing factor to their marital strife was Charles's sexual relationship with a young actor. When Charles Higham's biography of Charles Laughton was first commissioned, British tabloid newspaper *The People* reported that many of Charles's former sexual partners were concerned that they would be

11. *Morning Post*, August 25, 1943; *Pittsburgh Post-Gazette*, September 21, 1942.

12. Lanchester, *Elsa Lanchester, Herself*, 182.

13. Lanchester, 182.

14. Lanchester, 182.

15. "Charles Laughton," *Hollywood Greats*.

publicly outed. "Because many of Laughton's lovers are still alive in Hollywood, Elsa insists that biographer Charles Higham disguise their names," the newspaper reported. "But the homosexual community is still scared stiff. They feel they will still be recognisable because of particular situations and events."[16] If actor William Phipps had been worried then he had good reason to be, because despite calling him David Roberts, Higham provided a wealth of detail that makes Bill Phipps easily identifiable.

In many ways, Phipps represented the kind of man that Charles would become involved with repeatedly over the years to come. He was young, attractive, masculine, and bisexual rather than exclusively attracted to men, and he looked up to Charles for career guidance, appearing in Charles's acting classes, which began in the mid-1940s. He was dependent on Charles in other ways as well, according to Higham: "When David needed money, both Charles and Elsa, acting very humanely, agreed that he should be loaned various amounts."[17] Although their sexual relationship would fade over time and was never exclusive, the two men would remain close for the rest of Charles's life. Christopher Isherwood, a friend and later neighbor of the Laughtons, mentions Bill Phipps and Charles sharing a bed in 1960, and Phipps would be a pallbearer at Charles's funeral.[18] Elsa never expressed any hostility toward Phipps; indeed, although she was happy to keep her distance from the house during this time, Elsa was actually pleased with the effect the relationship had on Charles. "She was glad that Charles had found a more or less sustaining sexual and emotional relationship, that he seemed to be gaining a little in a sense of his own worth, that he hated himself just a fraction less."[19]

In an interview with Barry Norman, business manager and producer Paul Gregory would say that Charles had a Henry Higgins complex, that he delighted in helping handsome young men develop their acting skills.[20] Bill Phipps is the earliest example of this. He is also the most successful: from the late 1940s onward, he found regular work in westerns and science fiction films, and in 1950 he provided the voice for Prince Charming in Disney's animated classic *Cinderella*.

After several separations, Elsa and Charles would eventually reconcile, and they would even begin citizenship proceedings together, but there was a new distance between them that did not go unnoticed. Separation rumors would appear in the press regularly throughout the 1940s, often countered with indignant denials, declarations of happiness, and revoltingly self-effacing quotations allegedly from Elsa as to how to keep one's husband happy, such as "I don't think a

16. *The People*, December 8, 1974.

17. Higham, *Charles Laughton*, 110.

18. Isherwood, *Diaries*, vol. 2, 14.

19. Higham, *Charles Laughton*, 125.

20. "Charles Laughton," *Hollywood Greats*.

marriage can work very well if the wife's career becomes more important than the husband's."[21]

With feminism a dirty word in the 1940s, the newspapers praised Elsa for being happy in her husband's shadow. One particularly nauseating article demonstrates what successful women were up against: "Tiny, tireless, lighthearted Elsa Lanchester, goes from year to year on her pleasant, pleasing way, content to bask in the reflected glory of her actor husband, Charles Laughton," read the cloying prose. "Proud she is of the honors heaped upon her chubby spouse. Content she is to play second fiddle in the family orchestra. And yet Elsa Lanchester is one of the finest actresses of her time."[22]

She may have been willing to play the good wife in the press, but Elsa's career now became her retreat and her salvation. Between 1942 and 1945 she made seven films while performing six nights a week at the Turnabout and volunteering at the Hollywood Canteen on Monday evenings, the one night the Turnabout was closed. Keeping busy became Elsa's therapy.

Her time at the Hollywood Canteen also provided Elsa with a much-needed ego boost. The brainchild of Bette Davis, John Garfield, and Jules Stein, the Hollywood Canteen provided food and entertainment for servicemen free of charge from 1942 to 1945. Many movie stars volunteered their services, with some providing entertainment and others cooking and serving the food. One who accompanied Elsa on Mondays was former queen of Hollywood and America's sweetheart, Mary Pickford, now in her early fifties. For the servicemen, a dance with a Hollywood beauty such as Marlene Dietrich or Rita Hayworth was the highlight of their evening. In a 1960 interview with Phyllis Battelle, Elsa remembered that being the center of attention was a heady experience: "Soldiers crowded around me! And all the while the cute little blonde starlets, who wear all those false eyelashes in the cinema, went ignored. And it was only because they didn't look as good in person as on film, and I didn't look quite the horror they thought I was."[23]

A recurring theme in Elsa's interviews from the 1940s onward was that she was better looking in person than she often appeared on the screen; this fact was remarked on by reporters and, frequently, by Elsa herself. Although she was not a vain woman, as demonstrated by her early disregard for her appearance when meeting with Irving Thalberg, she nevertheless wanted it to be made clear that she was not *un*attractive. Doubtless, Elsa's insecurity in this regard was a result of being surrounded by Hollywood beauties and being rejected sexually by her husband. She also turned forty around this time, in a town obsessed with youth.

While the Turnabout and the Canteen kept her busy and away from home in the evenings, Elsa was also eager to find film roles to keep her occupied during the day. In 1942, in addition to *Tales of Manhattan*, she played a small part

---

21. *The Herald*, December 5, 1946.

22. *Hartford Courant*, March 6, 1944.

23. *Philadelphia Daily News*, February 17, 1960.

opposite Tyrone Power in *Son of Fury*, where once again her talents were said to be "wasted."[24]

Elsa made three films in 1943. First was another star-saturated anthology movie, *Forever and a Day*, described as "an All-Star, All-for-Charity medley in aid of war relief," in which all the performers donated their services.[25] Although Charles was also in the film, husband and wife did not appear together in the same scenes. The charitable ambitions of the film were certainly laudable, but it has not stood the test of time as a piece of entertainment.

A film that would retain its appeal for considerably longer was another of Elsa's 1943 vehicles, *Lassie Come Home*. The first—and some consider the best—movie in the hugely successful *Lassie* franchise saw Elsa back on the MGM lot in an unusually understated role for her as Roddy McDowall's mother. Considering that she was married to a Yorkshireman in real life, Elsa's accent in the film was patchy at best, although the *Yorkshire Post* would write that she "stands out for her clear-cut picture of a Yorkshire cottage woman."[26] She also received praise for rounding out what could have been a rather flat character by adding a "touch of bitterness, an assumed steeliness."[27]

Notable for being Elsa's first color film—allowing cinema audiences to finally see her famous auburn hair, which photographed beautifully—*Lassie Come Home* was a success on its release. Elsa, however, was not overly enamored with the movie. Years later she would expand on the old adage "never work with children and animals": "Never try to compete with a dog, horse, child or any other form of loveable animal life. It's a thankless job, unless you like to take the money and run."[28] It is interesting that Elsa here speaks of acting alongside others as a form of competition, which can perhaps be linked to the much-refuted accusations of scene-stealing that would occur later in her career. In *Lassie*, however, she lost the contest, being upstaged not only by the dog, but also by the wide-eyed and earnest child actors Roddy McDowall and Elizabeth Taylor.

24. *Sunday Post*, September 20, 1942.

25. *The Tatler*, June 16, 1943; *Liverpool Evening Express*, September 11, 1943.

26. *Yorkshire Post and Leeds Intelligencer*, January 5, 1944.

27. *Daily Oklahoman*, December 19, 1943.

28. Hadleigh, *Leading Ladies*, 94.

18 We Don't Know Who We Are

In the press, Elsa's hectic workload was beginning to attract attention, with one article dubbing her "Hollywood's busiest actress" and claiming that the twin demands of stage and screen meant that she was averaging five hours of sleep a night.[1] Another report claimed that the figure was closer to four hours, and went on to detail her demanding schedule: "Up at six, she works all day. . . . From the studio she goes straight to the Turnabout. . . . After midnight she goes to dinner—then home."[2]

Author Axel Nissen wrote of Elsa's film career, "As a general rule: The bigger the film, the smaller was Lanchester's part."[3] While the accuracy of this statement is debatable, the inverse notion—that Elsa's biggest roles came in smaller pictures—finds support in two wartime B-movies that she made in the early 1940s: *Thumbs Up* (1943) and *Passport to Destiny* (1944). The latter represents the only time in her entire career that Elsa would receive lead billing.

Made by Republic Pictures, a Poverty Row studio, *Thumbs Up* features a plot about an American singer (Brenda Joyce) who takes a job in a British munitions factory in order to further her career by means of a talent competition available only to employees, but who is humbled by the selfless spirit of her coworkers, led by Elsa. The film is notable for being one of Elsa's few musicals in which she actually sings, performing the duet "Love Is a Barmy Thing" with J. Pat O'Malley, and participating in several group numbers. The general consensus, as evidenced by the *Daily News* review, was that "though definitely a B picture, [the film] is satisfactorily entertaining."[4] Elsa's performance, however, proved more divisive. While the *Chicago Tribune* declared Elsa's to be the "best acting in the film, by far . . . a lifelike and three-dimensional portrait," *The Gazette*'s reviewer was of the opinion that she "overacts appallingly."[5] As usual, the truth lies between these two extremes.

---

1. *Miami News*, November 4, 1942.

2. *Tampa Tribune*, April 4, 1943.

3. Nissen, *Actresses of a Certain Character*, 92.

4. *Daily News*, July 10, 1943.

5. *Chicago Tribune*, July 12, 1943; *The Gazette*, July 24, 1943.

Passport to Destiny, an RKO movie, was originally called *Dangerous Journey*, and was rushed through production at breakneck speed, with the film company keeping a wary eye on world events. In a curious and ultimately unsuccessful mixture of drama and farce, the plot follows a Cockney charwoman who—believing herself invincible due to a lucky charm—sets out for Berlin to kill Adolf Hitler. With the Allies gaining ground across Europe, producer Herman Schlom hurried to complete the film before the war was over. In this he succeeded, but the quality suffered as a result, and the reviews were largely negative.

Passport director Ray McCarey echoed reports from two decades earlier when he referred to Elsa as "the female Charlie Chaplin," who championed the cause of the little woman as Chaplin had for the little man.[6] In the sequences where Elsa pretends to be unable to speak or hear, her clowning, silent-cinema skills are shown to be as good as they were in the 1920s Wells silent shorts.

Indeed, that the film does not work cannot be laid at Elsa's door. Her character's quirks and idiosyncrasies—based, she claimed, on a former servant—are funny and watchable. Critics at the time agreed that she was the only reason to see the film, with one review sniping, "If you like Elsa, you'll be able to sit through this third-rate Nazi thriller."[7] Another review, however, claimed she was miscast, demonstrating neatly the problems Elsa faced in image-obsessed Hollywood: "Miss Lanchester has always been a difficult actress to cast satisfactorily. For romantic roles she is a little plain; for Mrs. Muggins she is a little too young and attractive."[8] Sadly *Passport* would reinforce RKO's opinion that Elsa was "non-box office," and she would never again get star billing or a lead role.

Socially, Elsa and Charles continued their curious partnership that saw them pursuing separate interests and acquaintances. One occasion saw them dining in the same restaurant but at different tables; Elsa was with some of her Turnabout colleagues, and Charles was dining with pupils of his Shakespeare acting classes.[9] These pupils included actors such as Shelley Winters, Kate Lawson, Arthur O'Connell, Denver Pyle, and, of course, Bill Phipps.

In addition to their main home, in Pacific Palisades, Elsa and Charles also owned, at different times in the 1940s, two properties to which they could escape when real life became too stressful. The first was a wooden, three-bedroom cottage set on three acres of land in the mountainous community of Idyllwild. This log cabin, with its large stone fireplace and forest surroundings, brought back memories of their beloved and much-missed Stapledown. When circumstances forced them to sell the Idyllwild property, Elsa and Charles replaced it with a fifteen-acre plot of land on the Palos Verdes Peninsula. The property had previously been a millionaire's orchard and aviary; they had the former bird hos-

6.   *Shamokin News-Dispatch*, April 18, 1944.

7.   *Daily Times*, May 20, 1944.

8.   *The Gazette*, May 15, 1944.

9.   *Times Journal*, April 15, 1948.

pital building transformed into a small, two-bedroom retreat. There, among the peacocks and olive trees, they entertained famous friends such as director Jean Renoir. As their lives became less entwined, however, they began taking separate trips. Charles would frequently take his lovers to Palos Verdes, while Elsa was more likely to visit with a group of friends that often included her fellow Turnabouters. She remembered these as good times: "We'd have a barbecue or make a big pot of spaghetti, make silly movies, or take a lot of Polaroid pictures. We laughed a lot."[10]

Elsa claimed that Charles was envious of these friendly gatherings and would occasionally tag along, but when he did "he just couldn't participate. . . . Charles really didn't make friends very easily."[11] Ironically, in his recollections of these excursions, Turnabouter Forman Brown would remember it entirely the other way around, with Elsa as the more socially awkward of the pair. In his book *Small Wonder*, Brown wrote, "Charles was always much more at ease with strangers than Elsa." After a description of a typical idyllic stay at the Idyllwild property, Brown commented, "Charles was always the perfect host, and Elsa was more at ease with us, and we with her, during these brief interludes than at any other time."[12]

But after a while, the escape route offered to Elsa by the Palos Verdes property was cut off by Charles. A complex man, he suffered agonies of guilt regarding his lifestyle, and he told Elsa that their retreat was becoming "a regular love nest." He made it clear that he found this unacceptable, despite playing the main part in treating it that way. Just as Elsa had been indignant with what she saw as her mother's hypocrisy, Elsa was angry with Charles for his attempt, in her words, "to make me feel immoral in order to ease his own conscience."[13]

Although he continued to make films, Charles was increasingly dissatisfied with the work he was producing in Hollywood, much of which was far below the high standard he had set in *The Private Life of Henry VIII* (1933) and *Mutiny on the Bounty* (1935). His Shakespeare acting classes, conducted at the Laughtons' Pacific Palisades house, were an attempt at creative satisfaction that brought him great pleasure. Elsa was happy to see Charles enthused about a project, but once again she had to put up with people in her home who did not always treat her with respect. Chief among these was Shelley Winters, with whom Elsa would clash many times over the years. The cause of irritation on this occasion was Shelley's habit of parking her car crosswise behind Elsa's, meaning that Elsa had to interrupt the classes to request it be moved so that she could leave for her evening engagement at the Turnabout. This happened repeatedly. Elsa recalled that she

---

10. Lanchester, *Elsa Lanchester, Herself*, 200.

11. Lanchester, 200.

12. Brown, *Small Wonder*, 229, 231.

13. Lanchester, *Elsa Lanchester, Herself*, 200.

hated having to disrupt the class because "Charles resented interruptions and seemed to blame me, rather than Shelley."[14]

Another frequent visitor to the house connected with Charles's craving for artistic fulfillment was German theater practitioner Bertolt Brecht. Together, the two men translated, rewrote, and performed Brecht's *Galileo*, and although the final production fell short of expectations, their professional partnership was a rewarding one for them both. Simon Callow writes that the two men had much in common, personally as well as professionally: "each had a wife who ran the house, while lovers hovered in the background, occasionally awkwardly entering the domestic frame."[15]

Elsa empathized with Brecht's wife, Helene Weigel. A respected actress in her home country, Weigel was forbidden by her husband from taking small roles in American films. Elsa believed it was this, rather than Brecht's infidelities and temperament, that made Weigel an unhappy woman. "I think it might have changed her life . . . if she'd worked," Elsa wrote. "She must have been absolutely boiling inside."[16] Elsa could easily have been describing her own first stay in Hollywood.

Elsa's warm feelings toward Weigel did not extend to her husband, and her penned portrait of Brecht is a fine example of Elsa at her most irreverently savage. After claiming that he "didn't have a very strong personality," Elsa goes on to decry the foul odor of Brecht's cigars—"perhaps the passing through Brecht made the smoke come out with the sourest bitterest smell"—and his toothless "black hole" of a mouth. Even his mistresses, she claims, were unattractive: "More your stolid spinsters."[17]

In her autobiography *Elsa Lanchester, Herself*, Elsa scrutinizes Brecht and his collaboration with Charles for a full seven pages, yet she spends less than a quarter of a page discussing the death of her own father, Shamus Sullivan, which occurred in October 1945. A telegram from Biddy telling Elsa the news was followed by a letter that discussed Shamus's death only briefly. "It is difficult to know just what could have been done to help Shamus these last years," Biddy wrote. "That resentment against life seemed to grow on him and he was very stubborn in refusing any proffered help. . . . I feel it has happened for the best."[18]

Elsa, with her characteristic lack of self-awareness, draws attention to her mother's short and unemotional response in a remarkably brief passage of her book, during which Elsa expresses no emotion whatsoever. Later, she offers a little more, recalling that when the telegram arrived, "I said to myself over and

---

14. Lanchester, 177.

15. Callow, *Charles Laughton*, 169.

16. Lanchester, *Elsa Lanchester, Herself*, 194.

17. Lanchester, 193.

18. Lanchester, 219.

over again, 'Poor little Shamus . . . Poor little Shamus.'"[19] Steve Cockayne, in his biography of Elsa's brother, writes that Waldo felt a similar emotional distance from the event: "as the years had passed [Shamus] had retreated more and more into himself. While Biddy still commanded a significant presence in Waldo's life, Shamus had gradually dwindled into a bitter, shadowy ghost."[20] Her father, who had been a stranger for a long time, had quietly faded out of Elsa's life, "always having sent his love to me in Biddy's letters but never writing himself."[21]

Elsa had much to distract her from her bereavement. A new round of separation rumors appeared shortly before her and Charles's eighteenth wedding anniversary: "Writers better be careful what they say about Charles Laughton and Elsa Lanchester," one article warned. "They're seeing red because of the persistent rumors that they're tiffing."[22] As well as protesting too much about her marital problems, Elsa also made regular headlines in the *Los Angeles Times* in the postwar years for her ongoing and ever-changing performances at the Turnabout Theatre. "Anniversaries"—five hundred performances, six hundred performances—were marked with celebrations and promoted with puff pieces in the local press.

It was reported that the Theater Guild asked Elsa to appear alongside her husband in *Galileo*, but she turned down the role, saying: "I'm very much opposed to husband and wife appearing together in the same play or picture. It generally makes for professional jealousies."[23] The absurdity of this statement is obvious, although it went undiscussed at the time. By late 1946, when these words were printed, Elsa and Charles had appeared in many plays and films together, and it hadn't been all that long since it was being reported that Charles was actively seeking projects where he could appear alongside his wife.

Elsa's film work had slowed to an average of one or two pictures a year, and she worked for various studios, making *The Spiral Staircase* (1946) and *The Bishop's Wife* (1947) for RKO, *The Razor's Edge* (1946) for Twentieth Century-Fox, *Northwest Outpost* (1947) for Republic, and *The Big Clock* (1948) for Paramount. After her brief stint in B-picture leading roles, these films saw her back in character parts, supporting leading actors such as Tyrone Power, Cary Grant, Loretta Young, Nelson Eddy, and—despite her strongly stated aversion to such things—her own husband.

Elsa's appearance as the "enchantingly blowsy" inebriated housekeeper in the thriller *The Spiral Staircase* drew the ire of the censors.[24] In a Hays Office ruling that borders on farcical, it was decreed that Elsa could not belch to indicate

19. Lanchester, 315.

20. Cockayne, *Master of the Marionettes*, 177.

21. Lanchester, *Elsa Lanchester, Herself*, 315.

22. *Indianapolis News*, January 8, 1947.

23. *Lancaster Eagle-Gazette*, December 9, 1946.

24. *Des Moines Tribune*, February 22, 1946.

her character's intoxication, as that was considered unladylike. She was, however, permitted to daintily tap her diaphragm if she felt it necessary.[25] Given that the movie was about a serial killer who murders young disabled women, this censorial focus on Elsa's drunken portrayal was mocked in the press for its absurdity. As can perhaps be gleaned from the above, Elsa provided "needed humorous relief" in an enjoyably melodramatic movie that saw Ethel Barrymore nominated for the Oscar for Best Supporting Actress.[26]

The Razor's Edge was another high-quality production that gave Elsa a justifiable sense of pride. In an interview later in life, she would recall, "I repeatedly had tiny roles in very good movies, like Edmund Golding's *The Razor's Edge*, from the novel by Maugham. Alas, I did more watching than acting. Big stars on beautiful sets, speaking highly literate words."[27] While her role in *The Razor's Edge* was so small as to be labeled a bit part, rarely has so much been done with so little. Silencing those who dismissed her performance skills as limited to exaggerated grotesques, Elsa appears as the secretary Miss Keith, who is charmed by Tyrone Power in a scene that is less than two minutes in length and took only an afternoon to shoot.[28] Despite the brevity of her time on the screen, reviewers lavished praise on her performance. "Elsa Lanchester turns in a bit performance that will linger in everyone's memory as the standout work of the whole show," one critic enthused. Another went even further: "Elsa Lanchester, in one brief, single scene runs rings around the rest of the cast when it comes to superior acting."[29] This was praise indeed, for the talented cast included Gene Tierney, Clifton Webb, and Anne Baxter. Baxter would win an Oscar and a Golden Globe for Best Supporting Actress for this movie, while the film itself would get an Academy Award nomination for Best Picture.

Next Elsa played an exiled Russian princess in the operetta *Northwest Outpost*. Having appeared in Nelson Eddy's first movie—*Naughty Marietta* in 1935—Elsa now appeared in what would be his last. Once again playing the comic relief, she received good reviews, with the critics bemoaning the fact that they saw too little of her, something that was becoming a regular refrain. One such complaint read, "It strikes me that we'd have funny comedies if Elsa (Mrs. Charles Laughton) Lanchester were given more big roles."[30]

Having played royalty, Elsa was not eager to go back to playing maids and housekeepers, explaining to Sheilah Graham that she feared being typecast: "I had six offers to play a housekeeper part after *The Spiral Staircase*," she said. "But

25. *Lancaster New Era*, September 11, 1945.

26. *Lansing State Journal*, January 27, 1946.

27. Hadleigh, *Leading Ladies*, 94.

28. *San Mateo Times*, January 1, 1952.

29. *Atlanta Constitution*, November 24, 1946; *Dayton Herald*, November 20, 1946.

30. *Daily Oklahoman*, August 8, 1947.

it's like playing butlers, you get typed as a servant very easily."[31] Therefore, when a scheduling clash meant she had to choose between playing a housekeeper in *The Bishop's Wife* or an eccentric artist in *The Big Clock*, the choice was an easy one and Elsa picked the latter. However, delays in production meant that she was eventually able to play both parts.

The Bishop's Wife was a star-studded seasonal comedy, starring Cary Grant as an angel who helps a bishop and his wife (David Niven and Loretta Young) find purpose and happiness at Christmastime. Although Elsa was once again cast as a servant, she made the most of the part, giving a warm, soft performance and staring at Cary Grant with appropriate adoration whenever possible. However, despite the film's heart-warming themes of redemption and goodwill, the atmosphere on the set was decidedly uncomfortable. After a fortnight of filming, producer Samuel Goldwyn replaced the director and ordered a complete rewrite of the script at a rumored cost of $900,000, putting additional pressure on a cast that was already at breaking point. David Niven was originally contracted to play the role of the angel, but Cary Grant, as the bigger star, demanded the meatier lead role; this, combined with Niven's disapproval of his fellow Englishman's staying in America throughout the war while Niven returned home and enlisted, would have been enough to create a difficult working atmosphere, but Niven was also deep in mourning.

In May 1946, just months before filming on *The Bishop's Wife* began, Niven's wife, Primmie, had died at the age of twenty-eight. The circumstances of her death were tragically ludicrous, in the best Hollywood tradition. Primmie and David Niven had been attending a dinner party held by Tyrone Power and his wife, alongside other stars including Rex Harrison, Gene Tierney, Patricia Medina, and Cesar Romero. After dinner, as was fashionable at the time, these A-list stars decided to play party games, specifically one called Sardines, a hide-and-seek-style game that was played in the dark. "I was hiding upstairs with Ty Power," Medina recalled, "when we heard a thud. Ty rushed to put the lights on and we found that Primmie had mistaken the door to the powder room or closet and had fallen down all the stone steps into the cellar."[32] Mistaking the door to the cellar for a closet, Primmie Niven had fallen twenty feet, head-first down stone steps. She died a couple of days later of a fractured skull and brain lacerations.

Although the critics were lukewarm about *The Bishop's Wife*, the public enjoyed it—the film was even said to be a favorite of England's Queen Elizabeth and Princess Margaret—and it was nominated for an Academy Award for Best Picture.[33] Elsa, however, in her small supporting role did not attract much attention. *The Big Clock* would be an entirely different matter.

31. *Indianapolis Star*, March 21, 1947.

32. Lord, *Niv*, 136.

33. Lord, 146.

Despite her recent protestations that married couples should not work together, Elsa appeared alongside Charles in *The Big Clock*. It was reported that the Laughtons had made it clear to Paramount "that they like their working arrangements distinct and separate," but this may have been an attempt to save face, as Elsa received no direct payment for the picture: her fee was considered as included in the $100,000 payment that Charles received for his role.[34] Simon Callow considered this payment structure "as clear an identification as could be imagined of the disparity in their respective standings."[35]

It also seems certain that the couple worked on their parts together. Callow related an amusing story of Elsa and Charles visiting *The Big Clock* producer Richard Maibaum in his office. Elsa did all the talking, telling Maibaum that she and Charles would regretfully be unable to take part in the picture because "we don't know who we are, and we never take anything on unless we know who we are." Presumably accustomed to dealing with actors, Maibaum did not act on this information and was rewarded for his patience when the Laughtons returned a few days later having discovered who they were—their characters would be modeled on Dorothy Parker and Colonel McCormick, apparently—and therefore having decided to proceed with the film. This was strange behavior indeed, especially from Elsa. "Maybaum [*sic*] drily observes," wrote Callow, "that Laughton said nothing whatever at either meeting, and he was never certain how seriously [Charles] took it."[36] However, it was far more typical of Charles than of Elsa to walk away from a film because he couldn't find the character; he had done so, for example, with *David Copperfield* in 1935. Indeed, it was far more typical of Charles to bother searching for the character in the first place. It's also worth noting that Elsa's portrayal of artist Louise Patterson has nothing whatsoever of Dorothy Parker about it, having been based, according to interviews Elsa gave at the time, on her Aunt Mary.[37]

Whatever her inspiration, Elsa is marvelous in *The Big Clock*. Although she plays a scatterbrained eccentric, she invests her portrayal with a knowing undercurrent and a sly edge to her humor that make her enjoyable to watch. Simon Callow disagrees, considering her performance "out of key with both Laughton and the film," a criticism that perhaps makes sense if viewing *The Big Clock* as an example of film noir.[38] However, the movie is a curious—and successful—blend of comedic and noir elements, with Elsa and Charles playing at opposite ends of the scale but remaining in harmony.

The film itself, and Charles's appearance in it, garnered wildly mixed reviews in 1948, although today both are held in very high regard. However, Elsa's

---

34. *Philadelphia Inquirer*, February 8, 1947.

35. Callow, *Charles Laughton*, 188.

36. Callow, 188.

37. *Valley Times*, October 19, 1948.

38. Callow, *Charles Laughton*, 187.

contemporary reviews were exemplary. A critic who hated the film and thought Charles went "from bad to worse" opined that Elsa's was the "one very good performance." Those who loved the film also rated her highly, saying, "Even in an exceptionally good picture she almost helps herself to first honors."[39]

Even more exciting was a review that read, "Elsa Lanchester, as a bizarre painter, does a bit worth an Oscar."[40] This was a popular opinion, and when *Film Daily* attempted to predict the Academy Award nominees for Best Supporting Actress, Elsa featured in the list. The magazine prided itself on its ability to correctly anticipate who would be nominated, but in this case it was wrong. Elsa would have to wait a little longer for recognition from the Academy.

Although things were going well for Elsa, the reviewer who saw Charles as going "from bad to worse" was more accurate than they could have imagined. Morose regarding both his personal life and his career, and faced with the news that the cliff beneath their Pacific Palisades home was starting to slip, Charles struggled to cope. Elsa recalled that her husband was "in despair."[41] As it always had, property proved to be the cure as well as the disease.

The Laughtons' new house on Curson Avenue in Hollywood would remain Elsa and Charles's home until they died. It was smaller than their previous house, and it needed some work done, but when all the modernizations and improvements were made, including the addition of a pool, both Elsa and Charles were delighted with their new surroundings. The house even came equipped with a room perfect for Charles's Shakespeare classes, which the Laughtons would refer to as the "schoolroom."

---

39. *Oakland Tribune*, April 15, 1948; *Spokesman Review*, May 7, 1948.

40. *Spokesman Review*, May 16, 1948.

41. Lanchester, *Elsa Lanchester, Herself*, 183.

Although insecure about her unconventional beauty, Elsa enjoyed dressing up in custom-made designer gowns on several of her tours.

19 Boyoboy!

"By this time," Elsa claimed, "Charles and I had grown too far apart to be really honest with each other anymore."[1] She provided several reasons for this, including her own success at the Turnabout and the amount of time she spent there, even when filming. While the positive elements of appearing at the Turnabout far outweighed the negative, the endeavor did have its downsides. Time away from Charles could be viewed as either a good or a bad thing depending on their individual moods at the time, but a few other incidents provided cause for concern. On one occasion, Elsa contacted the police to report the loss of a gold broach valued at $1,950, which had gone missing somewhere between her dressing room and the stage at the theater.[2] This would not be the only time the police were called to the Turnabout.

In April 1946, Elsa left the theater after the show with fellow performer Lotte Goslar, a German comedienne, dancer, and mime, whom Elsa was providing with a lift home. Both women got into the car, but before Elsa could start the engine, the door opened, revealing a man brandishing a .45 caliber automatic. He demanded their valuables, and eventually ran away after taking $45 from Elsa and some papers from Goslar. Although the shaken women would provide a description of the robber, which was circulated in the local press, no one was ever charged with the crime.[3]

That Elsa and Goslar had a lucky escape was evidenced a few years later, when the theater itself was robbed at gunpoint on January 1, 1948. Yale Puppeteer and Turnabouter Roddy Brandon and a member of the theater staff, J. Gordon Amende, were in the cashier's cage at the closed theater when the gunman entered. The robber, later identified as career criminal George Donald Steel, demanded the keys to the safe and threatened to shoot the men if they ran.[4] According to Forman Brown, Brandon, "foolishly protecting the box office," at-

---

1. Lanchester, *Elsa Lanchester, Herself,* 188.

2. *Los Angeles Times,* July 12, 1947.

3. *Los Angeles Times,* April 27, 1946.

4. *Greenville Daily Advocate,* January 3, 1948.

tempted to flee, whereupon Steel shot him in the chest. Brandon was rushed to the hospital, where newspapers reported his condition as critical. Brown would later write, very briefly, of the incident and recalled that Brandon's life "hung in the balance for days."[5] Miraculously, however, he was to make a full recovery.

Every year, following the busy Christmas and New Year period, the Turnabout would close for a few weeks to give its hardworking performers a chance to relax and unwind. With her home situation as tempestuous as ever, Elsa decided that her holiday in January 1948 would be of the busman's variety. She secured a four-week engagement at New York nightspot Café Society Uptown, where she would perform a selection of Forman Brown's songs, with the composer himself accompanying her on the piano. Although his partner's shooting would doubtlessly have kept Brown from keeping this engagement, the venue itself closed down before the show could open. After spending hours rehearsing her first one-woman show, Elsa found the cancelation painful. "I was so disappointed," she told reporters. "I don't know of another place in the country where I could do my act. Of course, I'll never leave the Turnabout. But it would be fun to try a club next January."[6]

Elsa's career went through cycles of famine or feast, with lengthy quiet spells suddenly interrupted by relatively short periods of intense activity. As she moved into middle age, these busy periods would occur with less frequency. During a quiet spell in 1948, Elsa was once again considering other ways of advancing her career aside from making movies. An August 1948 gossip column announced that Elsa Lanchester had decided to "forsake Hollywood to do night club engagements, radio and television—good exercise for her wit and talent for mimicry."[7]

It's unlikely that Elsa ever seriously considered quitting the movies, however, and just a couple of months later the tide had turned once again. Columnist Hedda Hopper, always an advocate of Elsa's, wrote, "At last her good acting is paying off and she is set for five pictures. . . . I hope the parts won't all be bits. She deserves the best—it's what she always gives."[8] Remarkably, Elsa's career was about to hit another high point while she was in her mid-forties, typically a difficult age for actresses. Elsa was reaping the benefits of being considered a character actress rather than a glamour girl—a fact that was stated outright when her casting in *The Inspector General* (1949) was discussed.

Originally called *Happy Times*, *The Inspector General* was a Danny Kaye vehicle, for which his wife and manager Sylvia Fine produced song lyrics. Such was Danny Kaye's popularity in 1949 that he and his wife both apparently had some

5. Brown, *Small Wonder*, 253. See also *Muncie Evening Press*, January 2, 1948; *The News-Messenger*, January 3, 1948

6. *The Gazette*, March 1, 1948.

7. *Fort Worth Star-Telegram*, August 19, 1948.

8. *Los Angeles Times*, October 27, 1948.

say in the casting of the picture. Upon hearing that glamorous Eve Arden was no longer in the film, Hedda Hopper rang Fine to hear who Arden's replacement was to be, expecting it to be another screen siren, as names previously linked with the role included Marlene Dietrich and Joan Blondell. When she was told that the part had gone to Elsa, Hopper expressed considerable surprise, causing Fine to explain: "We wanted a glamour girl to costar with Danny, but the writing of her part never matched his. It always turned out to be a fine acting role with little glamor. It was Henry Koster, the director, who suggested Elsa. We all fell out of our chairs and onto our faces and said, 'She would be perfect.'"[9]

Koster had directed Elsa in *The Bishop's Wife* (1947) and would go on to direct her in the 1949 film *Come to the Stable*. He was another advocate of Elsa's, saying, "She's not just competent or adequate, she has that extra spark that fascinates you."[10]

During the period she was shooting *The Inspector General* at Warner Brothers, Elsa was also filming her scenes in *The Secret Garden* (1949) at MGM. Based on the book by Francis Hodgson Burnett—who also created Little Lord Fauntleroy, a character Elsa had played onstage two decades earlier—the film starred the accomplished child actress Margaret O'Brien. Also in the cast was a young actress called Susan Fletcher, who played the small role of the scullery maid. Fletcher appeared in several scenes with Elsa, who was back to playing the help, this time as the upstairs maid, Martha. Fletcher later recalled one occasion when she, Elsa, and Gladys Cooper were filming close-up shots of their reactions to a child's tantrum:

> It wasn't easy. Not that the scene was difficult, but because of an electric feeling of amusement on my left, that was Elsa Lanchester, right in character as Martha, the cheerful upstairs maid, laughing uproariously through the whole business. Her performance was so real, I could feel it without seeing her—and I had a terrible time keeping my own expression straight and stupid. Elsa has that certain magnetism which is purest theater—and makes her great in whatever role she plays.[11]

This onscreen magnetism, the "spark" that Henry Koster referred to, had often caused critics to remark on Elsa's scene-stealing abilities, but it had never been suggested that upstaging other actors was something that she did deliberately. Although such behavior was common in the industry, it was frowned on and regarded as unprofessional and somehow unsporting. One gossip column item regarding Elsa's view on the practice said, "Elsa Lanchester, a scene-stealer if there ever was one, says she's met her Waterloo. She's dividing her time between Mar-

9. *Los Angeles Times*, September 17, 1948.

10. *Valley Times*, October 19, 1948.

11. *Vancouver Sun*, November 10, 1948.

garet O'Brien and Danny Kaye, and says they're both impossible to steal from."[12] Admitting to being a deliberate scene-stealer, albeit in a rather roundabout way, would be something that Elsa would soon have cause to regret.

She was not wrong, however, about the screen presence of Kaye and O'Brien. Although Elsa received some good notices for both films, they were brief as the focus was always on the stars. *The Inspector General* was not well received, and it remains a tedious watch today for all but the most die-hard fans of Kaye. As the mayor's wife, Elsa is effective but underused. Reports at the time claimed that she and co-star Barbara Bates were angry because they felt much of their best work had ended up on the cutting room floor. "They should know by now," one columnist remarked, "when Danny is in a picture, there is not much room for anyone else."[13]

But Elsa had little time to dwell on such slights: within a few months of wrapping *The Secret Garden* and *The Inspector General*, she was back with director Henry Koster on the Twentieth Century-Fox lot to film *Come to the Stable*. Elsa was once again cast as an artist, but Amelia Potts was nothing like the sharp, witty Louise Patterson she had played in *The Big Clock*. Elsa would later describe Miss Potts as "one of my treacliest roles," and indeed the entire film is saccharine in the extreme, being the story of two nuns—played beatifically by Loretta Young and Celeste Holm—and their determination to build a children's hospital.[14] Miss Potts is a painter of religious scenes, who takes the nuns into her home. Although Elsa manages to find some slight humor in her character's airheaded tendencies, it is not a comedic role, being instead somewhat overly earnest.

Outdoor filming took place during an unusually cold California winter, which affected cast morale. Although Koster tried to cheer his actresses up by sending them flowers and arranging for long-distance phone calls from loved ones,[15] a gossipy item from columnist Edith Gwynn would undo all his good work:

> Boyoboy! You should hear about the scene-stealing that's going on over at 20th-Fox on the sets of *Come to the Stable*. Loretta Young and Celeste Holm are the stars of this one, but Elsa Lanchester, playing a colorful role in it, is nabbing the spotlight (and the camera!) to such an extent that the atmosphere is getting even cooler than the weather.[16]

This was a curious accusation. Certainly no upstaging is evident in the finished film—indeed, Elsa would remark decades later that friends of hers had seen the movie several times and yet forgot she was in it.[17] However, at the time, Elsa felt

12. *Long Beach Independent*, October 7, 1948.
13. *Spokesman Review*, January 14, 1950.
14. Hadleigh, *Leading Ladies*, 95.
15. *Shiner Gazette*, December 1, 1949.
16. *Tampa Bay Times*, January 11, 1949.
17. Hadleigh, *Leading Ladies*, 95.

so strongly about these claims that she addressed them at length in an interview with Virginia MacPherson. At first, MacPherson feigned ignorance as to why Elsa felt she had been insulted; to say someone "stole" a scene was considered by journalists to be a compliment, MacPherson explained, and it was certainly not meant to embarrass or offend an actor. Elsa shut this down in her typically direct fashion. "A scene-stealer is a bad actor or actress," she fumed. "This columnist called me a scene-stealer right in the middle of *Come to the Stable*. The next morning I had to go to the studio and face Loretta Young and Celeste Holm, the two girls I was supposed to be stealing scenes from." Both had read the article and let their unhappiness with Elsa be known. Elsa concluded angrily: "A scene-stealer doesn't help a movie star one bit. He spoils the whole mood everybody else has been working hard to set up."[18]

Although strongly cloying by today's standards, *Come to the Stable* was well received upon its release, with Loretta Young, Celeste Holm, and Elsa all drawing praise for their performances. Reviewers Kate Cameron and Marjory Adams and columnist Hedda Hopper, among others, predicted that Elsa would receive an Oscar nomination for "her very best characterization in a career of brilliant portrayals."[19]

They were correct. When the nominations were announced on February 15, 1950, Elsa was listed in the Best Supporting Actress category, as was her co-star Celeste Holm. Loretta Young received a nomination for Best Actress, and *Come to the Stable* was also in the running for four technical awards. The ceremony was held on March 23, 1950, at the RKO Pantages Theatre. Although the event was televised, the camera only shows the stage, so when Ray Milland—Elsa's *Big Clock* co-star— stepped up to the podium to announce the winner in her category, we do not have a close-up of Elsa looking nervous, carefree, or quietly confident. Nor do we have footage of her reaction to the announcement that the award went to Mercedes McCambridge for *All the King's Men* (1949). Elsa's disappointment was shared with all involved with *Come to the Stable*, which failed to win a single Oscar despite its seven nominations.

Was it a painful experience for Elsa when she returned home that evening to see Charles's Oscar for *Henry VIII* taunting her from its spot on the mantel? It is difficult to be sure how much value Elsa placed on the Academy Awards. Certainly Charles's statuette was not treated with any reverence; visitors were amused to notice that the naked golden figure had been partially clad in a loincloth-style undergarment fashioned from adhesive tape. "We had a very modest cook once," Elsa said by way of explanation. "We had to put pants on everything."[20] Fortunately they stopped short of clothing the figures in Renoir's *Judgment of Paris*. However, given Charles's well-known fondness for swimming naked, not

18. *Santa Fe New Mexican*, April 11, 1949.

19. *Boston Globe*, September 1, 1949. See also *Daily News*, July 28, 1949; *Chicago Tribune*, January 3, 1950.

20. *Dunkirk Evening Observer*, March 23, 1950.

to mention the extramarital visitors to the Laughton house, that cook probably didn't stay too long.

In February 1949, while she was filming *Come to the Stable*, Elsa celebrated her twenty-year wedding anniversary. Although relations between them remained strained, Elsa and Charles put on a good show for the press. Charles had been away in France and England over Christmas and New Year's, but he was home by February, and he brought back with him a large diamond for Elsa, said to have once belonged to the Mughal emperor Shah Jahan, the man who commissioned the building of the Taj Mahal. It was reported that the purchase of the gem served a dual purpose: "to celebrate their 20th wedding anniversary—and incidentally to squelch rumors of an impending separation."[21] This was not the only attempt the Laughtons made to try and quell speculations regarding their marital happiness. There is evidence that Elsa would sometimes call Louella Parsons personally to deny any reports of discord, while her Turnabout colleagues refused to answer when "spies from the Hopper and Parsons camp began coming to the theater and questioning anyone they could corner."[22] One evening, Hedda Hopper herself was to attend the show, so Charles—who was filming long hours and was exhausted—was summoned to be there to lovingly greet his wife when she emerged from her dressing room.

It is debatable how effective such measures were, for the separation rumors would continue through the years, although the true reason for their turbulent marriage would not appear in print until Elsa herself revealed it in the mid-1970s. Charles's sexual orientation became something of an open secret in Hollywood in later years, but there was nothing published to suggest that these powerful columnists were aware of it at this stage.

When asked how she felt about the separation speculation, Elsa could occasionally be flippant. Once, she claimed to enjoy the rumors. "We've averaged at least two such rumors every year during the 20 years we've been married," she stated. "They keep us feeling young. When the columnists stop separating us, we'll begin to consider ourselves old and stodgy."[23] It seems that both Elsa and Charles sometimes rather enjoyed the drama of the situation.

Her marriage was not the only aspect of Elsa's life that featured in the widely circulated newspaper columns, and there were often reports about her undertaking one project or another that would never come to pass. Some of these would fall through, while others only ever existed in the columnists' imaginations. In the late 1940s it was variously claimed that Elsa was to appear in a Broadway play called *Down the Hatch*, that she was to star in her own television series, and that she was going to pen her own gossip column. Her writing career was the focus of a lot of speculation, with rumors that *Charles Laughton and I* was being developed

21. *Republican and Herald*, November 22, 1948.

22. *Courier Post*, November 8, 1948; Brown, *Small Wonder*, 232.

23. *Lancaster New Era*, January 19, 1949.

into a screenplay by Charles Bennett, that Elsa had written a book called *Hollywood Can Be Human,* and that she had collaborated with Eugene Loring on a film script called *Ballet Oop,* which Columbia was said to be interested in.[24]

Even if Elsa was seriously considering these projects, at this stage in her life and career, it is difficult to see where she could have found the time. In addition to her ongoing work at the Turnabout—which included rehearsals and frequent new material, as well as nightly performances—Elsa continued appearing regularly in front of the camera, following *Come to the Stable* with four movies filmed within the space of a year. Once again, she worked for several studios, including Universal, MGM, and Columbia.

The first of these movies, *Buccaneer's Girl* (1949), saw Elsa back at Universal Studios for the first time since *Bride of Frankenstein* nearly fifteen years earlier. In that movie, her exposed cleavage had caused problems with the censors, and in *Buccaneer's Girl* it was a case of history repeating. However, this time director Frederick de Cordova addressed the problem during shooting, asking costume designer Yvonne Wood to add several inches of ruffles to the neckline of Elsa's gown.[25] Elsa's décolletage was not the only hurdle the picture faced with the censor. In the original script, Elsa's character had been a madam, and the star, Yvonne De Carlo, had played a runaway who ended up working for her. Clearly, this was never going to pass the morality code, and so Elsa's character was changed to a woman who runs a strange hybrid of talent agency and finishing school and sends her pupils out to sing and perform at parties for wealthy men. Faced with a watered-down character whose best lines had been cut by the censor, Elsa put her powers of suggestion—honed at the Cave of Harmony and further perfected at the Turnabout—into play. According to writer Virginia MacPherson, "She took a line about 'dressing properly,' added a knowing leer, and gave mental visions of a weekend orgy in Babylon. She used her face and her hips to fill in the words the morals boys chopped out."[26]

Another risqué-sounding subject—a stripper who poses for a painter—was toned down to musical respectability in Elsa's next film, *The Petty Girl* (1950, *Girl of the Year* in the United Kingdom). Author Clive Hirschhorn, in his encyclopedia of Hollywood musicals, wrote that "Third-billed Elsa Lanchester committed grand larceny in every scene she was in," a comment that certainly appears to be intended as a compliment.[27] The film itself is middling fare, but Elsa does seem to be enjoying herself. This enthusiasm continued when the cameras weren't rolling, perhaps encouraged by the presence in the cast of Melville Cooper, who had once been a regular at the Cave of Harmony. Occasionally the two would get to

24. *Los Angeles Times,* May 24, 1948; *Los Angeles Times,* October 19, 1949; *Valley Times,* June 8, 1948.

25. *The Dispatch,* September 26, 1949.

26. *The Dispatch,* September 26, 1949.

27. Hirschhorn, *The Hollywood Musical,* 313.

reminiscing on set, and they would entertain their co-stars Robert Cummings and Joan Caulfield with some of the sketches they remembered from decades earlier.[28] This was also the time when Elsa apparently wrote a script called *Ballet Oop* with Eugene Loring, who was the choreographer for *The Petty Girl*. It was said in a brief news snippet that Columbia, the studio that released *The Petty Girl*, was interested in the project, but it was never mentioned again, and Elsa was soon moving over to MGM for her next role.

Mystery Street (1950) was a change from Elsa's previous two films, which had both been Technicolor froth in which she played her usual light comedy. Now she showed her skill in a film noir concerning an investigation into the murder of a pregnant bargirl. Elsa played Mrs. Smerrling, the unfortunate girl's landlady, a truly revolting creature who schemes, blackmails, and contrives to turn the misfortunes of others to her own advantage. It is another example of the range of Elsa's talents, and contemporary reviewers agreed, writing once again that "Elsa Lanchester steals the picture as a gin-swigging landlady living behind bead curtains with her parrot and her memories."[29]

Elsa's final film of this burst of activity was for her the least successful and least enjoyable of them all. Dismissed in her autobiography as "an unimportant little Western," *Frenchie* (1950) starred Shelley Winters, with whom Elsa had already had several run-ins at Charles's Shakespeare class.[30] Although she provides few details, Elsa recalled that Winters was "nasty to me during filming and I really wasn't comfortable with her because I thought she was a tricky little thing."[31] However, any altercation with Elsa made so little impact on Winters that she misremembered which picture they appeared in together when discussing it in her own autobiography, where she said only that "Elsa Lanchester was my sidekick and was dressed in very bizarre outfits."[32]

At one point during this 1949/50 period of activity, Elsa had built up quite a number of unreleased films, ensuring that her name would continue to be in the press for months to come. When she was asked what she planned to do next, she cleverly retorted, "I think I'll sit around on my backlog."[33] It was a cute sound bite, but it couldn't have been further from the truth; Elsa had no plans to rest on her laurels in the 1950s.

---

28. *Lincolnshire Echo*, January 10, 1950.

29. *Rocky Mount Telegram*, June 5, 1950.

30. Lanchester, *Elsa Lanchester, Herself*, 239.

31. Lanchester, 239.

32. Winters, *Shelley*, 366.

33. *Corsicana Daily Sun*, December 14, 1949.

20 A Desperate Quality

The new decade began with what Elsa called "a moment of great fulfillment," when she and Charles officially became American citizens on April 28, 1950.[1] The citizenship ceremony at the Los Angeles Federal Building was conducted by Judge Jacob A. Weinberger. When he asked whether either of the Laughtons had been in any legal trouble, Elsa nervously blurted out, "I've had a speeding ticket!" which elicited laughter from the others present.[2] Press photographers and reporters were there, and the pictures show both Elsa and Charles looking relaxed and happy. When asked about what the ceremony meant to her, Elsa told the press: "There were 29 nationalities represented, and in all those eyes there was a look of restfulness and calm. We had all achieved something precious which had taken years of study and patient waiting. . . . I am most proud and excited to be an American today."[3]

The process certainly had taken a long time, with the Laughtons originally applying for citizenship in the early 1940s.[4] However, their lawyer Loyd Wright had advised them to delay proceedings until the war was over, to avoid ill feelings in England affecting the success of their films there. Despite this consideration, attitudes in Britain toward Elsa and Charles, already cooled by their absence during the war, were certainly not improved by their becoming American citizens.

Reporting on the citizenship ceremony, the British press sought out comment from Charles's family. His brother Tom acted as the family spokesperson, saying, "We think it was a very natural thing for Charles to do. He has lived and worked in the United States for many years and by this time he must have many more friends there than he has here."[5] However, *The People* reported

1. *Dunkirk Evening Observer*, May 1, 1950.
2. Higham, *Charles Laughton*, 153.
3. *Dunkirk Evening Observer*, May 1, 1950.
4. *Los Angeles Times*, November 10, 1942.
5. *Yorkshire Post and Leeds Intelligencer*, May 1, 1950.

that Charles's mother was "terribly hurt" by her son's decision to become an American.[6]

When the reporters spoke to Charles after the ceremony, besides the expected responses concerning his pride and happiness, he made several comments about the beauty of the Oath of Allegiance, such as, "It has a wonderful rhythm and a marvelous use of words. I would like to include it among my readings."[7] By speaking of his "readings," Charles was making reference to the new direction his career had taken, performing in one-man shows during which he would read from works including Shakespeare and the Bible. These performances were hugely successful and lucrative, and Charles found them more artistically satisfying than much of his film work in Hollywood. The person responsible for these speaking tours was Paul Gregory, who would play a large role in Elsa and Charles's lives in the coming years.

Handsome and intelligent, Gregory was an "agent, hustler, manager, promoter, producer, who leaped into Laughton's life from nowhere, and played at different times the rôles of fairy godmother and demon king."[8] His would have a disruptive and ultimately unsettling effect on Elsa's life, although her initial impressions were positive. "He was handsome," she recalled. "And he was full of ideas. Later, I learned to be more suspicious. And afterward, I learned to be afraid of him."[9]

However much of a malign influence Gregory would eventually prove to be, he introduced Elsa to Ray Henderson, who would become her longtime friend, lover, accompanist, and collaborator. Elsa was still performing at the Turnabout six nights a week, but she was beginning to get itchy feet; Charles's success touring the country inspired her to consider a similar undertaking for herself, and she and Henderson began to put together a nightclub act. Gregory encouraged this venture, and he arranged the venues and promotion, as he did for Charles. The tour opened in Montreal in October 1950, before moving to Boston and New York. It was the first long-term break Elsa had taken from the Turnabout since she opened there in 1941. During this time, she had only missed two performances: one was just after the United States joined the war, when there was a blackout in Los Angeles; and the other was shortly before her tour began, in September 1950. On this latter occasion, Elsa had gotten a black eye after running into a door.[10] When makeup proved ineffective in covering the bruising, Charles volunteered to cover for her. Forman Brown's account of this evening is delightful:

---

6.   *The People*, May 7, 1950.

7.   Higham, *Charles Laughton*, 153.

8.   Callow, *Charles Laughton*, 209.

9.   Lanchester, *Elsa Lanchester, Herself*, 202.

10. *The Mercury*, September 22, 1950.

Charles . . . went on—and on—and on. He told stories, he quoted Shakespeare, he read from the Bible and Thomas Wolfe, he recited limericks and delayed the finale by a good half hour. No one minded except Elsa, who stood in the wings muttering to herself, the principal sentence being "What a ham!" Charles would have been happy to appear the following night, or for the entire week, and was greatly disappointed at Elsa's firm veto of the idea.[11]

Elsa was back onstage the next night. Although Brown frames this as an amusing anecdote, Elsa may very well have been genuinely put out at being upstaged by Charles in this way in the place that she considered her own.

Alternatively, this may have been one of the periods where Elsa and Charles, united by a common interest, found enjoyment once again in each other's company. Charles was supportive of Elsa's ambitions to tour and insisted that she be seen at her best in glamorous outfits.[12] Much was made of this in the press, with columnist Erskine Johnson reporting that Elsa was "busting out as a beauty for her nightclub tour" in custom-made gowns by designer Valentina, and quoting Elsa as saying, "Up until now, I've been afraid of trying to look pretty. Before this, when I'd come out looking elegant, certain people around town would say, 'Poor Mrs. Laughton, is she trying to look nice?'"[13] This is a classic example of Elsa's insecurity about her looks, which at this point in her life were definitely beginning to fade a little, and her once-svelte figure was beginning to spread as she approached the end of her forties.

Elsa's first engagement was a weeklong run at the Normandie, a large supper club within the Mount Royal Hotel in Montreal, beginning on October 4, 1950. The local newspaper initially lavished praise on her performance—"Her bits of satire are delicious, her comedy subtle, her delivery perfect"—but after repeated viewings it tempered its opinion, writing that her act would do better in a smaller, more intimate venue. This later article also drew attention to Elsa's lack of experience using a microphone, which meant that occasionally "a particularly comical punchline is lost."[14] Elsa admitted to finding the microphone challenging after working without one for so long at the Turnabout. Microphones in this period came burdened with stands and wires, which Elsa found physically constraining. "I was trained as a dancer," she explained, "and I'm used to getting a lot of movement into my interpretations. It still bothers me not to be able to move around freely."[15] During one song, Elsa abandoned the microphone and leapt onto Ray Henderson's grand piano; she then proceeded to go through "more contortions

11. Brown, *Small Wonder*, 231–32.

12. Lanchester, *Elsa Lanchester, Herself*, 208.

13. *Marshfield News-Herald*, October 16, 1950.

14. *The Gazette*, October 7, 1950; *The Gazette*, October 9, 1950.

15. *Los Angeles Times*, November 12, 1950.

than a Yogi," "showing gams, rolling around and making generally like a juvenile delinquent."[16]

Following the Montreal run came engagements at the Copley Plaza Hotel in Boston and the Persian Room at the Plaza in New York. Although Paul Gregory was managing the tours of both Elsa and Charles, he had somehow neglected to notice that both Laughtons would be in New York at the same time in November 1950. When Charles arrived at the reception desk of the Plaza Hotel, where Elsa was staying, he was tired after a tour that covered 23,500 miles and over eighty performances, and he looked even more disheveled than usual. The receptionist rang Elsa's room and told her, "There's a man down here who claims he's Charles Laughton. What shall I do? Do you know him?" To which she replied, "Slightly. He's my husband. Send him up."[17] According to the various accounts of this incident, the hotel was full, and so it provided Charles with a truckle bed, which he sulkily occupied in the living room of his wife's suite.[18] If anyone at the hotel or in the press found it unusual that the Laughtons did not want to share a bed, and seemed unaware of each other's movements around the country, they left their opinions on the matter unpublished.

While at the Plaza, Charles attended Elsa's show at the Persian Room. According to Charles Higham, who can only have heard the story from Elsa, "Charles came to her performances, commenting unkindly on them, and hurting her deeply."[19] Without any further details it is impossible to say whether this was a case of Charles being cruel or Elsa being oversensitive—or even performing badly—but either way their relationship was back once again to being an adversarial one.

Although Elsa did garner some praise for her New York appearances, it was often conditional. "Preceded by a number of adverse reports," wrote *Billboard* reviewer Bill Smith, "Elsa Lanchester . . . turned in a surprisingly good job."[20] The *New Yorker* considered that her work had a "desperate quality" that transported her audience "into a disquieting place filled with sharp winds and unsteady laughter."[21] By December she was back in Los Angeles and at the Turnabout.

While Paul Gregory's focus was always primarily on Charles, he—or Ben Irwin, one of his employees—was also searching for opportunities for Elsa. An intriguing proposition was a British film called *Poor Nellie*, which would feature Elsa as a parlor maid who ends up owning her employers' house. Although this film never materialized, a trip back to England was planned for September 1951.

---

16. *Los Angeles Times*, November 12, 1950; *The Billboard*, November 4, 1950.

17. *Daily News*, January 7, 1951; Higham, *Charles Laughton*, 161; Lanchester, *Elsa Lanchester, Herself*, 219.

18. Higham, *Charles Laughton*, 161.

19. Higham, 161.

20. *The Billboard*, November 4, 1950.

21. Quoted in Lanchester, *Elsa Lanchester, Herself*, 208.

Elsa would come to view Gregory as a destructive force, someone who sought to get closer to Charles by sowing seeds of discord in the Laughtons' marriage, although by this time they were perfectly capable of creating such rifts themselves. His scheduling of the couple during 1950 and 1951 would ensure that they were often apart, possibly at Charles's request. Their diverging schedules began to attract attention, with one report saying "Elsa Lanchester goes to England just about the time husband Charles Laughton returns. But don't get any ideas of marriage trouble."[22] What this reporter was not privy to was the fact that when Elsa traveled to the United Kingdom and then on to France in 1951, she did so under the name Elsa Lanchester. As all her previous and subsequent travel was under her married name of Elsa Laughton, this is a clear indicator that her marriage was going through a particularly low period. Elsa's sexual affair with Ray Henderson—who accompanied her on this trip—may have been another reason for her choosing to use her maiden name.

Elsa's time in England would not provide a happy distraction. Although she had visited several times since the end of the war, this was to be her first professional engagement in the country since she filmed *The Beachcomber* back in 1938. Booked to perform at the Café de Paris—which was, rather confusingly, in London—Elsa was met with a frisson of excitement among those who remembered her nightclub performances from the days of the Cave of Harmony. Youngman Carter wrote in *The Tatler*, "Her return is an event for the survivors of the twenties to savour with a proper connoisseur's relish."[23] However, he and his fellow critics would not be impressed with what they saw.

Noel Whitcomb, writing in the *Daily Mirror*, was baffled by Elsa's material, comparing her to a gossipy housewife and complaining that she was "so bitterly cynical that the customers felt slightly uncomfortable."[24] This was high praise, however, when compared with the tirade that was Youngman Carter's review. He wrote that Elsa had disappointed her audience with her transformation from "a bright eyed Cockney sparrow into a plump, complacent American matron," who had lost her sense of humor and her comedic timing along with her figure. The anger felt in the country regarding Elsa's American citizenship was evident later in the review, when Carter wrote:

> It will be a great relief to us all when highly paid US citizens cease to try and entertain us with comical songs about folk who over-eat or who, poor souls, are overtaxed in their country. . . . If there is a moral to it, it is, I think, that foreign artists and prodigals would be wise to arrive in this country some weeks before their advertised appearance and acclimatize themselves to our contemporary ways of thinking, and to discover what will pass muster in the way of local jokes.[25]

22. *Calgary Herald*, June 15, 1951.
23. *The Tatler*, September 19, 1951.
24. *Daily Mirror*, October 3, 1951.
25. *The Tatler*, October 17, 1951.

This acclimation, of course, would not have helped matters at all; the British show business industry and press were upset at what they saw as Elsa and Charles's defection, and nothing she could have done would have gotten her favorable reviews from such an audience. The Café de Paris itself had suffered extensive damage during the war, with thirty-four people killed when a bomb exploded in front of the stage, and for Elsa to perform there was too much for some.

Elsa was devastated, and furious. Looking back on the event, she hit out at the critics for their "snooty, superior attitude," and claimed that it was the inclusion of American songs in her act that had been her downfall.[26] However, it was a British song from her Cave of Harmony days that would cause the most upset feelings. The management at the Café de Paris demanded that she remove the mildly saucy song "Somebody Broke Lola's Saucepan" from her act because it had apparently caused a member of the aristocracy to leave the venue. When a similar thing had happened during the Metropole *Follies* in 1926, Elsa had been fired from the show; this time she took matters into her own hands and refused to take out the song, thereby terminating her engagement halfway through the run.

With their newfound free time, Elsa and Ray Henderson parted ways for a while to spend time with friends and family before reuniting in London and then traveling to Paris, where they were to stay in the royal suite at the Prince de Galles Hotel. They would then fly home from Paris to New York. While they went their separate ways in England, Henderson went to stay with a friend, the composer Benjamin Britten, in Norfolk, while Elsa visited her mother in Brighton and Charles's family in Scarborough. During this visit Elsa informed Charles's brother Tom about her husband's sexual orientation, despite being fully aware of Charles's desire to keep it a secret from his family. The other Laughton brother, Frank, was in a relationship with a man, and the family knew of and accepted this, so perhaps Elsa felt that there was no harm in her revelation. While she insisted that she only told Tom in response to his suspicious queries about one of Charles's male companions, Tom disputed this claim. In a 1978 BBC documentary, Tom said: "I was never aware of it in any shape or form until Elsa told me. And I just was astounded."[27]

Whether or not her intention had been malicious, this conversation with Tom would have serious repercussions some years later, when Charles became convinced that Elsa had not only divulged his secret to his brother—something he found close to unforgivable—but also told his lawyer and perhaps others. With those around him fueling his paranoia, Charles finally did what he had threatened to do on many occasions and asked Elsa for a divorce.

Elsa played this situation down in her autobiography, basically dismissing it as a big misunderstanding that she somehow felt Paul Gregory was responsible

---

26. Lanchester, *Elsa Lanchester, Herself*, 217; *Public Opinion*, April 30, 1952.

27. Lanchester, *Elsa Lanchester, Herself*, 218, 226; "Charles Laughton," *Hollywood Greats*.

for. It was all settled, she claimed, after a meeting with the couple's lawyer, Loyd Wright, in which the truth of the matter was established. However, the speculation in the gossip columns ratcheted up a notch, with Sheilah Graham claiming, with some degree of accuracy, that "the Elsa Lanchester–Charles Laughton marriage is being held together by the distance they keep from each other," and Erskine Johnson informing his readers that their marriage "no matter what denials are made, is hanging by a slender thread."[28] Although they eventually reconciled to remaining married, Charles never apologized for his actions. Neither did Elsa.

28. *Tampa Times*, May 4, 1954; *Burlington Daily News*, April 26, 1954.

Both Elsa and Charles would receive Oscar nominations for their
performances in *Witness for the Prosecution* (1957).
Everett Collection Inc. / Alamy Stock Photo

21 No Middle Feeling

By this time, the always-uneasy working relationship between Elsa and Paul Gregory had ended acrimoniously. He had never managed to achieve for her what he had for Charles—largely, Elsa believed, due to a lack of effort on Gregory's part—although she did enjoy some smaller successes during her time under his management. To her regular six evenings a week at the Turnabout were added two shows a day at the Bar of Music, a supper club in Los Angeles. Elsa would perform a dinner show at the Bar of Music, then her spot at the Turnabout, then the supper show at the Bar of Music; across these three shows, she was singing twenty-three songs each night.

Following this, Elsa undertook a ten-week, sixty-performance tour with a modified version of her nightclub act, called *Private Music Hall*. Gregory insisted that in addition to her usual accompanist, Ray Henderson, Elsa be supported by a male quartet, the Mad Hatters, who would sing backing vocals and perform a couple of numbers on their own. Gregory also played a large part in selecting her material and insisted that Charles stay out of the rehearsal room: "Paul thought that he might interfere with rehearsals and give me complexes," Elsa recalled, suggesting that Gregory had accurately assessed the state of the Laughtons' marriage.[1] Playing colleges and auditoriums across the country, Elsa got an enthusiastic reaction from audiences, but the critics were less impressed. John K. Sherman wrote that the show was "only fitfully amusing," while, in an ironic twist, another review declared that "the Mad Hatters, a male quartet, stole the show."[2] By the time the show reached Ohio, a reporter concluded that "concert-goers are either thrilled by the performance of Elsa Lanchester . . . or they don't care for her at all. There's no middle feeling."[3]

Elsa blamed Gregory for the show's lukewarm reception, claiming that his selection of songs was weighted too heavily toward her Turnabout material, and therefore became monotonous. However, when she was informed that he had

---

1. Lanchester, *Elsa Lanchester, Herself*, 221.

2. *Minneapolis Star*, October 16, 1952; *Iron Country Miner*, October 17, 1952.

3. *The News-Messenger*, December 15, 1952.

canceled a planned second tour, Elsa was outraged. She left a message with Gregory's secretary, the content of which then prompted him to send her a telegram: "Will not tolerate your hysterical abuse. When you decide to go sane will be glad to talk with you."[4] It seems that Gregory never explained to Elsa his reasons for canceling the tour, but Elsa thought she knew what the problem was. "I thought, he really is a man with an ax, like Alexander Korda," she said. "They wanted to use Charles alone, to make him shine for them—but not with his wife around."[5] Although this had certainly been true of Korda, Gregory could have better kept the Laughtons apart by having Elsa tour the country rather than by preventing that from happening. Regardless, as had been the case with Korda, Charles continued his professional relationship with Gregory despite the ill treatment of his wife. Elsa was released from all contracts made with Gregory Associates, Ltd.

Back in Los Angeles, Elsa returned to her previous hectic schedule at the Turnabout and Bar of Music, although with a new accompanist as Ray Henderson was inducted into the army in February 1953. One evening, en route between the venues, Elsa collapsed. She was rushed to Saint John's Hospital, where it was discovered that she had a ruptured appendix, and a midnight operation was performed by Dr. Lyman Cavanaugh.[6]

Unable to appear onstage for a few weeks, Elsa decided to join Charles in New York while she recuperated. She told Hedda Hopper that she was hoping to renew her romance, but the reality of the situation was that Charles was accompanied on his reading tour by his boyfriend at the time, as Elsa was fully aware.[7] She refers to him as Charles's "road man," the latest in a string of attractive younger men who were paid to take care of Charles while he was touring. This particular young man did not seem to be earning his money, however, as Elsa found herself clearing away glasses and ashtrays when Charles and the road man returned to the room. Charles was carrying some heavy books and his overcoat, while the younger man held nothing; Charles then helped Elsa tidy, while the road man sat and smoked a cigarette. Eventually, Elsa lost her temper and dumped the tray of glasses and ashtrays in the man's lap, later telling him that he needed to put Charles first. "He is tired and he is getting older, and should be looked after," she told the younger man. "It's ugly to see this kind of behavior." The road man did not get the message, later saying of Elsa and Charles, "She just won't let him go, will she?"[8]

In the early 1950s, Elsa's career focus was firmly on live performance rather than film, although she continued making enough movies to remain in the public

4. Quoted in Lanchester, *Elsa Lanchester, Herself,* 226.

5. Lanchester, 226.

6. *San Francisco Examiner,* April 18, 1953.

7. *Daily News,* May 15, 1953.

8. Lanchester, *Elsa Lanchester, Herself,* 225–26.

eye. Her roles in such fare as *Androcles and the Lion* (1952), *Dreamboat* (1952), *Les Misérables* (1952), *The Girls of Pleasure Island* (1953), *Hell's Half Acre* (1954), and *Three-Ring Circus* (1954) were on the whole unsatisfactory, with some passing over into bad taste.

Her *Dreamboat* co-star Ginger Rogers would describe Elsa as "wonderful," but critics felt that her role as a sexually predatory college president was "nauseating" and "somewhat revolting."[9] They were even more horrified when she appeared in a cameo in Jerry Lewis and Dean Martin's *Three-Ring Circus* as the bearded lady. Kaspar Monahan remarked, "why this talented woman ever permitted such revolting indignities is a mystery to me."[10] It seems that Elsa was asking herself the same question. During shooting for the scene, she ate lunch at the Paramount commissary with her beard glued in place; "There were all sorts of jokes," she recalled. "Everybody was amused, but I had a terrible feeling inside of wanting to cry."[11] Always happy when making people laugh, Elsa felt this time that they were laughing *at* her rather than *with* her.

The old insecurity regarding her looks surfaced in a promotional interview she did for *Three-Ring Circus* with Aline Mosby. Speaking of her glamorous costume, which exposed her legs, she remarked: "If my face were dumb and pretty, I would have shown my legs long ago, but with features as twisted as mine, I was never asked to."[12] As if to challenge anyone to deny her lack of appeal, Elsa began the interview—which took place in a restaurant—by carefully removing the porcelain caps from her teeth while her fellow diners looked on, appalled. Years later, in 1961, when another interviewer asked her about this curious habit, she told him, "I don't do that anymore. Permanent caps now, and thank goodness they fit. Those Hollywood caps used to make me look like a horse."[13]

Although she was focused on her live performances, in July 1954 Elsa felt that her time at the Turnabout had come to an end after more than a decade, and she announced her intention to leave. Forman Brown suspected that Elsa "believed that our productions had perhaps lost some of their pristine freshness and spontaneity, and that not enough new songs were forthcoming."[14] Her importance to the theater was highlighted when the Turnabout suffered from falling attendance after her departure, and closed for good less than two years later.

In 1954, amid filming commitments, Elsa returned to the Blue Angel in New York, where she had first appeared in 1952. This time her material was more varied than it had been for the *Private Music Hall* tour, and it included a reading

9. Rogers, *Ginger*, 348; *The Observer*, August 24, 1952; *Philadelphia Inquirer*, September 4, 1952.

10. *Pittsburgh Press*, January 7, 1955.

11. *Press Democrat*, July 5, 1954.

12. *Press Democrat*, July 5, 1954.

13. *Asbury Park Press*, March 21, 1961.

14. Brown, *Small Wonder*, 252.

from T. S. Eliot's *Old Possum's Book of Practical Cats* and imitations of celebrities such as Zsa Zsa Gabor. The second of the Kinsey Reports, *Sexual Behavior in the Human Female*, had recently been released to much controversy, and Elsa included some mocking references to it in her act. When asked her opinion on the book's discussions of previously taboo subjects—including sexual orientation—Elsa cracked, "Wake me up when a book titled *The Sexual Behavior of Dr. Kinsey* rolls off the press!"[15]

After her run at the Blue Angel was over, Elsa returned to Hollywood to film *The Glass Slipper* (1955), with a screenplay penned by her friend Helen Deutsch, the woman who had been responsible for introducing Elsa to the Turnabout. The film was a musical retelling of the Cinderella story, with Leslie Caron and Michael Wilding in the lead roles. Elsa played the evil stepmother as a "well-adjusted witch," while Estelle Winwood was the fairy godmother.[16] Despite the quality cast, the film was not a success, and it lost money for MGM.

Elsa no longer had to depend on film work for national and international exposure: the world was changing. Television was rapidly gaining in popularity, and by the mid-1950s the Hollywood bigwigs were getting nervous. For actors, the new medium provided another avenue to pursue their craft, although it was looked down on as inferior to film stardom, just as acting in the movies had once been sneered at by those who considered acting on the stage to be superior. Film writer Christopher Isherwood, later a friend of Elsa's, would write in his diary: "Oh the horror of TV! It is so utterly utterly *inferior*, yet just enough to keep you enslaved, entrapped, on the lower levels of consciousness—for a whole lifetime if necessary."[17]

Much early television drama was broadcast live, so it presented a real professional challenge to those who were used to Hollywood's multiple takes and forgiving editing. Elsa appeared in a live drama as part of *Studio One in Hollywood* (1948–58) called "Music and Mrs. Pratt" (1953), in which her co-star was Philip Abbott. In an interview with John N. Gondas decades later, Abbott said that *Studio One* was one of his earliest experiences with television, and he found the experience terrifying. Abbott attempted to cover his nervousness until he realized that Elsa was also scared. He claimed that they supported each other through the "harrowing but exhilarating" ordeal.[18]

The experience did not put Elsa off television, and she followed *Studio One* with appearances on *Omnibus* (1952–61), *Ford Theatre* (1952–57), *Schlitz Playhouse of Stars* (1951–59), and an episode of *The Star and the Story* (1955–56) entitled "The Creative Impulse," based on a short story by Somerset Maugham.

---

15. *Daily Herald*, August 21, 1953.

16. *Miami Daily News-Record*, September 30, 1954.

17. Isherwood, *Diaries*, vol. 1, 829 (emphasis in original).

18. *Journal News*, June 16, 1974.

Such was the snobbery regarding television that it was written in the press at the time that Elsa had "succumbed to telefilms."[19]

Elsa was not the only member of her household trying new things; in 1954 Charles turned his hand to directing. Produced by Paul Gregory, and starring Robert Mitchum and Shelley Winters, *The Night of the Hunter* (1955) was not well received on its first release, and Charles would never direct again, although today the film is regarded as a classic. Elsa claimed that she had been offered the role that went to Lillian Gish, but she turned it down because she did not want to be around Charles when he was so nervous and emotionally invested in a project, and she didn't want to be around Gregory at all. Nor did she have a high opinion of the lead actors. Of Winters, Elsa wrote, with exquisite venom: "Many people saw in Shelley the temperament of an uncontrolled, bitchy, selfish, catty woman. I must say that I have always seen her as a good actress."[20] Mitchum had an equally low opinion of Winters, but Elsa did not think much of him either:

> Mitchum came to our house a couple of times to talk about his part, and in his anxiety to seem intelligent about it, he talked all through dinner. . . . I don't know, maybe Bob Mitchum is very bright, but I never heard such a lot of words—big, long words, one after the other. Perhaps he felt insecure with Charles and was trying to impress him.[21]

Mitchum's biographer, Lee Server, put this down to jealousy, writing that Elsa was "always prone to a snit when her husband was fawning over another man."[22]

Elsa and Charles's association with the hell-raising, rebellious Mitchum would have further curious consequences, which became public in 1957, when Paul Gregory appeared in court and swore under oath that he had been blackmailed by an agent of *Confidential* magazine.

Confidential was another example of the changing times. Once upon a time, badly behaving Hollywood stars feared only the catty comments of powerful newspaper columnists such as Hedda Hopper and Louella Parsons, but now there was a new level of dirt-dishing being published. *Confidential* paid for scandal and published salacious details that would make Hopper and Parsons blush, and it seems that sometime around 1954 or 1955, one of the magazine's representatives approached Gregory and informed him that they were in possession of a story that concerned him, Mitchum, and the Laughtons, and events that occurred at a party they had all attended. Informing Gregory that publication would be "scandalously injurious" to all parties involved, the magazine demanded $1,000 to kill the story.[23]

19. *Daily Herald*, August 10, 1954.

20. Lanchester, *Elsa Lanchester, Herself*, 239.

21. Lanchester, 237–38.

22. Server, *Robert Mitchum*, 325.

23. *Daily Mirror*, August 17, 1957.

It's unclear what the story was. *Confidential* did publish an article in July 1955 with the title "Robert Mitchum: The Nude Who Came to Dinner." This concerned Mitchum's supposed appearance at the Laughton home for dinner, to which he arrived late and drunk. He then, according to the article, proceeded to remove all his clothes, douse himself liberally with tomato ketchup, and declare, "This is a masquerade party, isn't it? Well, I'm a hamburger!" He followed this by dancing around a little, sprinkling ketchup around the room as he did so, before his date managed to convince him to get dressed.[24]

James Bacon, a friend of Mitchum's, would later tell Lee Server that the origin of that story was much more damning than the final article:

> Mitchum told me . . . he was with Charles Laughton and this other guy [Paul Gregory], and of course the two of them are both fags, and . . . they can't take their eyes off Mitchum, I guess. So Mitchum said he opened his pants, took his cock out, laid it on the plate, and poured ketchup over it. And he says to them, "Which one of you guys wants to eat this first?"[25]

Anything that threatened to reveal to the public Charles's true sexual orientation was certainly something Gregory would have wanted to keep hidden. (Despite Mitchum's insinuation, Gregory was not gay.) But when he testified in court, however, Gregory claimed that although the "Nude Who Came to Dinner" article wasn't true, that was not the story he was blackmailed over. Later in the proceedings, Gregory confused matters further by saying that it might have been Agnes Moorehead who was going to be mentioned in the "ruinous" story, rather than Elsa.[26]

The incident highlights how much of a risk Charles was taking as a famous actor with what was then considered a scandalous lifestyle, and why he stayed with Elsa even when they seemed to cause each other little but aggravation and hurt. Gregory, in an interview from the late 1970s, summed it up perfectly: "Elsa gave Charles a fixture in his life that he needed," he explained. "And as much as he spit and clawed and kicked at it, he still needed it. . . . He liked having a Mrs. Laughton."[27]

Charles's working relationship with Gregory, however, was not to be as long lasting as his marriage. In 1956, Charles officially dissolved their partnership and never spoke to or saw Gregory again. The final straw in their stormy union was Charles's discovery that Gregory had encouraged the "road men" to get all they could from the actor, including expensive gifts and cars.[28]

---

24. *Confidential*, July 1955.

25. Server, *Robert Mitchum*, 352.

26. *Tucson Daily Citizen*, August 16, 1957.

27. "Charles Laughton," *Hollywood Greats*.

28. Lanchester, *Elsa Lanchester, Herself*, 245; Callow, *Charles Laughton*, 243.

22 All Our Scenes Were Love Scenes

Although rumors circulated during 1954 that Elsa was to appear in a play—as Mary Queen of Scots, or as Anne of Cleves in a stage musical about Henry VIII—or else in a British picture where she would play a professional divorce co-respondent, her main source of income at this time was television.[1] Elsa was unconvinced of the quality of the medium, saying in 1960, "when I sign for a television appearance I don't expect good writing," and admitting that "some of the offers I took strictly for the money."[2] Not all her television performances were in forgettable shows, however. She reprised her role in a version of *Ladies in Retirement* (1954), about which a reviewer wrote, "TV really makes up for all the trivia when it comes through with something like 'Ladies in Retirement'... have you seen anything to equal Elsa Lanchester's performance as Emily?"[3] Moreover, she made an appearance in *I Love Lucy* (1951–57) that is a riot. In the episode entitled "Off to Florida" (1956), Elsa plays a motorist who picks up Lucille Ball and Vivian Vance's characters, Lucy and Ethel. After hearing a radio broadcast, the two passengers then suspect her of being an escaped murderess. She in turn suspects them of being the criminals. This kind of wacky humor, complete with wide eyes and double takes, was second nature to Elsa, and she made the most of every moment.

She also won praise for her appearance in the televised version of *Stage Door* (an episode of *The Best of Broadway*, 1955) and in a sketch called "The Flattering Word" on *Shower of Stars* (1954–58). When reviewing the latter, one critic asked, "Why isn't Elsa Lanchester on some regular TV top program? ... she was sensationally amusing."[4] Ironically, just a week or so before these words were printed, Elsa had started work as a permanent panelist on a weekly Los Angeles television show called *Words about Music* (1956), which ran on a local late-night slot for six months.

---

1. *Los Angeles Times*, August 2, 1954; *Daily News*, November 29, 1954.

2. *Valley News*, September 29, 1960.

3. *Boston Globe*, December 10, 1954.

4. *Evening Review*, March 21, 1956.

In costume for a photo shoot to promote her 1961
Elsa Lanchester—Herself show in New York.
Everett Collection Inc. / Alamy Stock Photo

The format consisted of composers presenting their new songs to four panelists—two guests and two regular members, Elsa and Oscar Levant—who then commented on what they heard. It was hosted by Frank DeVol, and guest panelists included Zsa Zsa Gabor, Raymond Burr, Natalie Wood, and Vincent Price, but the real star of the show was Oscar Levant, with his acidic sense of humor. He was described at the time as "a man with the wit of a near-genius wrapped up in the personality of a child. He has a way of putting his finger squarely on half-truths and speaking his mind with a child's disregard for the consequences."[5] Shelley Winters, who had been the recipient of Levant's cutting remarks, regarded him as "a very tortured man who sprayed his self-loathing on anyone within range."[6]

Elsa admitted that keeping up with Levant's wit and intelligence was exhausting, but she did have someone in her life at this time who helped her a little, a sexual partner who occasionally suggested clever lines for her to use on the show. Although Elsa would later publicly discuss many intimate details of her life, she remained secretive about her romantic activities with other men during her marriage. In a 1983 interview, in response to a question about her sex life, she stated:

> I think there were five, six, maybe seven men in my life. These affairs never lasted more than two years. At the end of each, the sex attraction had dwindled, and I was usually bored with the man. For the most part, Charles never said anything. . . . But I never fell in love with any of them, so it was largely a physical and psychological therapy that I periodically needed and enjoyed.[7]

In her autobiography, Elsa would write about her "nearly affairs" with Joe Losey and Jeffrey Dell, but she only discussed one of her actual affairs in any detail. This relationship, in the mid-1950s, was with a man she referred to only as "Leif." Elsa met him through a mutual friend, *Night of the Hunter* author Davis Grubb, and she describes him as a free spirit who indulged openly in his pleasures despite having a wife and children back home in Boston. Leif was a surgeon from a good family, whose parents had sent him to Los Angeles for psychiatric help, and he leaps off the pages of *Elsa Lanchester, Herself* as an eccentric personality who perhaps reminded Elsa of her wild, bohemian youth. On their first trip away together, she writes, he set fire to his pubic hair.

There is no suggestion that their relationship was anything more than what later generations would term "friends with benefits." Leif told Elsa about a threesome he had with two women he picked up at Ray Henderson's nightclub performance, one of whom was a famous comic, and Elsa enjoyed the story so much she retold it in her autobiography.

5.   *Democrat and Chronicle*, April 17, 1956.

6.   Winters, *Shelley*, 255.

7.   *San Bernardino County Sun*, May 15, 1983.

Leif seems to have made Elsa feel attractive again. He liked her to wear a fishnet top, and she declared, "I rather fancied myself in it." He also seems to have shared her cutting sense of humor, that strange ability to both wound and amuse, once announcing at a party that Elsa was "the best lay in Southern California." When Elsa asked why Southern California, he replied that he had never been to Northern California.[8]

Although Charles was away touring for much of the time, he did meet Leif and knew of Elsa's involvement with him. Elsa claims that Charles told Leif about his sexual orientation, which is curious if true. She also says that Charles warned her not to let Leif hurt her, although nowhere in her account of the affair does Elsa seem to be emotionally invested to the point where he could do so. Indeed, she would be the one to break things off between them after she accompanied Leif to a house that was equipped with "a sort of home traction apparatus hanging in the bathroom . . . with straps and ropes." Although certainly no prude, Elsa declared that such a contraption was "not for me" and beat a hasty retreat.[9]

Words about Music came to its own abrupt end after Oscar Levant walked away because the producers would not let him discuss politics on the show. He then started his own show with the same title, although an entirely different format, on which Elsa was an early guest, appearing alongside Eva Gabor.

Elsa's film output in the late 1950s was a triumph of quality over quantity. Although she would only make two films in this period—*Witness for the Prosecution* (1957) and *Bell, Book and Candle* (1958)—they are two of her best parts and performances. That she does not discuss either of them in her autobiography is a frustration to many fans, leaving some to wonder whether Elsa was the source of the opinion expressed in Charles Higham's biography of Charles Laughton, that *Witness for the Prosecution* was "a farrago, the characters mere paper cut-outs or mere caricatures, the plot development so convoluted that it finally became laughable."[10] If she felt this way, then she was in the minority, for the film was a huge success at the time, and it remains popular today.

Directed by Billy Wilder, *Witness* would be a landmark film for several reasons. It would be Tyrone Power's final completed movie; the actor would suffer a fatal heart attack on the set of *Solomon and Sheba* in 1958. More than that, though, and although none knew it at the time, it would be the last film that Elsa and Charles would ever make together. It is certainly one of their best pairings. Charles is magnificent as the defense barrister Sir Wilfred, who takes on a murder trial at the Old Bailey despite the doctor's orders, as he has just been released from the hospital after suffering a heart attack. Elsa plays Miss Plimsoll, his henpecking, fussing, relentlessly chirpy nurse, and their banter is a delight. They manage to convey adversaries who would be lost without each other. "In the

8.   Lanchester, *Elsa Lanchester, Herself,* 243.

9.   Lanchester, 243.

10. Higham, *Charles Laughton,* 204.

nicest sense of the phrase," Elsa would later reflect, "all our scenes together were love scenes."[11]

Journalist Joe Hyams was tasked with interviewing Charles on the *Witness* set. He wrote of the experience: "Press agents on his pictures always have a hard time guessing the temper of the temperamental Laughton and arranging an interview with him is a problem of studying signs, portents and the humidity." His interview with Charles went badly, with the actor coming across as arrogant, childish, and petulant, refusing to answer questions and emitting sudden expulsions such as, "What is talent? What is God? What makes a good performer? I don't know."[12] However, Billy Wilder would say that Charles was in good spirits during filming; indeed, the great director was a fan of both the Laughtons. He would later say of Elsa, "She was one of the most original actors I ever worked with, the other being Charles Laughton. I loved her deeply."[13]

Despite Charles's irritation with reporters, he was said to be an upbeat and positive presence during production, once more enjoying movie making after some less pleasurable experiences. Without a "road man" around, Elsa took care of her husband on set, cooking his meals on a stove in his dressing room.

The film won rave reviews, and although it featured stellar performances from Marlene Dietrich and Tyrone Power, and a wonderful cameo from Una O'Connor, it was Elsa and Charles who received the lion's share of the praise. Their performances in scenes together attracted particular attention, with one critic writing, "This brilliant pair of duelists puts everybody else into the background."[14] When the Academy Award nominations were announced in February 1958, the film received six nods, including Best Picture and Best Director. Both Elsa and Charles were nominated, for Best Supporting Actress and Best Actor, respectively.

With Elsa's previous Oscar nomination for *Come to the Stable* (1949) back in 1950, she had been considered unlikely to take the prize, with most pundits correctly predicting Mercedes McCambridge's win for *All the King's Men* (1949). In 1958, however, Elsa was the front-runner in a strong pack that included Hope Lange and Diane Varsi (both for *Peyton Place*, 1957), Carolyn Jones (*The Bachelor Party*, 1957), and Miyoshi Umeki (*Sayonara*, 1957). Columnists and commentators including Bob Thomas, Glen Graham, and Dan Lydon had Elsa as the odds-on favorite, and reported that she had been "favored in pre-award polls of Academy members to win."[15] But Oscar is a contrary fellow who likes nothing more than to upset expectations, and everyone was duly shocked when the award went to the underdog, Miyoshi Umeki. Charles also missed out, although Alec Guinness's win for *The Bridge on the River Kwai* (1957) had been

---

11. Hadleigh, *Leading Ladies*, 95.

12. *Orlando Sentinel*, July 19, 1957.

13. Callow, *Charles Laughton*, 247; *Napa Valley Register*, December 27, 1986.

14. *Illustrated London News*, February 22, 1958.

15. *Journal Herald*, March 27, 1958; *Windsor Star*, March 27, 1958.

the expected result. Like *Come to the Stable* before it, *Witness* would not take home any Academy Awards.

Neither of the Laughtons attended the Oscar ceremony in March 1958, as they were in London rehearsing a play. Elsa had attended the Golden Globes the month before, however; indeed she had hosted the event along with Red Buttons and Rossano Brazzi. *Witness for the Prosecution* was nominated for five awards: Best Motion Picture (Drama), Best Director, Best Actor (Drama) for Charles, Best Actress (Drama) for Dietrich, and Best Supporting Actress for Elsa. It won in only one of these categories, with Elsa taking home the Golden Globe for Best Supporting Actress 1958. This was the only major acting award she would win in her entire career.

Between August 1957, when *Witness* wrapped, and March 1958, when the Academy Awards took place, Elsa was not idle. In this brief period she released an album, rehearsed a Broadway show, visited the United Kingdom, came back to film a movie, and then returned to the United Kingdom to appear in a play.

The album, *Songs for a Smoke-Filled Room*, featured many of the Forman Brown songs that Elsa had performed at the Turnabout, such as "If You Can't Get in the Corners" and "Fiji Fanny," as well as numbers like "The Ratcatcher's Daughter," which dated back to her Cave of Harmony days. Charles also featured on the recording, providing a brief introduction to each song. "Elsa, who is my wife, will liven up any gathering she gets into," he intones at the beginning of one number. "It isn't so much *what* she says but *how* she says it."

Despite what must have seemed overly dated material in the rock 'n' roll era, *Songs for a Smoke-Filled Room* received largely positive reviews. One fan was Willie Wax, who wrote in his Platter Patter column, "Elsa Lanchester—that wonderful woman—has finally brought out an album on HiFi records. Called 'Songs for a Smoke-Filled Room.' She is assisted, and she needn't have been, by her husband Charles Laughton. But it is Elsa's show all the way." Another reviewer agreed, writing, "If she had not been around so long she would be a major discovery."[16] A second album, *Songs for a Shuttered Parlor*, would be released the following year to similar acclaim.

Sadly, Elsa's Broadway appearance would be less successful, despite the involvement of legendary producer and director George Abbott. Abbott—known for such stage successes as *A Tree Grows in Brooklyn* (1951), *The Pajama Game* (1954), and *Damn Yankees* (1955)—approached Elsa in May 1957 with a script called *Too Many Doctors*, written by Claude Binyon. Elsa had worked with Binyon before when he wrote and directed the 1952 movie *Dreamboat*, in which she had appeared with Clifton Webb and Ginger Rogers, and this *Doctors* script was for another farce. Elsa told Hedda Hopper that it was one of the liveliest plays she had ever read, in which her character was a hypochondriac millionaire admitted to a hospital, where high jinks ensue.[17]

---

16. *Altoona Tribune*, September 5, 1957; *San Francisco Examiner*, October 20, 1957.

17. *Newark Advocate*, May 24, 1957.

With the play's title changed to *A Soft Touch*, rehearsals began in September 1957, for a planned opening date of November 13. During the rehearsals, Elsa was interviewed by Jian Hanauer, to whom she praised the show's collaborative nature. "It isn't a complete vehicle for anybody," she said, "and I like that. I don't think I'd ever want to sustain a big drama. I don't think I like acting that much. The first ladies of our business just live for that sort of part, but I'm not constructed that way."[18]

However, after two weeks of rehearsals, Abbott announced that *A Soft Touch* would be postponed indefinitely. The show's producers, Harold Prince and Robert Griffith, were told that the script required major revisions, and the cast members were released from their contracts. John Chapman, in his Curtain Going Up! New York theater column, speculated that the show might have closed sooner but for Abbott's unusual directorial methods. "He never goes near a play until the actors have become familiar with their lines and have a rudimentary notion of how and where to move," claimed Chapman. "Then he steps in and begins applying 'the Abbott touch.'"[19]

Suddenly and unexpectedly cast adrift, Elsa immediately boarded an airplane to London, where Charles was visiting on a promotional tour for *Witness for the Prosecution* with Billy Wilder and Tyrone Power. When she landed, Elsa was greeted by her husband with his typical overcompensatory enthusiasm, as was reported in the inimitable style of the British tabloid press: "It was a Laughton-esque scene—full-blooded, heavy-lipped," wrote the *Daily Mirror*. "The biggest smacker seen at London Airport for many a long day." After his passionate display, Charles boomed at reporters, "I refuse to kiss my wife on the cheek—what kind of relationship do you think we have?"[20]

Elsa found her husband in good humor, having accepted an offer to act in a West End play—*The Party* by Jane Arden—the following year. He had also appeared on British television as guest master of ceremonies on a popular variety show called *Chelsea at Nine* (1957–60), which had been well received.[21] Thrilled to have another Hollywood movie star to boost ratings, the show's producers quickly signed Elsa up to perform her act, but once again the work of Forman Brown went unappreciated by a transatlantic audience. One television critic opined that Elsa's showing "would have fallen with a wet thud at a Women's Institute weekly meeting," and claimed that her rendition of "If You Peek in My Gazebo" was "screamingly unfunny."[22] Possibly there were still some ill feelings toward Elsa in the British press; indeed, the reviews for the Laughtons' performances in *Witness* had been less enthusiastic on this side of the Atlantic. Elspbeth Grant in *The*

18. *Fort Worth Star-Telegram*, October 8, 1957.

19. *Daily News*, October 27, 1957.

20. *Daily Mirror*, October 15, 1957.

21. Higham, *Charles Laughton*, 207–8.

22. *Liverpool Echo*, October 23, 1957.

Tatler dismissed Elsa's Miss Plimsoll as "ludicrously agitated" before remarking with incredible pomposity, "I do not myself consider cardiac trouble a laughing matter, nor do I care to see the nursing profession held up to ridicule." However, even this humorless reviewer had to admit that the general public felt differently: "but perhaps I am being stuffy: the greater part of the audience seemed to find it all vastly entertaining."[23]

While in England, Elsa traveled to Brighton to see her mother. Now in her late eighties, Biddy was finding her loudly proclaimed independence a harder pretense to maintain. Elsa and Charles had been financially supporting her for decades; as Elsa pointed out, Biddy could not receive a widow's pension after Shamus's death because she was not technically a widow.[24] On this visit, Elsa would help move Biddy from a third-floor flat to one at ground level at Highcroft Villas in Brighton. Despite Biddy's crotchety protestations, the flat was equipped with "luxuries" such as heating, and a rope to help her get out of the bath. "It was always a hopeless task to try to get her to change to a life with a few more comforts," Elsa would remember. "Any room she lived in was without any order at all. Boxes full of letters and snapshots and old bills, scraps of cloth—all shoved under the bed or sofa—and something or other on every table and chair."[25] The mother-daughter relationship, although mellowed by distance, still floated uneasily on an ocean of misunderstandings and stubbornness. When Elsa's cousin Marjorie heard that Elsa was in England, she arranged a family gathering in Wilmcote, which would reunite Biddy with her brothers Frank and George for the first time since they assisted in kidnapping her more than six decades earlier. Steve Cockayne quotes Frank's granddaughter as saying, "To see Biddy with her brother Frank was lovely. They were chatting away. It had been a long time since the lunacy business."[26] Sadly, despite being the catalyst for the event, Elsa did not attend. Cockayne does not provide her reason for missing the gathering.

23. *The Tatler*, February 21, 1958.

24. Lanchester, *Elsa Lanchester, Herself*, 316.

25. Lanchester, 220.

26. Cockayne, *Master of the Marionettes*, 255.

23   You've Killed Everything

Filming for *Bell, Book and Candle* took place at Columbia Pictures between February 3 and April 7, 1958, although Elsa had completed her scenes and was back in England by late March, causing her to miss the Oscar ceremony where she was nominated for Best Supporting Actress. *Bell, Book and Candle* was a major picture for Columbia, and it featured a suitably star-studded cast, with Kim Novak and James Stewart in the lead roles. The supporting cast was of exceptional quality, comprising Elsa, Jack Lemmon, Ernie Kovacs, and Hermione Gingold. Based on the hit Broadway play by John Van Druten, the film was a supernatural romantic comedy about a family of modern-day witches. Novak played Gillian, who casts a spell on Stewart's businessman to make him fall in love with her. Elsa played Gillian's Aunt Queenie, who is also a witch, albeit a less successful one. Although Elsa had played flighty, scatterbrained characters before, rarely had she achieved such an endearing characterization. Queenie is ditzy and childlike, and Elsa's trademark giggle is very much in evidence, but there is none of her usual strident, haughty accents. This is one of Elsa's softer performances, and her Aunt Queenie is immensely likable; it is definitely, as Gregory William Mank writes, "one of her finest roles."[1]

The atmosphere on set was pleasant, "great fun, very relaxed," with Elsa saying that Kim Novak was "easy to work with. She didn't have the typical star ego or condescensions."[2] Jack Lemmon, who played Gillian's warlock brother Nicky, spoke to Hedda Hopper about his respect for his fellow supporting actors Elsa and Hermione Gingold. "With those two old girls you have to watch your step," he said. "They're great scene stealers and both are hysterically funny."[3] The reviewers agreed with him, writing that "Misses Gingold and Lanchester are perhaps the greatest witches to brew a stew since *Macbeth*."[4]

---

1.   Mank, *Women in Horror Films*, 311.
2.   Hadleigh, *Charles Laughton*, 97.
3.   *Los Angeles Times*, May 11, 1958.
4.   *Valley Times*, November 13, 1958.

Elsa attended the film's premiere in October 1958 with writer Christopher Isherwood and his friend Ella Corbin, the future Countess of Sandwich. This is the first time Isherwood mentions Elsa in his diaries, which would prove to be a valuable source of information regarding Elsa and Charles for the next few years. As well as being a friend, Isherwood would become a neighbor of the Laughtons and a prospective collaborator with Charles. He would detail the frictions in Elsa's marriage with the insight of an insider, and his barbed entries sometimes make uncomfortable reading.

Although Elsa was very fond of Isherwood—who was her age and shared her sharp, occasionally spiteful sense of humor—she intensely disliked his long-term boyfriend, the artist Don Bachardy, who was thirty years Isherwood's junior. Bachardy was well aware of Elsa's enmity toward him. "Her loathing of me is really quite phenomenal and on such a deep primitive level that I can't take it personally," he wrote in a 1970 letter to Isherwood. "It goes so far beyond me or anything I've done that it would be sheer vanity to assume any responsibility for it."[5]

When Elsa finished filming *Bell, Book and Candle* in March 1958, she was an Oscar-nominated actress with a major movie awaiting release. She would have been shocked had she known that she would not make another motion picture until 1964—although she would certainly not be idle in those years. Her first order of business was another trip to England to begin rehearsals for *The Party*, in which she had agreed to appear with Charles, who was also directing, although the couple would not appear in any scenes together. The play was a serious drama in the fashionable Angry Young Man genre exemplified in John Osborne's *Look Back in Anger* (1956), and it featured a risqué, potentially incestuous subtext between father and daughter. Charles was to play the alcoholic father; Elsa had a character part as a nylon-stockings saleswoman.

Although Charles had been excited by the project as soon as he read the script, Elsa was much less enthused, a direct contrast to how she had felt about her failed Broadway venture, *A Soft Touch*. Elsa had previously explained that the difference between their preferred acting styles created a balance in their careers. "He has the drive and the talent for the big things, and I tag along on the flighty side," she said. "It's dreadful the other way around."[6] She agreed to appear in *The Party*, despite her misgivings, because Charles asked her to, and, as she told journalist Bob Thomas, "if just one of us did it, we would be apart for a year or so. There's no sense in that; you might as well be divorced."[7] Elsa wasn't the only reluctant cast member; Joyce Redman was so unhappy in her part as Charles's wife that she tried constantly to get out of doing the play.[8] Rounding

---

5.   Isherwood and Bachardy, *The Animals*, 437.

6.   *Fort Worth Star-Telegram*, October 8, 1957.

7.   *Boston Globe*, March 11, 1958.

8.   Lanchester, *Elsa Lanchester, Herself*, 248.

out the cast were Ann Lynn, John Walsh, and Albert Finney. Finney had been selected personally by Charles, who had seen him play Macbeth in Birmingham, and had reportedly told him, "You were bloody awful, but what can you expect at your age?" Despite this, Charles saw the potential that would result in Finney's celebrated career, with *The Party* providing the young actor's West End debut.[9]

The play opened in Edinburgh in April 1958, then went on to Manchester, Liverpool, and Newcastle, before opening in London on May 28. Considerable publicity was made from the fact that this was the first time Elsa and Charles had appeared onstage together since *Peter Pan* in 1936, so audiences and critics alike were understandably disappointed that the two never appeared in a scene together. This was not the only unsatisfactory aspect of the "grim drama," with reviewers panning the writing and Charles's direction.[10] "The play is dull," declared the *Daily Mirror*, "much of it is repetitive and unimaginative." Elsa was accused of overacting, her usual exaggerated comedic style at odds with the gritty realism that this style of production required, a fault that the critic from *The Observer* blamed on Charles's inadequate direction. However, most commentators agreed that it was good to have Charles back on the London stage where he belonged.[11]

Despite the poor reviews, Charles's star power was enough to keep ticket sales steady, and the cast settled into a run that would eventually last six months. During their time in England, Elsa and Charles spent more time in each other's company than they had done for many years, socially as well as professionally. They lived in a flat near Baker Street and took trips to the English countryside as they had done when they were courting, being so charmed with their rediscovery of England's rural beauty that they entertained fantasies of returning permanently, although nothing would come of this. They also attended a garden party given by the Queen at Buckingham Palace, and they journeyed to Stratford-upon-Avon, where Charles met with director Glen Byam Shaw. Shaw was eager for Charles to appear onstage in some big Shakespearean roles, and the actor was happy to be convinced. Charles would eventually agree to play the lead in *King Lear* and Bottom in *A Midsummer Night's Dream* for the Royal Shakespeare Company's centenary season in 1959.

A new acquaintance made around this time was *National Velvet* author Enid Bagnold, whom Elsa would describe delightfully as "still handsome, though rather weighed down in front with a bust that had probably always been there."[12] Charles and Bagnold would become firm friends, and he would lunch with her in Brighton often, although Elsa preferred to visit Biddy on those occasions, rather

---

9.   Hershman, *Strolling Player*, 70; Lanchester, *Elsa Lanchester, Herself*, 248.

10. Lanchester, *Elsa Lanchester, Herself*, 248.

11. *Daily Mirror*, May 29, 1958; *The Observer*, June 1, 1958; Callow, *Charles Laughton*, 250.

12. Lanchester, *Elsa Lanchester, Herself*, 251.

than having to make polite conversation with Bagnold's husband, Sir Roderick Jones, and her son, a train enthusiast.

Their stay in England also gave Elsa and Charles the chance to reconnect with Iris Barry. Previously employed at New York's MoMA, where she had been the first curator of the film department, Iris had retired and by 1958 was living in the South of France with an olive oil smuggler called Pierre Kerroux. Elsa did not hold out high hopes for Iris's new flame—describing him as "very rough"—but she would later admit that "he turned out to be a nice fellow."[13] Charles paid for Iris and Pierre's travel to England and their accommodation, and Elsa described their visit as a highlight of her time in London. Although Iris still enjoyed a drink, she remained as forthright and witty as ever—and although her drunken quarrelsomeness would lead to remorse the next day, Iris retained her ability to laugh at herself. Charles remained uncomfortable with Iris's excessive drinking. He had hated drunkenness since his early days in the hotel trade, when it would often fall to him to turn out rowdy drunks from the bar. However, he was beginning to drink more himself. "And Charles suffered remorse too," recalled Elsa. "But he never laughed about it."[14]

The Party would continue its run at London's New Theatre until November 1958, but in September, Elsa "got fed up with co-starring with her husband on the London stage," according to journalist Mike Connolly, "and flew back to Hollywood—leaving Charles Laughton to find a new leading lady."[15] *The Stage*, England's newspaper for the theater industry, confirmed that "Renée Houston took over Elsa Lanchester's part in *The Party* at the New, on Wednesday of last week, so that Miss Lanchester can fulfil previous professional commitments."[16] Never a fan of "the depressing play," Elsa was presumably grateful for the chance to jump ship when she was offered the title role in "Mother Goose" (1958), a television film aired as part of the series *Shirley Temple's Storybook* (1958–61).[17]

Former child superstar Shirley Temple was now thirty years old and a mother. *Shirley Temple's Storybook* featured adaptations of fairy tales that starred well-known actors, with Temple narrating and sometimes acting. Her three children would make their acting debuts in the final episode of the first season, "Mother Goose," in which Elsa appeared. This resulted in a wary atmosphere on the set. When a crew member swore during a "Mother Goose" rehearsal, Temple fired him and told the shocked cast—including Elsa—that such language was inappropriate on a children's show, although there had been no children present at the rehearsal.[18]

---

13. Sitton, *Lady in the Dark*, 8, 384; Lanchester, *Elsa Lanchester, Herself*, 249.

14. Lanchester, *Elsa Lanchester, Herself*, 250.

15. *Desert Sun*, September 10, 1958.

16. *The Stage*, September 11, 1958.

17. Lanchester, *Elsa Lanchester, Herself*, 250.

18. Windeler, *The Films of Shirley Temple*, 255.

Elsa would follow this with a few more television appearances, guesting several times on Jack Paar's various talk shows, and once in a skit about witches on *The Dinah Shore Show* (1951–57) to promote *Bell, Book and Candle*. She also continued working on her live performance skills with her longtime friend and accompanist Ray Henderson. In addition to playing the piano during Elsa's act, Henderson was also a composer. In late 1958, Elsa made a private recording of two operettas that Henderson had composed for her, one of which had lyrics by the acclaimed science fiction writer Ray Bradbury.

As previously mentioned, Bradbury had been an enthusiastic Turnabout Theatre fan in the 1940s. His writing career had taken off in the following decade with the publication of *The Martian Chronicles* in 1951 and *Fahrenheit 451* in 1953. For a while in the mid-1950s, Charles Laughton considered the possibility of adapting *Fahrenheit 451* into a stage play, and he approached Bradbury to discuss the matter. Although nothing would develop professionally from this encounter, Ray Bradbury and his wife, Maggie, would form a close friendship with Elsa and Charles, taking their young daughters over to swim frequently in the Laughtons' pool. It was while reminiscing with Elsa about the Turnabout that Ray Bradbury was inspired to experiment with a new writing style. "I tried my hand at writing a small science-fiction operetta for Elsa," he recalled, "but, let's face it, I was no Forman Brown. Writing such deceptively simply lyrics takes a very special talent. I went back to my short stories and novels."[19]

When Elsa played the recordings of her two Henderson-scored operettas for Christopher Isherwood, he recorded in his diary that Bradbury's was the better of the two, with the other one being "The Duke and the Dairymaid," with lyrics by Sam Rosen.[20] Although there had been rumors for years that Elsa was to appear on Broadway with these works and maybe also a one-act play, it was not to be.

In fact, Elsa's primary interest in late 1958 would not be her own career. Rather, she would devote the majority of her energy toward helping Charles ready himself for his upcoming appearance as King Lear. Charles Higham writes, quite correctly, that these preparations began when Charles returned from England in late 1958. However, it could also be said with equal accuracy that this performance had been years in the making, as Charles had harbored ambitions to play Lear since the 1920s, speaking about it frequently in interviews. Film critic Barry Norman would say that King Lear was "a character with whom [Charles] felt a great affinity, a shared sense of being persecuted by others of smaller stature than himself. This ambition, an obsession almost, was finally realized in 1959."[21]

Knowing how much this role meant to her husband, Elsa agreed to help him in his exhaustive and consuming preparations, but she demanded certain

19. Bradbury, "What Else but Elsa?," 10.

20. Isherwood, *Diaries*, vol. 1, 786; *Variety*, October 3, 1956.

21. "Charles Laughton," *Hollywood Greats*.

conditions first. She must be able to speak freely, she insisted, and he must agree to listen to her advice and—importantly—to her criticism. "You're not going to like all the things I say," she told Charles, "but I cannot go ahead with this huge project unless I speak my mind. I love this project. And I cannot be gentle, I cannot be a hypocrite. I must be able to speak without fear."[22] Charles agreed, and they set to work.

After some time spent studying the script of *King Lear* in the schoolroom of their Hollywood home, the Laughtons traveled to Hawai'i, where their work would not be interrupted by the pesky realities of daily life. For five weeks they were "entirely inseparable" as they battled with the meanings and interpretations present in *Lear*.[23] They took inspiration from the elements and their surroundings, with Charles recalling that stormy ocean crossing of 1935, and Elsa connecting it to the script: "the extraordinary connection and repetition of references to water, climaxed by the great storm scene. It was like an outburst of tears, that storm."[24]

Whether this creative partnership contributed in any positive way toward Elsa and Charles's personal relationship is questionable. The counterargument—that it damaged any residual fondness that remained between them—has several points to recommend it. Elsa confided in Christopher Isherwood that during their work on *Lear*, she and Charles had very little conversation. "She says that she hardly speaks when Charles is in the house—he's so domineering," Isherwood wrote. "Sometimes she is useful to him."[25] By the time Charles was preparing to take to the Stratford stage as Lear, they had descended to recrimination, name calling, and blame.

The pressure on Charles was intense. The centenary season was a star-studded one, featuring performances from such luminaries as Paul Robeson, Laurence Olivier, Edith Evans, and Sam Wanamaker. The cast of *Lear* was also impressive, with Albert Finney, Zoe Caldwell, and Angela Baddeley appearing alongside Charles. *A Midsummer Night's Dream* had been well received, but *Lear* was the acid test, and Charles knew it.

Elsa attended all rehearsals, sitting at a desk surrounded by preparatory notes, always ready to remind Charles of the decisions they had made regarding important emphasis and phrasing. One of these decisions was to drive director Glen Byam Shaw to distraction, and it may have originated with Elsa. During their work on the play's history, Elsa went back and looked at the original folios and discovered that there were discrepancies between the punctuation and capitalization of the text as it appeared in the originals and in Charles's modern working script. Charles—if not at Elsa's suggestion then certainly with her approval—be-

---

22. Lanchester, *Elsa Lanchester, Herself,* 258.

23. Lanchester, 258.

24. Lanchester, 259.

25. Isherwood, *Diaries,* vol. 1, 811.

came convinced that a word beginning with a capital letter in the original folio indicated that Shakespeare intended that word to be stressed, and so he set about doing just that. "No arguments about the capriciousness of Elizabethan printers could sway him," Simon Callow commented drily.[26]

The final screaming showdown came as opening night approached. Charles's relief following what his director had declared to be a wonderful dress rehearsal was immediately undone when Elsa burst into his dressing room bubbling over with anger, blame, and indignation. She told him that he had been dreadful, that he had reverted back to all his old irritating mannerisms and forgotten or ignored everything she had worked on. "I don't know what we've been spending this last year doing!" she yelled in his face. "I've just wasted my time. It was not worth it at all!" Charles's reaction to Elsa's outburst was equally dramatic and deliberately hurtful. "You've ruined it! I'll never do it now, it's hopeless," he told her. "You've killed everything."[27]

Years later, Elsa seemed smugly confident that her "brutality" (as Charles called it) had its desired effect: "I hadn't ruined a thing because the actual performance was the best thing Charles ever did. It was marvelous. No tricks, none at all. And he got wonderful reviews."[28] Actually, Charles's reviews were mixed, with some—including the *Sunday Times* and the *News Chronicle*—being particularly merciless.

Charles suffered mentally and physically during the run of *Lear*. He had never been in the best of health, due to his weight, and the following years would see his body destroyed by various conditions—heart problems, gallbladder, cancer—all of which had already begun to make themselves known during the physically strenuous production. Elsa recalled that he wore a bottle-green robe during rehearsals, and he perspired so much that when he dropped the robe to the floor, it was too heavy for her to pick up. Nor was she able to pick Charles up mentally when he started having nightmares, which his cousin Jack Dewsbery, a psychiatrist, concluded were linked to his inability to philosophically accept the idea of death. "Once *King Lear* had opened," Elsa concluded, "I think Charles was a sick man." However, she did not stick around to nurse him, flying back to the United States shortly after opening night. Less than a week after she left, Charles would meet and begin a relationship with Terry Jenkins, a model many years his junior, which would last until Charles's death.

Once the experience was over, and tempers had cooled, Charles did acknowledge Elsa's sacrifice of her time to help his career. He bought her a car to say thank you, although newspaper reports at the time claimed that the Lincoln Continental and the Hawaiian "vacation" had been gifts to celebrate the couple's thirtieth wedding anniversary. Charles's second gift of appreciation was his

---

26. Callow, *Charles Laughton*, 264.

27. Lanchester, *Elsa Lanchester, Herself*, 265.

28. Lanchester, 266.

promise to create and direct a one-woman show for Elsa to take on tour. This was to be an autobiographical show, with Elsa telling amusing tales from her life, as well as performing her usual songs, for which she would be accompanied by two pianists, Ray Henderson and Don Dollarhide. The show had several different working titles, among them *The Private Wonderland of Elsa Lanchester* and *Elsa Lanchester Censored by Charles Laughton*, before ultimately being dubbed *Elsa Lanchester—Herself*. It was scheduled to open in Los Angeles in October 1960, but much was to happen before then.

24 Vain Old Hams

In March 1960, Jane Wyman presented a television show called *Academy Award Songs*, "a musical salute to motion picture songs that have won Oscars," featuring performances from Nat King Cole, Tex Ritter, Kay Starr, the Four Aces . . . and Elsa Lanchester and Charles Laughton.[1] The Laughtons' performance of "Baby, It's Cold Outside" was deemed by the press to be "a minor disaster," and a modern viewer might consider that opinion overly generous; Charles comes across as lecherous, Elsa as overly coy, and neither of them make any attempt at the tune. Journalist Dick Shippy wrote that "both Charles and Elsa acted a little ashamed of themselves; and truthfully I felt ashamed for them."[2]

Things did not improve for Charles over the months that followed. He suffered a heart attack in May, for which a diseased gallbladder was found to be the cause. The doctors put him on a strict diet and scheduled him for an operation in August. Frightened and depressed about his failing health, Charles made several big decisions about his lifestyle, telling Elsa and others that he wanted to be among his "own people," meaning gay men. He had sent for Terry Jenkins to come to America, and he intended to live with him in the house next door to where the writer Christopher Isherwood lived with his partner, Don Bachardy. Elsa describes the purchase of this Santa Monica property as a joint project, but Charles made it clear to Isherwood that his primary reason for buying the house was "to have a place to get away from Elsa," where he and Jenkins could live as a couple.[3]

When Jenkins arrived in Los Angeles, the new property was not finalized, and so he moved into the Curson Avenue house with Elsa and Charles. By all accounts, Jenkins was a pleasant, amiable man who was genuinely fond of Charles. Charles Higham describes their situation as "Socratic," and Charles enjoyed adopting once again his Henry Higgins persona—only this time his efforts were appreciated by a young man genuinely in awe of his intellect.[4] "I had never known

---

1. *Tampa Bay Times*, March 13, 1960.
2. *Pittsburgh Sun Telegraph*, March 16, 1960; *Akron Beacon Journal*, March 16, 1960.
3. Isherwood, *Diaries*, vol. 1, 857.
4. Higham, *Charles Laughton*, 219.

such a person in my whole life," Jenkins would later say of his lover and mentor. "His mind overpowered me. . . . Being with Charles, I now realize, was better than attending the best liberal university in the world."[5]

Isherwood would describe Jenkins as "handsome, unexciting, and, I really think, a very nice boy," and that seems to have been the general consensus.[6] It is harder to ascertain what Elsa made of this attractive interloper. The evidence suggests that Elsa liked Jenkins, was even fond of him, except for when she hated him, envied him, or pitied him. She made snide comments about him, certainly ("He was very good-looking, but a little bit jowly"), but she did that about everybody.[7] She thought that maybe he was a bit scared of her, and considering the stories he must have heard about her from Charles, this could well have been the case.

Such a variety of responses reflects the conflicting emotions the unusual situation was bound to create. When Charles lavished money and gifts on Jenkins, including a Thunderbird automobile, Elsa felt resentment stirring, which she openly acknowledged. But there was another feeling that Elsa connected to Terry, one that was infinitely sadder: gratitude. Such was Charles's temper and overbearing personality that Elsa felt safer when there was a third party around. Her fear was not of physical violence, but of the mental cruelties that she and Charles now inflicted on each other regularly and yet were reluctant for outsiders to witness. Their mutual animosity was clear to those closest to them, however: "Elsa says she feels that Charles hates her," Isherwood wrote in his diary in August 1960. "Maybe she hates *him*."[8]

Jenkins would not remain permanently in the United States, and he traveled frequently back to England for lengthy periods. Without his romantic distraction, and still in poor health, Charles slid into a black mood, which resulted in an intensification of his cruelty to Elsa. In earlier, happier times, during their courtship, Elsa had enjoyed Charles's taking an interest in her appearance, even when his suggestions had carried the implied slight that what she wore was not quite right or somehow unsuitable. These suggestions might have been an early manifestation of his Henry Higgins complex, but Elsa relished the attention. When he insisted, decades later, that she wear glamorous dresses during her *Private Music Hall* tour, she complied delightedly, defying staid middle age in custom gowns. But his interest in her appearance now, as she approached sixty, was not flattering. Always a lover of beauty—and with a corresponding hatred for its counterpart, which he considered himself a repellant example of—Charles berated Elsa for losing her looks, aging, gaining weight, and letting herself go. He suggested forcefully that she should get a face-lift; she vehemently refused.

5.   Quoted in Lanchester, *Elsa Lanchester, Herself*, 270.

6.   Isherwood, *Diaries*, vol. 1, 887.

7.   Lanchester, *Elsa Lanchester, Herself*, 267.

8.   Isherwood, *Diaries*, vol. 1, 899 (emphasis in original).

With these venomous outbursts, Charles was likely projecting his fear and disgust about his own aging and rapid decline—and his terror of dying—onto Elsa. Despite being upset at this new avenue of attack, Elsa did not share Charles's morbid dread of the advancing years. Back in 1938, in *Charles Laughton and I*, she had marveled at the lengths her fellow actresses would go to in order to stay desirable and relevant in a town and industry that fetishized youth, writing, "A life devoted to trying to keep the cradle at a convenient distance from the grave is hardly a life at all."[9] This was an easy position to take in her mid-thirties perhaps, but Elsa maintained a similar attitude toward the outward signs of aging throughout her life. Although she would bemoan the physical pains and emotional losses that inevitably accompanied old age, her expanding waistline and deepening laugh lines were not of concern. Her only concession to vanity was the maintenance of her red hair with dye. In her late sixties, she would claim that her lack of glamour in her youth had helped ease her passage into seniority. "I have no complex about growing old," she said. "I was not a beauty and never exploited my looks or my youth. This has its compensations."[10]

Except for filming an episode of the television show *Adventures in Paradise* (1959–62) in August, Elsa directed all her professional attention in 1960 toward the upcoming *Elsa Lanchester—Herself*. Charles's involvement was less than he had originally intended as complications from his gallbladder surgery saw him rehospitalized the month before the show was to open. Elsa claims that despite his enthusiasm for the project, Charles initially refused to put his name to it, but when he realized how good it was, he conceded to the credit "Censored by Charles Laughton." This claim is flagrantly untrue; "Censored by Charles Laughton" appeared in the press when the show was first announced, long before its quality could be ascertained, and was even given by some reporters as the show's title. His name meant increased publicity and ticket sales, and Elsa was never too proud to take advantage of such perks, reasoning that she put up with enough of the disadvantages of being Mrs. Laughton and had earned her share of his spotlight. Charles seemed to agree, and he posed for promotional pictures alongside Elsa in her "Pearly Queen" costume from the show, despite being visibly tired and unwell.

For Elsa, *Herself* represented a combination and culmination of all the shows that had come before it; highlights from her Turnabout and Cave of Harmony acts would be remixed with some of the formatting from the *Private Music Hall* tour. What was new were the anecdotal inserts, which transformed the performance into a deeply personal experience for Elsa. She would discuss her parents, their socialism, and her time with Isadora Duncan all those years ago in Paris. In an interview with the *Los Angeles Times* to promote *Herself*, Elsa tried to get across just how important this show was to her:

---

9.   Lanchester, *Charles Laughton and I*, 173.

10.   *Los Angeles Times*, November 1, 1970.

I am very enthusiastic about this concert. I am gambling everything on myself. All my life I've dissipated my talent—I've done songs, I've done acting. . . . Now some people will say, "What is it that you're doing on the concert stage?" It's vaudeville. You're selling everything you do directly to the audience. It's that audience contact, I suppose, that I prefer.[11]

Knowing how important it was to her, Charles rose from his sickbed and traveled to Stockton, California, for the show's tryout, although the journey exhausted him. When Elsa was taking repeated curtain calls from an enthusiastic audience, Charles suddenly decided that he wanted a share in the adoration and made his way from the auditorium, through the bowels of backstage, and into the spotlight. By the time he had completed his journey, the audience had left. This might have remained just a funny little aside, but the attitude it represented—Charles's inability to allow Elsa to shine without him, his desire to remind everyone who the *real* star was—would lead to much more serious events just a few days later.

Shortly before *Herself* was to officially open, at Royce Hall, on the campus of the University of California, Los Angeles, Elsa was at home at the Curson Avenue property when she heard screaming coming from the front of the house. When she ran outside, Elsa found Charles, seemingly suffering some kind of psychological breakdown, trying to throw himself down the stone steps that led to the road. His former lover and longtime friend Bill Phipps was struggling with him to prevent him from doing so. It would later transpire that prior to this, Charles had shouted to Phipps that he wanted pills in order to end his life. Elsa, acting instinctively, drew back her arm and slapped her hysterical husband hard across the face. It worked, and Charles became calm and quiet.

That Charles had been ill, depressed, and worried about the future for months would all seem, to an outsider, to be contributing factors to this episode—whether it was a genuine mental break or a curious cry for attention. However, both Elsa and Charles believed that *she* was somehow to blame, with Elsa convinced that Charles was trying to sabotage her upcoming performance. Immediately after the event, she rounded on him accusatorily. "You are trying to kill my show," she told him. "You want to destroy it and me. How can I possibly stand on that stage now and be light and cheerful as if nothing happened?"[12]

When Christopher Isherwood heard about these events the following day, he dismissed both Elsa and Charles as self-centered attention seekers ("Really, the fuss these vain old hams make!") and accused Phipps of stirring up animosity between them.[13] This assessment appears to ring true with a curious passage in Elsa's autobiography in which she describes an encounter with a psychologist that Charles's doctor had recommended she talk with after the suicide attempt.

---

11. *Los Angeles Times*, September 25, 1960.

12. Lanchester, *Elsa Lanchester, Herself*, 274.

13. Isherwood, *Diaries*, vol. 2, 14.

According to Elsa, this conversation was a "horrifying experience," during which the psychologist said something to her that was so devastating that she blanked it out from her memory entirely. All she could recall was her vehement response: "Either Charles said that—and he's a goddamned liar if he did," she screamed at the shrink, "or you just invented it and you're a goddamned liar. And even if Charles did say it, you have no business repeating it to me!" She later mused, "I still wonder what could have been so offensive. Something beyond human endurance."[1] Of course, we can never know, but it is reasonable to speculate that Charles had told the psychiatrist the same thing he told Isherwood: that Phipps had told him that Elsa had said that she wished Charles was dead, "as he had nothing left to live for."[2] This corrosive gossip and backstabbing destroyed any remaining affection in the Laughtons' long-suffering marriage.

Although two nurses were assigned to ensure that Charles did himself no further violence, and Phipps slept beside him to make doubly sure, Charles declared just a couple of days after the incident that he felt fine. Now, however, he expressed a concern that Elsa was preparing to have him committed to an institution. Isherwood recognized the meddling of Phipps in this new paranoia, and patiently assured Charles that such a thing was impossible. Clearly, however, it would be best for Elsa and Charles to have some distance between them, and it must have been a relief to all concerned when Charles flew to Japan with Terry Jenkins less than a fortnight after his attempt to end his own life.

Meanwhile, despite her concerns, Elsa's show opened on time, and to good reviews, with Frank Mulcahy writing in the *Los Angeles Times* that Elsa "was in her usual excellent form"; he was especially impressed with her "wonderfully casual and seemingly unrehearsed stories."[3] Proving the adage that one man's trash is another man's treasure, Isherwood, who attended the very same performance as Mulcahy, felt that the worst part of the show—none of which he enjoyed—was its *lack* of spontaneity. He provided the reason for this in a derisive diary entry that also demonstrated Charles's ongoing habit of putting Elsa down behind her back:

> Charles says she had to learn every word she says on the stage—all the asides, everything—by heart. "She couldn't even say, 'Hello, Santa Barbara,'" says Charles, "because if she learnt that line, she'd have to say it in Stockton and Miami as well—all over the country."[4]

As Elsa toured with the show around the United States, her reviews varied greatly, proving unequivocally that people either loved or hated her act, there was

---

1. Lanchester, *Elsa Lanchester, Herself,* 275.

2. Isherwood, *Diaries,* vol. 2, 14.

3. *Los Angeles Times,* October 4, 1960.

4. Isherwood, *Diaries,* vol. 2, 15.

no middle ground. In Calgary she was accused again of sticking too rigidly to what had been rehearsed, but not because she had memorized it, as Charles via Isherwood had suggested: "Busily reading the cue-cards obviously spread on the floor before the microphone, Miss Lanchester didn't once show any spontaneous humor," the reviewer wrote. Another criticism came in Boston, where Kevin Kelly, remarking on the show's "Censored by Charles Laughton" tagline, sniped, "The best thing Mr. Laughton could have done for his wife was to have kept her at home where I'm sure she'd be a smashing entertainer in the living room."[5]

The positive reviewers called her "bewitching" and "a true daughter of the British music hall." The most poetic among them, Sydney Rosen, wrote, "She has a bit of American Gothic about her, she is hard and tender, scared and rather loveable all at once."[6] It is impossible not to notice, however, that the positive reviews are clustered more toward the beginning of the tour, demonstrating that the stresses of being on the road took their toll on the fifty-eight-year-old performer. Elsa would arrive at a venue a few hours before curtain up, tired and dirty from traveling. After checking the lights and finding someone to press her costumes, she might—if she was lucky—have time for some food and a nap in her motel room before heading back to the venue for makeup and final checks. "Swearing and cursing about the lights. Furious because the stage is dirty, and balls of fluff sweep onto the costumes. No bathrooms some places," Elsa said in a typically candid interview at the time.[7] After the show was over, it was often a struggle to find anywhere that was open to get a hot meal, and sometimes Elsa found herself back in the motel room, washing down Ritz crackers with lemonade.

But it was all worth it, she claimed, for those moments in the spotlight, making the audience laugh and applaud. "When the music starts and I come floating out onto the stage, something happens," she said. "Something cleans me out. I feel alive." In a telling insight regarding her sense of offstage self-worth around this time, she concluded: "It's like a butterfly coming out of a dirty old chrysalis."[8]

The exhausting yet exhilarating tour ended in late November, and Elsa headed back to Hollywood. Without the adrenaline of regular performances, she was restless and out of sorts, her mood not improved by the impending marriage of her accompanist Ray Henderson. Elsa keeps the exact nature of her relationship with Henderson vague in her writings. He is cattily described by Isherwood as "a strange fat boy . . . smiling, campy, maybe a little sinister," and Katherine Bucknell (the editor of Isherwood's diaries) calls Henderson Elsa's "friend and lover," while noting that he was "much younger than she was."[9] Bucknell's description is accurate as far as it goes, but while their sexual relationship was fleeting and

5.   *Calgary Herald*, October 15, 1960; *Boston Globe*, November 7, 1960.

6.   *Times Colonist*, October 12, 1960; *Sacramento Bee*, October 21, 1960.

7.   *Detroit Free Press*, November 8, 1960.

8.   *Detroit Free Press*, November 8, 1960; Lanchester, *Elsa Lanchester, Herself*, 223.

9.   Isherwood, *Diaries*, vol. 1, 786; Isherwood, *Diaries*, vol. 2, 643.

unimportant, their friendship would prove to be a long-lasting one from which Elsa would draw much strength in the difficult years to come. In addition to completing many tours together—occasionally sharing a hotel room—Elsa and Henderson would take short breaks to Palos Verdes and frequently interacted socially. The culmination of their three-decade friendship would be when Elsa left $250,000 to Henderson in her will, although he ultimately predeceased her.[10]

Henderson's marriage inevitably meant that Elsa felt like she was losing him; when he married again a decade later, Isherwood wrote, "I think Elsa is more upset about this than she'll admit."[11] With Elsa and Charles stuck at home together over Christmas and New Year's, their bickering and antagonism quickly resumed, and Charles complained to friends that Elsa was "hysterical and obstructive," without clarifying what exactly she was obstructing.[12] His path would be clear soon enough, however, because in February 1961, Elsa would again be away from home, this time for the start of the *Elsa Lanchester—Herself* New York run.

On opening night the city was hit by a blizzard of such intensity that finding a taxi to take her to the venue proved impossible, and Elsa arrived at the Forty-First Street Theatre in the back of a police car. Despite the streets outside being covered with more than a foot of snow, she played to a full house. The reviewer for *The New York Times*, Milton Esterow, declared that the journey had been worth it: "If there's anyone who can make you forget about 17.4 inches of snow, it's Elsa Lanchester," he wrote, before concluding, "even if you have to use dog sleds, skis, or bulldozers, drop in on Elsa. She won't let you down."[13]

A warm reception in the cold weather was not enough to convince Elsa of the city's charms. She felt that New York had lost the freshness and sparkle that she had enjoyed when she first visited the city back in 1931. This may have been a case of rose-tinted glasses, for her letters to Jeffrey Dell from this time merely relate her longing to return to London. Whatever her original opinion was, Elsa expressed it only in her private correspondence at the time; three decades later she would not be so discrete. Interviewed by Mel Heimer in her room on the eleventh floor of the beautiful Algonquin Hotel, Elsa announced that New York was "beyond rescue." She decried the smog, the traffic, the dirt, and the noise, and claimed that the people just shoved and scowled. "No one smiles anymore," she said. "Whatever New York had, is gone."[14] Elsa later expanded this opinion to include all cities, expressing frequently when away from home her desire to return to her garden in the sun. "How anyone can live in a city, I'll never understand," she said.[15]

---

10. *Los Angeles Times*, January 6, 1987.

11. Isherwood, *Diaries*, vol. 2, 598.

12. Isherwood, 32.

13. *The New York Times*, February 6, 1961.

14. *Kane Republican*, March 15, 1961; Lanchester, *Elsa Lanchester, Herself*, 276.

15. *The Courier-Journal*, June 10, 1962.

Fortunately there were theaters in California too, and *Elsa Lanchester—Herself* would play three times at the Ivar Theater, Hollywood, in the early 1960s, with the run extended each time due to demand for tickets. The audience frequently featured movie stars and columnists, who praised Elsa's onstage antics. One who was less impressed was Jayne Mansfield, a 1950s blonde bombshell whose own career was nose-diving fast in this new and confusing decade. An anonymous gossip item in June 1961 reported that Elsa had given Mansfield "a good dressing down" when she had the audacity to walk out in the middle of Elsa's performance.[16]

Tempers also flared when Elsa and Charles attended a dinner at Romanoff's in honor of the journalist Randolph Churchill, although for once it was not the volatile Laughtons who were the antagonists. Charles was making a movie, *Advise and Consent* (1962), and Churchill—son of former British Prime Minister Winston Churchill—was in town to write a story about the film. Joining them for dinner were *Advise and Consent* director Otto Preminger; *Witness for the Prosecution* director Billy Wilder and his wife, Audrey; and writer I. A. L. Diamond. The trouble started when a drunken Churchill began, in the newspaper parlance of the time, "tossing verbal brickbats with the carefree abandon of an old-time vaudeville juggler." Preminger recalled that Churchill then "insulted everyone at the table."[17] According to the more sensational reports, an enraged Audrey Wilder then smacked Churchill across the face, although it seems more likely that she threw a napkin in his face before storming out of the restaurant, quickly followed by Elsa and the rest of the guests. When approached to comment on the incident, Churchill refused to discuss the matter, berating those who asked him by saying that he didn't think journalists should interview journalists. Audrey Wilder was more forthcoming, eagerly admitting to throwing the napkin, and saying, "Young Churchill is a colossal bore and I feel sorry for his father."[18] As well she might: a similar display during a meal on board Aristotle Onassis's yacht saw Sir Winston on the receiving end of Randolph's "verbal brickbats." Enraged, the elderly statesman ordered that his son be removed from the boat as soon as possible, and Onassis complied.[19]

---

16. *Indianapolis Star*, June 11, 1961.

17. *San Francisco Examiner*, October 19, 1961.

18. *Sacramento Bee*, October 19, 1961.

19. Montague Browne, *Long Sunset*, 299–300.

25   As Sick as Charles

Despite the growing distance and animosity between them, Elsa and Charles endeavored to maintain the illusion of a happy marriage in public. They attended several events together, including the premiere of Charles's film *Advise and Consent* (1962), in which Charles played a homophobic southern senator. According to Louella Parsons, watching the film at its premiere caused Charles to openly weep.[1] It would be his last film appearance.

Still unwell, Charles set out on a reading tour in early 1962, accompanied by Terry Jenkins and a road man—a real one, not a lover—Bob Halter. Elsa stayed in California with another run at the Ivar and some television work planned. At this time she was often in the company of former actor turned arts and antiques dealer Michael Hall, whom Christopher Isherwood—a former lover of Hall's—described in a letter as her "constant companion."[2] As Charles left, Elsa claims that she was struck by a premonition. "Sometimes you have a sudden flash that you're not going to see someone in health ever again," she recalled—although how much Charles could have been described as "in health" at this point is highly questionable—"and I had the feeling that I was a free woman. That's a terrible thing to say, in a way. But at that moment, that's how I felt."[3] The curious mixture of emotions that Elsa acknowledged here were in evidence during Charles's final illness and after his death, and led to Elsa being regarded by many observers as heavy-handed, unfeeling, and wildly inappropriate. Some of her actions and reactions can be understood with reference to her complicated marriage and the brusque awkwardness she inherited from her mother; others defy explanation entirely, and frame Elsa as an emotionally underdeveloped woman, who lacked the skills to deal with terminal illness in the socially acceptable manner.

---

1. *San Francisco Examiner*, December 13, 1961.

2. Isherwood and Bachardy, *The Animals*, 121.

3. Lanchester, *Elsa Lanchester, Herself*, 278.

Elsa was filming an episode of the television show *Follow the Sun* (1961–62) with Cesar Romero when she received a call that Charles had fallen in the bath and broken his collarbone. An operation on his shoulder and a stay at a New York hospital revealed that matters were far more serious—Charles had cancer.

During his early hospitalization, Charles was replaced on some dates of his reading tour by his friend Burgess Meredith. The remaining dates were covered by Elsa and Ray Henderson with a modified version of *Herself* minus Don Dollarhide, much to Charles's displeasure. It was not Elsa playing his dates that her husband objected to, or so Elsa claimed, but that his careful crafting of the show for three people was being tampered with. From his hospital bed, Charles went so far as to forbid Elsa from participating. She, of course, ignored him completely. The audience who booked tickets expecting Charles's sonorous readings of classical texts must have experienced quite a culture shock when presented with Elsa's bawdy music hall.

Around this time, Elsa also provided some voice work for composer Igor Stravinsky's television special *The Flood: A Musical Play* (1962). This work in seven parts contained music, ballet, songs, and spoken dialogue, this last created by Robert Craft from source material including medieval mystery plays and the Book of Genesis. It was highbrow stuff, and although Elsa's brief turn as Noah's wife was her usual comic light relief, she confessed herself baffled by the material: "I read a total of five lines and I don't have the vaguest idea what they mean," she said. "After I read the lines Maestro Stravinsky announced that I was perfect. It was a lovely compliment but I would have preferred it if they had told me what I said."[4] She had other things on her mind.

When her work was over, Elsa left Michael Hall and joined Terry Jenkins and Bob Halter at the Hotel St. Moritz in New York, where Charles would also stay when he wasn't being treated at the hospital. It's uncertain whether Charles knew how serious his condition was at this point, as his fear of thinking about or discussing his own morbidity was such that much remained unspoken. "He faced illness bravely," documentary maker Barry Norman would later say of Charles, "but not death, because death he wouldn't face at all."[5] Before his fall, Charles had been approached by Billy Wilder for the role of Moustache in *Irma la Douce* (1963), and while at the hospital he began to grow a mustache for the role that he still believed he might play.

Another delusion, brought about by the medication Charles was taking, would lead to some of Elsa's most inexplicable actions. Charles believed that he was going to travel to France in order to attend the Cannes Film Festival, and he spoke enthusiastically about the forthcoming trip, telling Elsa that they must meet up with Iris Barry while they were there. Instructed not to let Charles give up hope, Elsa was determined to keep up the pretense. She bought

4.   *Ashbury Park Press*, June 2, 1962.

5.   "Charles Laughton," *Hollywood Greats*.

a new dress for the occasion and a new set of luggage, and then she went one step further and had herself inoculated against smallpox. Elsa had never had any vaccinations—her brother, Waldo, had taken badly, so Biddy refused to let Elsa have them—but Elsa *had* traveled to France previously without getting the shots. Doctors had apparently faked certificates for her rather than risk a bad reaction. So why have the smallpox inoculation now? No reasonable explanation presents itself, and when Elsa unsurprisingly did have a reaction to the completely unnecessary vaccination, she took to her bed and relished her illness as providing a distraction from the grim realities and responsibilities of Charles's treatment. Her discussion of this episode in her 1983 autobiography demonstrates no awareness of how strange her actions were, instead offering a breathtakingly self-centered narrative:

> I had a high temperature and was as sick as Charles, in a way, for about a week. It was strange thinking of him coming into my room and saying "How are you to-day?"—when I knew that it was Charles who was dying. . . . In a funny way I was even glad to be so ill. It was one way to kill time and to kill some of my thinking about Charles. . . . I was occupying myself. It was more therapy.[6]

Meanwhile, Charles was deteriorating fast. The decision was made for him to return to California, with extra seats purchased on the plane so he could lie down. He was sedated for the entire journey.[7]

Although Charles managed to spend some time in the Curson Avenue house, much of his remaining life was spent at Cedars of Lebanon Hospital. His visitors included Billy Wilder and Albert Finney, and once news of Charles's condition was reported in the press, letters, cards, and flowers flooded in from friends, fans, and former co-stars. Some of these were kept from Charles, lest he realize quite how ill he really was.

But Elsa knew, and although she would cooperate with efforts to keep Charles's hopes up, she refused to sugarcoat the unpalatable truth in conversations with others. This led some to believe that she was actively looking forward to Charles's death. Chief among these was Christopher Isherwood, who was revolted when Elsa began discussing her plans for what she would do when Charles was gone, where she would live and who she would live with. "She seems to think only of the future, after his death," he wrote in his diary. "I will never forget the obscenity of Elsa's determination to see him buried."[8] This is the pinnacle of Elsa's social awkwardness, her inability to act in the expected manner, which was a legacy from her mother. Isherwood took her practicality and realism as ghoulish heartlessness, but Albert Finney saw the vulnerability

6.   Lanchester, *Elsa Lanchester, Herself,* 284.

7.   Higham, *Charles Laughton,* 227–28.

8.   Isherwood, *Diaries,* vol. 2, 208.

that lurked beneath. In a letter to John Beary, his understudy in *The Party*, Finney wrote:

> [After visiting Charles] I then went home with Elsa and talked to her for about an hour. She seems absolutely accustomed to living with the reality of Charles's illness. However, I think when he dies she will break.
>
> I find it difficult to tell with Elsa, really, because she always was so strange, but I think through all the difficulties of their marriage, there has remained a very strong bond between them and when that breaks it will affect her very badly.[9]

Finney had visited Charles in the hospital with Elsa's blessing; she felt that seeing someone so near death would be beneficial to Finney as an actor. Not all visitors were as welcome, however. Charles's former co-star and onetime protégée Maureen O'Hara, for example, claimed that she stayed away from Charles during his final weeks because she and Elsa had argued. According to O'Hara, Elsa "had accused me of sneaking into his hospital room and pinning St. Christopher medals under his bed. I hadn't done any such thing and the accusation was ludicrous."[10]

Family rallied round. Charles's brother Frank was staying with Elsa at the Curson Avenue property. His other brother, Tom, had flown over to see him, but work demanded his return to the United Kingdom after a couple of weeks. Frank and Tom were still practicing Catholics, and it was important to them that Charles return to the church before he died. One evening, when Elsa was at the ballet, Frank brought a priest to see Charles. The last rites were delivered, his sins were forgiven, and Charles was accepted once more into the fold of the faithful; he was also persuaded to sign his will—which left everything to Elsa—something he had previously prevaricated about doing, such was his reluctance to consider his own demise.

Elsa was livid when she discovered Frank's actions, claiming, correctly, that Charles was not in his right mind, and had always prided himself on his fervent anti-Catholicism. She was eventually mollified by Frank's gentle explanations, and the consideration that this deathbed return to the faith of his childhood—and the accompanying forgiveness and alleviation of the guilt that weighed so heavily on him—may have offered Charles some comfort and solace. Elsa would later call the devoutly Catholic Maureen O'Hara to let her know that Charles had seen a priest and had been given extreme unction. "I know it took a lot for her to admit that to me," said O'Hara, "and, in my eyes, it made her ten feet tall."[11]

When Frank initially informed Elsa of the priest's visit, she had reacted in her typically direct and brusque manner. But rather than dismiss her as unfeeling or selfish, Frank Laughton recognized that Elsa was frightened and incapable of

---

9.   Lanchester, *Elsa Lanchester, Herself,* 299.

10.   O'Hara and Nicoletti, *'Tis Herself,* 237.

11.   O'Hara and Nicoletti, 237.

showing or even acknowledging her fear. He provided Elsa with the support and attention that she desperately needed at this time, that all her unusual actions had been crying out for. "Frank was a great comfort to me," she recalled, "when all I needed was a little tolerance from others."[12]

In the hospital, Charles was receiving cobalt treatments and morphine for the pain, but by the end of November it was clear that nothing was helping, and that Charles's time remaining could be measured in weeks rather than months. On November 30, 1962, Charles unexpectedly left Cedars of Lebanon, accompanied by Elsa. A spokesperson for the hospital stressed that he had not been released for medical reasons. "We don't want anyone to get the idea that there has been any miraculous recovery," the spokesperson announced. "There has not. He is still seriously ill." The spokesperson told reporters that "no reason was given for the departure other than Laughton wanted to go home."[13] This seems logical on the face of it—most people prefer home to a hospital bed—but Christopher Isherwood claimed that this was not the case for Charles. He wrote in his diary that he visited Charles at Cedars on November 29 at Elsa's behest: "Elsa wanted me to go, to influence him if possible to agree to come back to the house, which he has violently refused to do."[14]

We can never know why Elsa would want Charles back at the house against all medical advice and seemingly against his own wishes. Frank may have recommended it; he had nursed his partner through terminal cancer and perhaps felt that the home environment would provide comfort in the tough days ahead. All reasoning can only be speculation at this point, but Charles eventually agreed to the move home.

He died in his beloved schoolroom on December 15, 1962.

12. Lanchester, *Elsa Lanchester, Herself*, 296.

13. *Spokesman Review*, December 1, 1962.

14. Isherwood, *Diaries*, vol. 2, 246.

26 Born Again

Elsa's immediate reaction upon hearing of Charles's death was an inability to focus. "For that short time I was a child," she would remember.[1] Frank Laughton, in his own quiet, efficient way, managed things; he sent Elsa upstairs, he contacted the doctor, he arranged for the body to be taken away.

The complex reality of the situation caught up with Elsa a few days later, the night before Charles's funeral, and she broke down violently. Happiness that Charles was no longer suffering was acceptable, but the unavoidable, undeniable relief she felt at being released from what had at times been a torturous union led her to feelings of guilt and disgust. Charles had been Elsa's anchor—sometimes holding her steady, sometimes dragging her down. For better or worse, she was adrift without him. And so, for an hour or two, she let go of all her self-control, and she wept. She cried for the man she thought she'd married and for the life that might have been, and she wept for the happiness that they had shared. She raged against fate until she had exhausted her anger, shame, and guilt, washed them away, and drowned them in a flood of tears and recriminations. Frank came and sat beside her. "You would not have done that if you hadn't been a nice person," he reassured her. "Now, come downstairs and we'll have a cup of tea."[2]

Charles's funeral was held at Forest Lawn Cemetery on December 19, 1962, and was performed by Reverend John Cantelon, who angered Elsa by ignoring several of her requests. Despite her expressly forbidding its inclusion, the hymn "Death, Where Is Thy Sting" was performed. The press reported that the ceremony was conducted with "quiet dignity," but the journalists' very presence prevented this from being true.[3] Christopher Isherwood—who was a pallbearer and read from *The Tempest* when Elsa's first choice, Burgess Meredith, couldn't make it—wrote about the "truly obscene contrast between the nicey-nice church behavior and all the cameras and newsmen outside, sticking their lenses

---

1. Lanchester, *Elsa Lanchester, Herself*, 301.

2. Lanchester, 302.

3. *Des Moines Tribune*, December 20, 1962.

At Charles's funeral in December 1962, Elsa speaks with actor
Raymond Massey, one of the pallbearers. An attendee recalled that the
funeral was marred by "all the cameras and newsmen outside, sticking
their lenses practically down Elsa's throat."
Everett Collection Inc. / Alamy Stock Photo

practically down Elsa's throat, even while the service was still going on."[4] James
R. Bacon, from the Associated Press, seemed disappointed at the lack of famous
mourners, filing copy that claimed "only a handful of celebrities, from among
scores invited, showed up."[5] That handful included Norma Shearer, Don Mur-
ray, Eddie Quillan, and Bob Newhart.[6] The pallbearers were Charles's agent and

4.   Isherwood, *Diaries*, vol. 2, 252.

5.   Associated Press release, December 20, 1962.

6.   *Liverpool Echo*, December 20, 1962.

his lawyer, as well as actor Raymond Massey, director Jean Renoir, and Charles's friend and former lover Bill Phipps, who struggled to keep his emotions under control. Ray Henderson played the organ for the nondenominational service.

Terry Jenkins, the last great passion of Charles's life, did not attend the funeral. He had stayed in New York, and he played no part in the final weeks of Charles's life, at the recommendation of Isherwood and others. Jenkins would marry shortly after Charles's death, having met his wife when she was a nurse looking after Charles in New York. According to Elsa, Charles had been thrilled when the pretty nurse had shown an interest in Jenkins and had begun flirting with him: "The fact that she liked Charles's friend showed Charles that his boyfriend was a man," Elsa recalled, "a masculine man, which was very important to him."[7]

Elsa presented a dignified and composed presence at the funeral. There are several anecdotes that seem to suggest she was treating this as a performance, probably as a way to cope with a social situation in which she did not naturally know how to behave correctly. Whenever she made a move, such as putting flowers on the coffin, she worried whether those watching would think the move was calculated. The weather was clear and fine, causing Elsa to make one of her typically awkward jokes. "I wish it had been a grey day," said the grieving widow at her husband's funeral. "It softens the face in the newsreel shots."[8]

Once the funeral was over, Elsa attended to all the necessary business, with friends like Frank Laughton and Ray Henderson at her side. She knew, though, that she needed to leave America for a time, in order to distance herself—mentally and physically—from the strains and responsibilities of the previous months. "I have to get away, make the break so I can come back and be born again," she told James Bacon of the Associated Press. "I am a comedienne and I must go on. But here in the house that Charles and I lived in for so many years, I find I haven't quite got the spirit yet to be funny."[9] Despite all the years of discord and misunderstanding with Biddy, Elsa knew that at this time of vulnerability and change, she needed to be with her mother.

In her autobiography, Elsa goes into minute detail about this visit to Brighton, describing even the bead of condensation on the taxi driver's mustache. Clearly this was a significant moment for her. It was here, Elsa claimed, that she became who she was to be for the rest of her life. No longer half of a pair, and the lesser half at that, she was now her own whole person: "the pleasant feeling that I was on my own and that decisions were suddenly mine, completely mine, gave me a fiery glow. . . . I had become a single person, an alone person, and a re-excited person. I never did like pitiful people and I decided not to be one."[10]

7.   Lanchester, *Elsa Lanchester, Herself,* 281.

8.   Isherwood, *Diaries,* vol. 2, 252.

9.   Associated Press release, January 29, 1963.

10. Lanchester, *Elsa Lanchester, Herself,* 306.

Elsa found Biddy much as she had left her, although a little older and now spending much time with Blanche Ward, Elsa's cousin, who now acted as Biddy's unofficial carer. Blanche was another direct and strong-willed Lanchester woman, who took Elsa to task for acquiring the American citizenship that took her so far away from her mother, although Biddy herself waved away such accusations. This ill feeling between Blanche and Elsa would simmer slowly for several years, before boiling over in spectacular fashion.

Once back in Hollywood, Elsa began establishing her new normal, slowly emerging back onto the social scene. She was interviewed on the *Tonight Show* with Johnny Carson (1962–92), and she accepted a Grammy on Charles's behalf for a spoken-word recording he had made. She and Ray Henderson resumed their professional partnership, and *Elsa Lanchester—Herself* played a few shows in Medford, Oregon. Elsa attended the premiere of the movie *Cleopatra* (1963), which starred her *Lassie* co-star Elizabeth Taylor, and told Hedda Hopper that it was "vulgar" and "aimed at low taste."[11] She attended a meal at Isherwood's house, where she and celebrity photographer Cecil Beaton nearly came to blows during an argument about Isadora Duncan. Isherwood sided with Beaton, and wrote the devastating observation in his diary that "Don [Bachardy] says she is absolutely evil. . . . But all I see is a miserable stupid half-crazy uneducated old bag, who can't help bitching."[12]

Despite this new socialization, Louella Parsons would write about how lonely life had been for Elsa "since she lost her beloved Charles Laughton."[13] Elsa's friends had been worried about the amount of time she spent alone, Parsons claimed, so they were relieved to hear that she had decided to return to work. The project was to be a horror-comedy for James H. Nicholson and Samuel Arkoff's American International Pictures (AIP). Originally established in 1954, AIP created low-budget films, usually released as double features, designed to appeal to teenagers. By the 1960s the company had decided to take advantage of the new demand for horror films—created by regular showings of the original Universal monster movies on television—and signed contracts with stars such as Vincent Price, Peter Lorre, Basil Rathbone and Boris Karloff. Elsa signed a three-picture deal in 1963. The first film she was scheduled for was *It's Alive!*, co-starring Peter Lorre, the plot of which involved Elsa turning into a spider. Although this project was announced in May 1963 and received sporadic mentions in the press over the following months, it was repeatedly delayed and was finally canceled when Lorre died following a stroke in March 1964. Seemingly unsure what to do with its elderly scream queen, AIP decided to use Elsa in its other money-spinning enterprise, beach party movies, a genre the company had

11. *Chicago Tribune*, June 22, 1963.

12. Isherwood, *Diaries*, vol. 2, 277.

13. *Springfield News-Leader*, May 10, 1963.

created with its 1963 hit *Beach Party* and the follow-ups, *Muscle Beach Party* (1964) and *Bikini Beach* (1964).

Elsa was cast in the science-fiction musical *Pajama Party* (1964), playing an eccentric widow who encounters a teenage alien named Go-Go and saves him when his jet pack malfunctions. Her character is also the victim of a plot by her neighbors to try and part her from her inheritance, while other subplots in the film involve motorcycle gangs, volleyball, and beach parties. The cast was solid, with Annette Funicello and Tommy Kirk in the lead roles, and a truly impressive—if somewhat dated—supporting cast that included Buster Keaton and Dorothy Lamour. Actress Bobbi Shaw, who played one of Elsa's scheming neighbors, saw an opportunity to learn from the more experienced members of the company. "I played opposite Buster Keaton in this picture," she recalled, "and watching him work—and also Elsa Lanchester—taught me more, I think, than I got out of two years of college . . . watching these old pros was an education in itself."[14]

One reviewer praised this as a return to form for Elsa, writing that she "comes close to stealing every scene in which she appears."[15] Long-term fans, however, did not like seeing her in such a vehicle after the majesty of *Witness for the Prosecution* and *Bell, Book and Candle*. "Elsa Lanchester, a great actress in my book, has such a silly role I turned from the screen," the *Boston Globe* critic wrote. "They shouldn't have done this to her."[16]

Pajama Party would be the only film that Elsa would make for AIP. Although she was reported in the press as being cast in several films—including *Beach Blanket Bingo* (1965), *How to Stuff a Wild Bikini* (1965), *Sergeant Deadhead* (1965), and *The Ghost in the Invisible Bikini* (1966)—Elsa did not appear in any of them. This may have been due to her distaste for the material; she had signed the contract with the intention of appearing in comedy-horror movies, such as the company's series of Edgar Allan Poe films made by Roger Corman and starring Vincent Price and Boris Karloff, not as the elderly support in silly teen comedies. However, there was one planned project for Elsa that was a cut above the others, a slapstick comedy with Buster Keaton.

Keaton had been a giant of silent and early sound cinema, and one of MGM's most bankable stars, but his career had suffered due to his alcoholism and troubled personal life. Now in his late sixties, he was enjoying something of a resurgence in popularity as younger generations became aware of him through television, and his genius work in silent films was rediscovered and appreciated anew. During his time at AIP, Keaton would make a total of four beach party movies, but the planned film *The Chase* (sometimes referred to as *The Big Chase*), in which he and Elsa were to star, would have been something very different. In-

---

14. *Austin American*, November 10, 1964.

15. *Great Bend Tribune*, January 17, 1965.

16. *Boston Globe*, November 19, 1964.

tended to be released to coincide with Keaton's seventieth birthday, the film was to be "a feature-length silent picture (except for music and sound effects) which will also involve 50 other prominent comedy stars." The story, as AIP explained, would revolve "around Keaton being mistaken for an espionage agent and a bizarre plot to kidnap the Statue of Liberty."[17] This is a mouthwatering prospect for fans of silent cinema, or those who enjoy the kind of slapstick, pratfall humor that is best created in this medium. Elsa had proved herself a master of the genre in her H. G. Wells–penned short films, and the prospect of her and Keaton both participating in a silent comedy is delicious. Sadly, it wasn't to be; Keaton went back to work at AIP on *How to Stuff a Wild Bikini* (1965), and he died a year later of lung cancer.

However, Elsa was not reliant on her AIP contract to get work, and she went directly to the press to complain about her lack of job offers. In a United Press International interview she claimed that nobody wanted to employ a widow. "It's been a bit sticky getting started again," she said. "There has been a tremendous backwash of sympathy for me, but not many offers for work."[18] By the time this was reported, Elsa had already filmed several television shows—including episodes of *Burke's Law* (1963–66) and *The Eleventh Hour* (1962–64)—as well as a feature film. This was the sex comedy *Honeymoon Hotel* (1964), the plot of which concerned two bachelors staying at a hotel reserved exclusively for honeymooning couples, and the farcical escapades that ensue from this premise. Unusual for its time in featuring an (uncommented-on) interracial romance, the film nevertheless left Elsa on familiar ground, playing a chambermaid. The film also reunited Elsa with director Henry Levin, who had been the stage manager on *They Walk Alone*, her 1941 Broadway show.

17. *Ottawa Citizen*, March 13, 1965; *Daily News*, March 21, 1965.

18. UPI press release, March 1964, quoted in *Coventry Evening Telegraph*, May 9, 1964.

27 Antique Charm

AIP might not have been able to find a use for Elsa, but another studio was looking for just her type: Walt Disney Studios. Between 1964 and 1969, Elsa would appear in four Disney movies, and a two-part episode of *The Magical World of Disney* (1954–97). Although the studio system was a thing of the past, these Disney films frequently employed a company of actors and technicians, which often created a congenial working environment. All but one of Elsa's Disney outings were directed by Robert Stevenson, and actors Richard Deacon, Dean Jones, and Ed Wynn were frequent co-stars. "Working at the Walt Disney Studios was different," co-star Hermione Baddeley would write. "There was a very special atmosphere there."[1] Elsa, ever practical, remembered that "the Disney people were a bit stodgy, and the pay wasn't the best in town, but they treated their stars well, and they liked to use you again and again. They liked knowing what they could expect from you."[2]

Elsa started out at the Disney Studios with a small but pivotal role in *Mary Poppins* (1964), as the nanny whose departure prompts the Banks family to hire the titular character. She is only in one scene, during which the maid (Hermione Baddeley) begs her to stay, the cook (Reta Shaw) sees her off with a cheery "good riddance," and the children's mother (Glynis Johns) sings a rousing song about being a suffragette, which Elsa's Katie Nanna tries in vain to interrupt. It was a role that must have brought back many memories for Elsa: of London, of the suffragism of her mother, and of the Margaret Morris dance school, where both she and Baddeley had been students. "The atmosphere was almost like being back in London, at the turn of the century," she recalled, before adding quickly, lest people start questioning her age, "Or rather, what I *imagined* the turn of the century to be like."[3] Actually, the film was set in 1910, a time when Elsa was eight years old and living in London. Although the film's reviews were good, one

---

1. Baddeley, *The Unsinkable Hermione Baddeley*, 204–5.

2. Hadleigh, *Leading Ladies*, 97.

3. Hadleigh, 97 (emphasis in original).

213

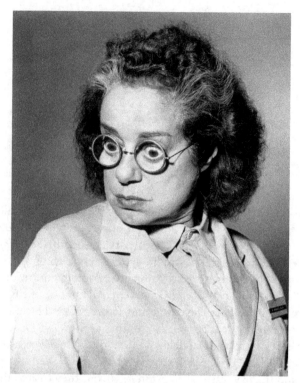

Elsa's appearance on *The Man from U.N.C.L.E.* in 1965 was lauded by fans, producers, and critics as a high point in the show's history. Her hair featured two gray streaks in homage to her role as the Bride.

Everett Collection Inc. / Alamy Stock Photo

critic felt that the "genuine comic talent" of Elsa was "absolutely thrown away" on such a small role.[4]

Mary Poppins was at the time Disney Studios' most expensive live-action film, and it remains one of the most successful in terms of Academy Awards, winning five Oscars from thirteen nominations. It was also Walt Disney's pet project, a film that he had tried for years to get permission to make from P. L. Travers, the author of the books on which it was based. It was filmed entirely on the company's Burbank lot, and Disney himself visited the set nearly every day. Karen Dotrice, who played one of the children in the movie, remembered Walt Disney "making sure that everybody was happy. That was the thing—he wanted everybody to enjoy the experience."[5] It seems he was successful. Hermione Baddeley described *Mary Poppins* as "a very happy film to make," and Elsa agreed,

---

4.   *Illustrated London News*, January 9, 1965.

5.   Gabler, *Walt Disney*, 598–99.

saying that the film was "lovely" to work on.[6] "I could only have hoped that my part were bigger, and perhaps a bit less cantankerous," Elsa would later say. "I don't mind so much playing nags and scolds, but then the public assumes that's what I'm like!"[7]

She would not escape this typecasting in her next Disney film either, playing a nagging, nosy neighbor in *That Darn Cat!* (1965), a comedy starring Hayley Mills and Dean Jones. The plot—a cat becomes an informant to the Federal Bureau of Investigation (FBI) after a kidnapping victim uses the creature to send a message—was typical Disney fare for this period, and although her character is thoroughly unlikable, Elsa does good comic work as she spies on the girls living next door while pretending to do housework. She is used more in this movie than in *Mary Poppins*, and her cantankerous character gets a hilarious comeuppance in the end, which sees a return of Elsa's infamous *Bride of Frankenstein* scream.

Blackbeard's Ghost (1968), her next Disney outing, provided a more sympathetic part for Elsa as the leader of the Daughters of the Buccaneers, descendants of Blackbeard (Peter Ustinov) who run a hotel that is at risk of being taken over by mobsters, until Dean Jones's track coach and Blackbeard's ghost save the day. If Elsa enjoyed her time at Disney for the first three movies, however, the bloom was definitely off the Disney rose by the time she made *Rascal* (1969), a movie based on the book by Sterling North about a boy and his raccoon. In an interview at the time, held to promote another movie she was making, Elsa was openly dismissive of *Rascal*. "In my next movie," she said, "they walk into the sunset with a raccoon. Isn't that extraordinary? You'd think writers would have got beyond walking into the sunset." Although she doesn't refer to the film by name—she doesn't need to, sunsets may be unoriginal but the presence of a raccoon helps narrow things down—this might have been because she didn't even remember it. Just a few years later, after her final job for the company (a two-part episode of *The Magical World of Disney* called "My Dog, the Thief" in 1969), Elsa would be asked for a comment on what the interviewer called her "Disney potboilers." "I really should remember the names," is all Elsa had to say on the matter.[8]

Of course, Disney Studios was not Elsa's only employer during the 1960s. She continued her live performances, although these were intermittent rather than part of a grueling tour. *Elsa Lanchester—Herself* played in Medford, Oregon, and in Santa Barbara, California, in 1963 and returned to the Ivar in 1966 for an extended run. Although the reviews for *Herself* remained mostly positive whenever it played, a revival of Elsa's *Private Music Hall* show in 1965 did not fare so well. The occasion was the grand opening of the McPherson Playhouse in Victoria, British Columbia, and Elsa—accompanied, of course, by Ray Henderson—was booked in as the opening act, the inaugural show at the new theater.

---

6.   Baddeley, *The Unsinkable Hermione Baddeley*, 205; Hadleigh, *Leading Ladies*, 97.

7.   Hadleigh, *Leading Ladies*, 97.

8.   *The Glens Falls Times*, September 19, 1970.

The reviews were scathing. The politest of them suggested that Elsa's act would have been "a decided hit, had she presented it 30 years ago," while another claimed it was embarrassing to witness, "like watching a favorite aunt who has been to the elderberry wine once too often."[9] The most vitriolic criticism came from a reviewer who had once been a fan of Elsa's, James Barber, writing in *The Province*:

> It was a sad performance . . . she chose to offer us the pathetic spectacle of her complete inability to accept the passage of time . . . we were left with an elderly lady supported by a mediocre pianist, unsuccessfully attempting the perpetuation of an anachronistic image. . . . The major embarrassment was not her material but herself . . . she continued for two hours with the merciless destruction of an illusion which I have cherished for 30 years.[10]

While she could perhaps be forgiven for the crime of aging, Elsa had clearly fallen out of step with the times. Her act had always been a throwback to the past, but the uniform negativity of these reviews suggests that an event such as the opening of a theater, which looks to the future, was entirely the wrong fit for a dated nostalgia act like *Private Music Hall*.

The wheel of fortune, however, continued to turn. Barely a week after this debacle in Canada, on March 8, 1965, Elsa appeared on television in an episode of *The Man from U.N.C.L.E.* (1964–68) entitled "The Brain-Killer Affair," which was lauded by fans, producers, and critics as a high point in the show's history. Elsa was in her element as Dr. Agnes Dabree, an evil scientist who has created a brain-draining machine. In a cute nod to *Bride of Frankenstein*, Elsa's "mad scientist" hair features two strategically placed gray streaks. "There has not been such a thoroughly enjoyable heavy since Sherlock Holmes met up with Professor Moriarty," gushed one review.[11] Executive producer Norman Felton agreed. In fact, Felton liked Elsa's portrayal so much that he rewrote the ending of the episode so that Dr. Dabree survives her fall down the elevator shaft and swears revenge, leaving the way open for a return appearance.[12] It was even rumored that producers wanted Elsa to return as the head villain for an entire season of the show, but by the time they got around to asking her, she had already committed herself to a new project.[13]

Elsa signed up for her first regular role in a television series in May 1965. Originally called *The Mr. and the Misses*, the program was retitled *The John Forsythe Show* (1965–66) to take advantage of the fame of its leading man, who had found previous television success with *Bachelor Father* (1957–62). Elsa had previously been wary of making such a long-run commitment, telling Hedda Hopper

9. *Nanaimo Daily News*, February 27, 1965; *Vancouver Sun*, February 27, 1965.
10. *The Province*, March 1, 1965.
11. *Reno Gazette-Journal*, March 9, 1965.
12. *Shreveport Journal*, April 23, 1965.
13. *The Daily Item*, May 14, 1965.

that "joining a series is sort of like getting married, but this was so right I couldn't resist," and saying to Vernon Scott that she took the part "because I need a family, and I wanted to see people every day."[14] Sadly, like Elsa's real marriage and family, her union with *The John Forsythe Show* would not turn out as she'd hoped, and would result in a degree of personal turmoil.

The premise for the show was the inheritance of a girls' school by a retired Air Force major (Forsythe), who has no experience with this sort of thing whatsoever. He is helped out by his equally clueless friend and former sergeant (Guy Marks), and the two men clash with the headmistress of the school, played by Elsa. Forsythe commented wryly on Elsa's scene-stealing abilities, saying, "It might be called *The Elsa Lanchester Show* after a while."[15] The critics agreed that Elsa was the best thing in it, but the reviews for the show as a whole were dismal. It was dismissed as "clichéd" and "pathetically weak," with several reviewers commenting that Elsa provided "the only bright spot on the show."[16] Television columnist Bob MacKenzie wrote: "The only point I can muster in favor of *The John Forsythe Show* is that it brings Elsa Lanchester back into public view. She's a dear little elf, pudgy as a pillow and full of antique charm. I'm crazy about her."[17]

Elsa enjoyed the "regular connection with life again" and was grateful for the steady salary and the scripts, which she regarded as funny and well written. However, she did not enjoy the 5:30 a.m. wake-up calls, the "degrading agony" of line learning, or the cast of thousands of teenage girls.[18] "Working with 2,120 girls on the show makes me thankful that Charles and I never had any youngsters," she said in one interview, with what the reporter regarded as "startling frankness."[19]

The John Forsythe Show was not renewed for a second season. While filming still continued on the first, Elsa received a steady stream of letters from England regarding the worsening state of Biddy's health. As she entered her mid-nineties, Biddy was growing weaker, and was being cared for by a team of nurses, under the watchful eye of Elsa's cousin Blanche Ward. Blanche wrote to Elsa, berating her for not coming home as Biddy's life neared its end. "Believe me, Elsa," she wrote, "if I had my mother alive, and were in your financial position, even the beckoning finger of fame and fortune would not keep me from her side!"[20]

Elsa wrote back, saying that the money she was earning from the television show was what enabled her to pay for Biddy's care, that she couldn't break her contract, and that she was on an income from Charles's estate and could not af-

---

14. *Los Angeles Times*, May 8, 1965; *San Bernardino County Sun*, October 9, 1965.

15. *The Courier*, July 28, 1965.

16. *Los Angeles Times*, September 14, 1965; *Minneapolis Star*, September 15, 1965; *Sonoma West Times and News*, September 23, 1965.

17. *Oakland Tribune*, September 21, 1965.

18. Lanchester, *Elsa Lanchester, Herself*, 313.

19. UPI press release, October 9, 1965.

20. Lanchester, *Elsa Lanchester, Herself*, 313.

ford to leave America. Although these were all valid reasons, it cannot be denied that Elsa ultimately chose to stay away because she did not want to witness her mother's final moments. She had endured the agonies of Charles's final illness and was not ready to go through more of the same. She admitted as much in her autobiography, writing, "I have a very strong feeling that if death cannot be a quiet celebration, then save others the sorrow of waiting and watching."[21] So it was that Elsa was in Hollywood when Biddy died of bronchopneumonia and senility on March 26, 1966, at the age of ninety-four. She died at home in Brighton, and the death was registered by Waldo. In her autobiography, Elsa misremembered the date, claiming that "Biddy faded away in April 1966."[22]

A letter from Blanche to Elsa following Biddy's death demonstrates the contempt her cousin felt for Elsa's excuses and absence. Despite the fact that it casts her in an unappealing light, Elsa would include the letter in her autobiography.

> Well Elsa,
>
> You have got what you wanted—Biddy's death—and I hope that you are thoroughly ashamed of yourself, sacrificing a wonderful person, worth twenty of you, to the mirage of Hollywood respectability! . . . it did not need a modicum of psychology to know she needed affection more than any of the other frost-bitten Lanchesters, of whom you are a fit scion . . .
>
> She wanted to see you before she died, but you found the Medusa of Hollywood to turn you into stone, and preferred the flicker of Television fame to your own mother in the end.
>
> I can only hope, and anticipate *your* own last year of life prove as harassed and unfriended as you caused your mother's to be.[23]

This would turn out to be a disturbingly accurate premonition of Elsa's own final years, one penned two decades before they came to pass.

Elsa did not return to England after Biddy's death, nor did she return for her brother Waldo's funeral in 1978. She couldn't have, even if she'd wanted to; Waldo's widow, Muriel, told no one the details of his funeral and cremation, and so was the only one who attended. According to a family friend, after Waldo's death Elsa invited Muriel to come and live with her in America—an invitation that was firmly refused.[24] This invitation seems unlikely, as the two women barely knew each other, but perhaps it speaks to how lonely Elsa had become by that time.

Biddy's death in 1966 is the last event of importance in Elsa's autobiography, written in 1983. The death is recorded on page 314, and the book finishes on page 318, yet the remaining two decades of Elsa's life would contain various forays into publishing as well as her continued work in film and television.

---

21. Lanchester, 314.

22. Lanchester, 314.

23. Lanchester, 314 (emphasis in original).

24. Cockayne, *Master of the Marionettes*, 297–98.

28   Today They Want the Truth

In a profile of Elsa written during the run of *The John Forsythe Show*, journalist Bob Lardine opined that there was "something a little sad about the little red-headed actress and her seemingly lonely existence without Charles Laughton." In the accompanying interview, Elsa described herself as living in Charles's shadow, saying "Charles, you see, was a larger than life kind of man. His impact on the outside world was so great people still speak of him all the time. And I live with that." She also said that her social life was now nonexistent, claiming, "Charles and I never went out much. Now I never go out at all."[1] Whether she was aiming for sympathy or just feeling sorry for herself, Elsa's situation in the mid-1960s was not significantly different from how it had been during Charles's lifetime. She had always been overshadowed by her more-famous spouse, and had frequently complained that people only sought her out in order to discuss Charles or to use her to get to him.

Although the house was emptier without Charles in it, their marriage had endured frequent absences and lengthy separations, so living alone was perhaps not quite the shock to the system for Elsa that it would be for other recent widows. Additionally, despite what she said in the interview, she did go out occasionally. Christopher Isherwood records in his diary seeing her at the opening of an art exhibition, "looking almost ladylike in a dark dress, gracious and bitchy-grand," and she attended the premiere of Vincent Price's AIP movie *The Tomb of Ligeia* (1964) alongside other horror icons such as Vampira and Carroll Borland (from *Mark of the Vampire*, 1935).[2]

Elsa also continued to work, filming her part in the musical *Easy Come, Easy Go* (1967) shortly after the final episode of *The John Forsythe Show*. The movie is notable for the fact that Elsa not only sings onscreen, but performs a duet with the King himself, Elvis Presley. Before being cast in a Presley movie, Elsa had already gone on record as not being a fan of rock 'n' roll music; when she had to sing one such number in a *Forsythe Show* episode, she spoke of the "inhuman

---

1.   *Daily News*, December 5, 1965.
2.   Isherwood, *Diaries*, vol. 2, 387.

sound of electronic machines" in reference to electric guitars. "It's not that I dislike the idea of a new sound for a new generation," she said later. "But after a day of listening to it on a film stage my ears were humming as if I had just returned from a transatlantic jet flight."[3]

By October 1966, when *Easy Come, Easy Go* was filmed in a matter of weeks, Presley had traveled far from his original rock'n'roll roots. To satisfy contracts he deeply regretted signing, the once-innovative performer had been churning out his kitschy romantic musicals at a rate of about three a year for six years, with the quality declining a little more each time. In *Easy Come, Easy Go*, he played a navy frogman, diving for buried treasure with the help of a go-go dancer (Dodie Marshall), who also happens to be a yoga student. Elsa played her yoga instructor, who berates the amusingly inflexible Elvis when he interrupts her class, with the song "Yoga Is as Yoga Does." As an Elvis Presley number, the song is a travesty, with a cutesy melody and lyrics such as "I can see lookin' at you, you just can't get settled / How can I even move, twistin' like a pretzel?" and "You tell me just how I can take this yoga serious / When all it ever gives to me is a pain in my posteriors." As a comic performance, though, it's a hidden gem. Elsa, in her flowing garments, strings of beads, and wild ginger hair, is so entertaining that even Presley struggles to keep a straight face at times. Although she never claimed to be inspired by Isadora Duncan for this performance, there is definitely an element of the same ridiculous pretentiousness that Elsa describes her former teacher as demonstrating. Unfortunately, reviewers of the time did not agree, claiming that she was "far from hilarious," and the film's sound track holds the dubious honor of being Elvis Presley's lowest-selling album ever.[4]

Around the time she filmed *Easy Come, Easy Go*, Elsa was also preparing to exhibit and then sell Charles's art collection, which she had inherited when he died. In her autobiography, the sculptures and paintings that she and Charles purchased are discussed at length, and are frequently the cause for arguments, especially when it comes to Charles's habit of giving away valuable paintings to friends—she gives examples including Tyrone Power and Paul Gregory—without asking Elsa, or even informing her. By far the most serious incident, one that reveals the deep fractures of communication in their relationship, was when Elsa returned from her first *Private Music Hall* tour to find that Charles had sold a jadeite mask that Elsa had purchased. This mask had been strong-featured and, to Elsa, powerfully erotic. She had been proud that whenever people visited, they complimented the mask, although Charles never gave her the credit for choosing it. When he exchanged the mask for four terra-cotta figures, Elsa felt the act as a personal betrayal. "I really hated Charles for parting with it," she would remember, "and I would nurse that hatred through all the years."[5] Despite her

---

3.   *Star-Gazette*, January 1, 1966.

4.   *Oakland Tribune*, March 29, 1967.

5.   Lanchester, *Elsa Lanchester, Herself*, 205.

deep hurt and anger, however, Elsa did not tell her husband how she felt. In fact, she allowed the incident to become something of a joke between them years later, when she discovered that the mask was worth a great deal more than she had paid for it and had pride of place in an important collection of pre-Columbian artifacts.

Even so, Charles's action of selling something that Elsa valued had a long-term effect on her behavior. "Since that time," she claimed, "I have never bought anything like that of value—I dared not. Selling the mask was part of a killer thing in Charles, and it killed my taste and initiative. To this day I cannot bring myself to fall in love with objects or something I might want to possess."[6]

To be able to own and then dispose of Charles's precious art collection must have felt like a form of retribution, and Elsa threw herself into the task. To give the exhibition and sale extra publicity, Elsa appeared on talk shows and gave newspaper interviews discussing the works and their significance. She was asked about her reasons for parting with the collection, and her answer demonstrated how Charles and his memory still held a strong power over Elsa, keeping her—in her own eyes at least—from moving forward: "They were so valuable that I was almost afraid to leave them alone. I was afraid . . . some disaster would befall the mementoes. Caring for Charles' art treasures became a full-time responsibility. . . . It was almost as if I had become an instant mother and was no longer free to live my life."[7] Elsa did not attend the sale at the Parke-Bernet Galleries in New York, which fell short of raising the hoped-for amount, revealing that Charles may not have possessed the keen eye that he prided himself on and had sometimes been duped into overpaying by unscrupulous collectors and galleries. Although the dispersal of Charles's art collection could have begun a period of healing and looking toward the future for Elsa, it appears to have done quite the opposite, and soon there were reports in the press that Charles Laughton's widow was writing a "shocking, tell-all biography of her late spouse."[8]

Similar rumors of Elsa writing a follow-up to her 1938 (auto)biographical account of life with Charles had cropped up several times over the years since his death, but nothing further had come of them. This time, however, Elsa was serious, and she hired Dr. Ned Hoopes to co-author the book, visiting the library to read through newspapers and magazines, and appealing in the press for photographs and letters.

Hoopes wore many hats, having worked as a teacher, psychiatrist, editor, anthologist, and television presenter over the years, none of which was sufficient to impress Christopher Isherwood, who dismissed Hoopes as a "gushy sob sister" with "a vulgar little mind."[9] It was claimed in the press that Hoopes was helping

6.   Lanchester, 206.

7.   *Press and Sun-Bulletin*, November 14, 1970.

8.   *San Francisco Examiner*, December 3, 1967.

9.   Isherwood, *Diaries*, vol. 2, 514; Isherwood and Bachardy, *The Animals*, 311.

Elsa access powers of total recall through hypnosis, but in truth he helped with the more mundane tasks of research and structure, as well as writing.[10]

Controversially, Elsa made the decision that Charles's sexual orientation—which was not yet public knowledge—would be revealed and discussed in the book. However, this information was only hinted at in the press. Sheilah Graham wrote in her column, "From what Elsa has told me of the book it will be absolutely candid, and some areas will surprise you. Today they want the truth and the truth is what the authors are writing."[11] Elsa embellished on this in various interviews, dropping hints left and right, but always stopping short of revelation. "It's a serious book about a person who had terrible guilts and problems and strange relationships," she told journalist Nancy Woodward. "No, people who knew Charles won't be surprised. For others, it will be up to the reader. We will present various facets. Rather like a detective story and you can jump to your own conclusions."[12]

Elsa's use of Charles's fiercely guarded secret as a teaser to promote interest in her book was considered by those in the know to be in poor taste—Isherwood referred to it as "truly horrible" and "revolting." Elsa continued regardless, with the book becoming a passion project that occupied all her time and attention.[13] The interview with Nancy Woodward quoted above was actually arranged to promote Elsa's appearance in *Me, Natalie* (1969), a comedy-drama for which Patty Duke won a Golden Globe, and in which a twenty-nine-year-old actor called Al Pacino made his film debut. When Woodward arrived to conduct the interview, she was warned by the press agent that Elsa was far more interested in discussing the upcoming book than in promoting the picture. The poor press agent then sat helplessly by as Elsa dismissed her role in the film as a cameo. She only took these bit parts, she claimed, to keep her name before the public while she worked on the book. "But I don't like doing them. They're dull one-sided performances. The film can do very well without them."[14] Elsa would later claim that she had filmed several scenes for the movie, but that her part had been cut down to a bit in editing.[15]

But despite Elsa's initial enthusiasm, the Hoopes collaboration would never result in a published volume. After Elsa withdrew her support from the project due to clashes with her co-author, Hoopes carried on alone for a while, using copies of interviews he and Elsa had done together, while telling Elsa that he had abandoned the project entirely. When she found out that Hoopes had pro-

10. *San Francisco Examiner*, December 3, 1967.

11. *Valley Times*, March 21, 1968.

12. *San Francisco Examiner*, December 1, 1968.

13. Isherwood, *Diaries*, vol. 2, 514.

14. *San Francisco Examiner*, December 1, 1968.

15. Hadleigh, *Leading Ladies*, 97–98.

duced a finished volume—which he titled *A Public Success, a Private Failure: The Unauthorized Biography of Charles Laughton*—Elsa was so upset that she took to her bed.[16] However, Hoopes's book would remain unpublished, and Charles was to be allowed to remain in the closet of the public imagination for a little while longer.

Every now and again, Elsa's personal life would flicker into the gossip columns. Ed Sullivan wrote that she was dating Don Abbott in 1965, while Walter Winchell had her "rendezvousing with a social worker" a couple of years later.[17] Christopher Isherwood pondered whether Ned Hoopes was "making love" to her, and also mentioned actor Jack Grinnage as an occasional overnight guest of Elsa's in 1968, although by 1971, Isherwood claimed that Grinnage had paired off with "another of [Elsa's] male attendants."[18] Ray Henderson remained a regular companion, although his 1969 marriage meant that he was not as available to Elsa as he had been previously. He was, however, present at one gathering that Elsa hosted in April 1969, where other guests included Jim Bridges, Tony Harvey, and Rita Hayworth. Isherwood, who dropped in briefly, wrote in a letter to Don Bachardy that "Ray and Rita clicked which didn't please Elsa."[19]

Evidence that Elsa was active socially can be juxtaposed with stories of wrenching loneliness. Author Wendy Moffatt discusses one such incident, when publisher John Lehmann visited the home of Isherwood and Bachardy in 1970, where the latter was to paint his portrait. Hearing of his visit, Elsa drifted over from next door. "Lanchester had lived alone for a decade," writes Moffatt with slight exaggeration. "She was capable of drinking too much. Her large brown eyes could grow pathetic with storms of emotion. But that night, 'very affectionate and gentle,' she reminisced about John's sister Beatrix, a friend and fellow actress with whom she had worked in England long ago. The men delicately escorted Lanchester home."[20]

Beatrix Lehmann had been Elsa's understudy in *The Way of the World* back in 1924, and at the time her mother had worried that friendship with the worldly Elsa would corrupt the innocent girl. Those heady days—when Elsa was the toast of London town, changing costumes in taxis and charming the literary elite—must have seemed like another life to Elsa by 1970. But although she was unquestionably entering the twilight of her career, Elsa still had some strong performances to give, and a whole new fan base waiting to appreciate her.

---

16. Isherwood, *Diaries*, vol. 3, 211.

17. *Daily News*, April 9, 1965; *San Francisco Examiner*, March 6, 1967.

18. Isherwood, *Diaries*, vol. 2, 514, 533; Isherwood, *Diaries*, vol. 3, 132.

19. Isherwood and Bachardy, *The Animals*, 393.

20. Moffatt, *Great Unrecorded History*, 7.

29 Wonderfully Weird

It was on television that Elsa would find her creative outlet and earn her best notices of the late 1960s and early 1970s. She writes very little about her television work in her autobiography, but she does consider three appearances to be worthy of mention. After dismissing her movie work during this time as "large parts in lousy pictures and small parts in big pictures," Elsa wrote: "I have been in a few rare, well-etched parts in segments of a series that were of quality: *Then Came Bronson*, *To Catch a Thief*—uh, yes, and *The Lucy Show*."[1]

Then Came Bronson was a single-season show, airing between September 1969 and April 1970, in which Michael Parks starred as a disillusioned reporter, Bronson, who sets out on a soul-searching mission on his motorcycle. Each episode saw him encounter someone in need of help, which Bronson would provide. Elsa appeared in the third installment, "A Circle of Time," as Hattie Calder, a *Titanic* survivor in her eighties. When reporters commented on the curious casting of a sixty-seven-year-old British woman as an octogenarian Colorado pioneer, Elsa replied, "Age and national origin needn't limit an actress if she has any talent range at all. I'm not even wearing special make-up."[2]

The episode was filmed in the Colorado mountains, seven thousand feet up, causing some concern among the crew for Elsa's health at that altitude. Despite her constant assurances that she never felt better, she knew that they were keeping a close eye on her, and assistants would run over to give her oxygen between takes. Whatever went on behind the camera, the result was one of Elsa's best and most moving performances. Although her accent is perhaps more British than anything else, and she had a familiar haughty tone, her Hattie Calder is a tired fighter, a lonely survivor, much like Elsa herself. Her performance was haunting and heartbreaking, and her reviews were excellent, with one saying that "not even the sparse grandeur of a Colorado ghost town set against the Rockies could take away from the impact of guest star Elsa Lanchester's acting in this hour."[3]

---

1. Lanchester, *Elsa Lanchester, Herself*, 311.
2. *Wellsville Daily Reporter*, August 11, 1969.
3. *Star-Gazette*, October 8, 1969.

It Takes a Thief (1968–70) starred Robert Wagner as a cat burglar recruited by the government, and was known for featuring many big names as guest stars, including Bette Davis, Ida Lupino, Frankie Avalon, and Fred Astaire, who had a recurring role. The show's producer, Paul Mason, had the idea of creating a series for Elsa to star in as a meddling old woman who solves crimes, similar to the Agatha Christie character of Miss Marple. In an attempt to convince the powers that be at Universal to commission the series, Mason cast Elsa as a meddling former British spy in *It Takes a Thief*. Although he told television columnist Joan Crosby that if nothing happened on the series idea, he would bring Elsa back in the same role on *It Takes a Thief*, nothing further would develop in either of these directions. However, Elsa enjoyed her time on the show, noting that the cast and crew treated her well, and that she was given some form of script and wardrobe approval, which made her feel more kindly toward all involved.[4] Again, her reviews were uniformly positive.

The third show that Elsa mentions in her autobiography—*The Lucy Show* (1962–68)—is not one that she ever appeared in, although her confusion is understandable considering the number of shows Lucille Ball made with her own first name in the title. Having previously appeared in an episode of *I Love Lucy* (1951–57) in 1956, Elsa also appeared in an episode of *Here's Lucy* (1968–74) in 1973, where her comic talents were once again shown to their full potential. In the episode, Lucy goes undercover in a women's prison to try to find out where Mumsie Westcott—an erratic bank robber played by Elsa—has hidden the money she stole. However, Mumsie's memory, always shaky, is made worse by her drinking habit. Elsa plays up this delightful character to the hilt, singing to herself, talking to plants, and peppering her speech with Cockney slang. At one point her antics prove too much for Lucy, who can be seen attempting to smother her genuine laughter.

Other notable television appearances for Elsa at this time were two episodes of *The Bill Cosby Show* (1969–71), and a recurring role in the final season of *Nanny and the Professor* (1970–71). In the latter—which had a *Mary Poppins*–like premise of a British nanny with magical powers—Elsa played the eccentric Aunt Henrietta in three episodes, "Aunt Henrietta's Premonition," "Aunt Henrietta and the Jinx," and "Aunt Henrietta and the Poltergeist."

The Bill Cosby Show featured its eponymous star as Chet Kincaid, a high school teacher. In her first episode on the series, "The Elevator Doesn't Stop Here Anymore," Elsa exploited the comic potential of her character being trapped in an elevator with Bill Cosby and Henry Fonda (she played the school cleaning lady, while Fonda played one of the faculty). Although Cosby's spectacular fall from grace would see him incarcerated in 2018 for aggravated indecent assault, it was her other co-star that Elsa held in low regard. In her autobiography she claims that Fonda was prejudiced and cruel to Charles Laughton when they

---

4.   *Santa Maria Times*, December 6, 1969; *Star-Gazette*, December 20, 1969.

worked together on a Broadway play, *The Caine Mutiny Court-Martial* (1954), which starred Fonda and was directed by Charles. She quotes Paul Gregory, who produced the show, as saying: "During one rehearsal, Henry Fonda behaved miserably and insulted Charles like I have never heard anyone insult him or anybody else in all my life—and in front of the whole company. Right from the stage, Fonda looked at Charles and said, 'What do you know about men, you fat, ugly homosexual.'. . . It crushed Charles." Elsa affirms that Charles had told her the same story, but insisted that the actual word Fonda had used to berate him was "faggot."[5]

Elsa's second appearance on *The Bill Cosby Show*, "The Power of a Tree," featured an environmental message, which Elsa embraced in her promotional interviews for the show. In a 1971 quote that sounds well ahead of its time, Elsa linked the emerging environmental awareness to her old familiar themes of Malthusian overpopulation and childlessness. "We have to educate the generation now in its teens to practically not reproduce anymore," she told the *Los Angeles Times*. "Zero population growth. It's more and more people that cause problems like pollution. Along with the profiteers who make millions of dollars turning out products that aren't biodegradable."[6]

As the new decade began, Elsa was being linked more often in the public imagination to her iconic 1935 role as the Bride of Frankenstein. This reassociation had begun in the 1960s as the Universal monster movies made their way to television, capturing a new audience along the way and inspiring such sitcoms as *The Addams Family* (1964–66) and Universal's own *The Munsters* (1964–66); Elsa's hair in her *Man from U.N.C.L.E.* appearance in 1965 had featured two gray streaks in homage to her iconic role. Although AIP had been unwilling or unable to capitalize on Elsa's creepy credentials in the previous decade, she did make three horror films in the early 1970s: *Willard* (1971), *Terror in the Wax Museum* (1973), and *Arnold* (1973), as well as an episode of the macabre television show *Night Gallery* (1969–73).

Directed by Daniel Mann and starring Bruce Davison in the title role, the "wonderfully weird" *Willard* was based on the novel *Ratman's Notebooks* by Stephen Gilbert.[7] The plot concerned a young, socially awkward man who develops a disturbing and ultimately deadly affinity with rats. Elsa played Willard's mother, Henrietta, who lives with him and is an unsettling character, both domineering and coy. It is an unnerving piece of acting from Elsa. "I like to make people laugh," she said, "but on the other hand, in *Willard* I am kind of very happy to do a mixture of a nice woman and a nasty woman. Variety is really what any actor likes."[8] Sadly she did not have much chance to develop her character, as Henri-

5. Lanchester, *Elsa Lanchester, Herself*, 234, 235.

6. *Los Angeles Times*, February 26, 1971.

7. *Kensington Post*, November 26, 1971.

8. *Glens Falls Times*, September 19, 1970.

etta dies about half an hour into the film. Reviews were lukewarm, but audiences liked it, and the film was the twelfth highest-grossing movie of 1971.[9] Elsa would later speak disparagingly of *Willard*, saying, "I don't really have much of an excuse for that one, except that it was a first of its kind, and I always like to try something completely, mind-bogglingly new."[10]

If *Willard* was "a pathological study of loneliness," as Elsa termed it, then *Terror in the Wax Museum* and *Arnold* were horror-comedies of the kind she had perhaps expected to make with AIP.[11] Both were directed by Georg Fenady, produced by Bing Crosby Productions (the Old Groaner himself was not personally involved in either movie), and distributed by Cinerama Releasing Corporation, as was *Willard*. Although they were relatively low-budget offerings, both featured a collection of well-known names, with some perhaps past their best: Roddy McDowall, Victor Buono, and Stella Stevens appeared in *Arnold*, while Ray Milland, Maurice Evans, and John Carradine were in *Terror in the Wax Museum*. Shani Wallis appeared in both.

Terror in the Wax Museum featured a murder mystery plot with apparent supernatural elements, which appears in retrospect more like an episode of *Scooby-Doo* than a gory horror movie. Elsa gets plenty of screen time as a scheming guardian, out for profit and financial gain, once more enjoying performing at the more strident and domineering end of her register. In contrast, her character in *Arnold* was that of a twittery, birdbrained spinster, whose brother—the titular Arnold—appears to be committing multiple murders from beyond the grave. Although the plot was ridiculous and the production values were low, in *Arnold* Elsa demonstrated more skill and character development than she was able to do in other, better movies.

In her *Night Gallery* episode, entitled "Green Fingers" (1972), Elsa gave a deliciously creepy performance as a widow who refuses to sell her home to a ruthless tycoon, and who is content to remain busy in her garden where, as she says, "Everything I plant grows." Her initial sweetness contrasts superbly with episode's dark climax that is still remembered as nightmare-inducing by adults who first watched it as children decades ago.

Elsa's appearances in horror films ended with *Arnold*, but she would continue to receive plaudits for *Bride of Frankenstein* throughout the decade. In 1974 she was the special guest at the Count Dracula Society's annual awards dinner, and five years later she was given a Golden Scroll for her work as the Bride by the Academy of Science Fiction, Fantasy and Horror Films.[12] There was even a rumor in 1974 that Elsa would appear alongside Ricardo Montalbán in a remake of *Dracula* to be directed by Frank Dunlop, but nothing came of it. Although

9.   Nash Information Services, "Annual Movie Chart—1971."

10. Hadleigh, *Leading Ladies*, 98.

11. *Glens Falls Times*, September 19, 1970.

12. *Los Angeles Times*, February 23, 1974; Mank, *Women in Horror Films*, 314.

horror films in general were becoming gorier and more violent—her own work providing rather old-fashioned exceptions—Elsa still defended the genre, saying that "if it weren't for horror films a lot more people in this country would be lying on psychiatrists' couches and blabbling about their repressed desires or what have you." She explained that, in her opinion, "the sight of so many bizarre murders and such actually help a person who has a lot of repressed hostilities building up inside him. They're a form of therapy and the pent-up viewer can lose his real hostility by replacing it with the hostility he sees on the screen. In this way no one gets hurt."[13]

As the decade progressed, Elsa's health took a turn for the worse, and she was briefly hospitalized at St. John's Coast Hospital in August 1974 for an operation following a cancer scare. Although she slowed down her performing work, Elsa was once again busy with the writing of a biography of her late husband.

---

13. *Independent*, August 6, 1973.

Die Laughing (1980) was Elsa's final role. She found the filming
experience disheartening, degrading, and lonely.
Everett Collection Inc. / Alamy Stock Photo

30   It Might Help People

After the planned biography of Charles Laughton with Ned Hoopes fell through in the late 1960s, Elsa continued to search for another author with whom to collaborate on the project. In 1970, Allen Drury was considering taking the job, but it wasn't until 1973 that Charles Higham was commissioned. "She told me that she had been through several writers, looking for a man who could manage an authorized life of her late husband," Higham recalled of his first meeting with Elsa; "she told me that these authors had disappeared into bars on drunks, and/or run off with other men."[1] By this time, Elsa had decided that she would not involve herself in the actual writing of the book—and would therefore receive no credit for authorship—although she would remain deeply involved in the research and structuring process.

When Elsa approached him, Higham was still early in his career as a biographer, having published work on Orson Welles, Florenz Ziegfeld, and Cecil B. DeMille. He would later become famous for his works claiming that Errol Flynn was a Nazi spy (*Errol Flynn: The Untold Story*, 1980) and that Cary Grant was a wife-beating gay man (*Cary Grant: The Lonely Heart*, 1989), but there is nothing shocking or sensational in his biography of Charles Laughton beyond the fact that he openly discusses Charles's sexual orientation. As a gay man, Higham might have been expected to sympathize with the Laughtons' situation—despite his own sexual orientation, he had previously been married to a woman, from who he separated in the 1950s.

Although Higham would present a rosy picture of his working relationship with Elsa in his author's prologue to *Charles Laughton: An Intimate Portrait*, he would later claim that he had focused on Charles's career rather than his personal life in the book because of his distaste at what he saw as Elsa's desire to "revenge herself on Charles."[2] Higham claimed that Elsa had a filing cabinet filled with reports and photographs from the private detectives she had hired to spy on Charles, material that she used to keep her husband from leaving her.

---

1.   Higham, *In and Out of Hollywood*, 167.
2.   Higham, 168.

While the book was being written, an article appeared in the *Los Angeles Times*, in which Joe Losey—who had been the stage manager on *Payment Deferred*, with whom Elsa had a flirtation, and who later worked with Charles Laughton and Bertolt Brecht on *Galileo*—claimed that it was Charles who had denounced Brecht and himself to the FBI, leading to their being subpoenaed by the House Un-American Activities Committee. When asked why Charles would have done such a thing, Losey replied, "Laughton was a naturalized American, so maybe they threatened to have his citizenship revoked. . . . In his authorized biography, he claimed that he had been duped by Brecht and me."[3] This was clearly inaccurate—Charles did not become a citizen until 1950, long after the run of *Galileo*, and the only remotely authorized biography of him was Elsa's *Charles Laughton and I*, written years before these events. Elsa sprang to her husband's defense in a letter to the newspaper, which was published on March 30, 1975. She pointed out the obvious factual problems in Losey's version of events, claimed that Charles had no political interests whatsoever, and rebuked Losey for his "gratuitous remarks about Mr. Laughton's frailties."[4] These remarks of Losey's—which included calling Charles "a coward" and "schizophrenic . . . definitely a Jekyll and Hyde"—were not dissimilar to claims that Elsa would make, via Higham, in the upcoming biography.[5] Indeed, it may seem odd that Elsa would be so fierce in defending Charles at the very time she was contributing to what some saw as a desecration of his memory. Elsa's retort, should she have been challenged on this, would presumably have been on the theme of accuracy: Losey had made accusations that were false, and that was simply unacceptable to her. The truth, however painful or unwanted, was another matter.

Teasers began to appear for *Charles Laughton: An Intimate Biography* in late 1974, and Charles's sexual orientation began to be openly discussed in the press. Columnist John J. Miller was typical of many when he speculated who might be outed as a result of the publication. "Elsa isn't going to name names," he wrote (inadvertently acknowledging that Elsa, not Higham, was the force behind the book), "but aside from that she isn't going to do anything to disguise identities—which should make some of those famous names very easy to figure out."[6] The British tabloids, as was their tendency, played up the potential for possible scandal, claiming that "panic-stricken male film stars and directors in Hollywood are bracing themselves for a brisk round of malicious gossip . . . for the secret homosexual love-life of British actor Charles Laughton is to be published."[7]

Elsa was asked many times why she had decided to make the reality of her marital situation public knowledge, and she gave several different answers. She

---

3.   *Los Angeles Times*, March 9, 1975.

4.   *Los Angeles Times*, March 30, 1975.

5.   *Los Angeles Times*, March 9, 1975.

6.   *San Francisco Examiner*, January 19, 1975.

7.   *The People*, December 8, 1974.

claimed, doubtlessly correctly, that someone else would do so if she didn't, and at least this way she could control the narrative. Also, times were different now, and such things were no longer dirty little secrets to be hidden away, but could be discussed openly and honestly. And finally, "because it might help people who are faced with the same kind of problem and must deal with the terrible guilt that Charles felt most of his life."[8]

Reaction to Elsa's revelations was mixed when the book was published in 1976. Some felt that she was extremely brave, and admired her for her honesty and for her devotion to Charles during his lifetime. Others, of course, felt that she was acting in the worst possible taste, trading in her husband's secret for publicity and financial gain. Shelley Winters, speaking at the San Francisco Film Festival, said she could never forgive Elsa for "saying such terrible things about him in her recent book. He was a kind and lovable man and all I can think is that she's very old and bitter."[9] Stanley Eichelbaum wrote a damning piece in the *San Francisco Examiner* that is worth quoting at length:

> Something nasty and reckless comes out of Elsa Lanchester's confession, after all these years, that her late husband, Charles Laughton, was a homosexual. . . . [The news] got the widest possible coverage, with Elsa being lauded by some for her courage and honesty. But what about her disloyalty to Charles, who must be tossing in his grave to know that his wife had pushed him out of the closet? . . .
>
> That Elsa has now spilled the beans strikes me as a gross indiscretion and can't really be justified by her saying that . . . she hoped men in the same predicament as Charles might benefit from his story. . . . In view of Laughton's erratic unhappy sex life, one wonders why Elsa felt her disclosures might help any of today's homosexuals.[10]

Of course, any opinion worded as strongly as this invites counterarguments. Perhaps Charles's experience could teach people to be more honest with themselves, to live truthfully rather than remain in a harmful, hurtful double existence. Perhaps a reader's sympathies could extend to seeing both Charles and Elsa as victims of a society that caused such deep feelings of shame to be associated with any lifestyle that wasn't the accepted heteronormative standard. In his prologue, Higham stressed that Elsa and Charles's marriage was a roller coaster, and that although there were "moments of severe tension and unhappiness between them," there was also much that was positive in their relationship.[11] This assessment was echoed by Ben Irwin, who worked for many years on public relations for Charles. "It was a marriage of convenience, to be sure," said Irwin, "but it was also one of warm respect for each other's gifts, of honesty, of supportiveness in

---

8. *San Francisco Examiner*, May 28, 1976.

9. *San Mateo Times*, October 26, 1976.

10. *San Francisco Examiner*, June 27, 1976.

11. Higham, *Charles Laughton*, xviii.

times of stress, and, if you buy the definition of love being total acceptance of your mate, warts and all, yes, love."[12] Elsa herself was warier of such a romanticized portrait of her marriage, preferring instead to say that they were "totally comfortable together. In love? Certainly in the first years, yes. But when he was around with other people—and I was around with other people—I don't think in love is quite the word you use."[13] She also admitted that she missed Charles more a decade after his death than she did immediately following the event.

Other than its revelations of Charles's sexuality, Higham's book was considered by many to be rather dull, and Higham himself admitted that Elsa was unhappy with the result.[14] Mel Gussow, writing in *The New York Times*, opined that *Charles Laughton: An Intimate Biography* was "a disappointment." He went on to say that "Laughton really deserves a good book, and his widow, Elsa Lanchester, herself a fine character actress, apparently offered the author complete cooperation and access to letters. She wrote the introduction—and I wish that she had written the book."[15]

The *Intimate Biography* would take up most of Elsa's time between 1974 and 1976, but she did manage to appear in one film during that time, the star-studded murder mystery spoof *Murder by Death* (1976), which was written by Neil Simon and directed by Robert Moore. The plot concerned a millionaire who gathers the world's most famous detectives—each a parody of a fictional sleuth—at his home and arranges for them to compete to solve a murder. Elsa played Jessica Marbles, based loosely on Agatha Christie's Miss Marple, who was accompanied by her elderly nurse, played by Estelle Winwood. Others in the cast included Truman Capote, Alec Guinness, David Niven, Maggie Smith, Peter Sellers, and Peter Falk.

After making her professional stage debut in 1903 at the age of twenty, Estelle Winwood undertook a career that would last an incredible eight decades, only ending a year before her death in 1984, at the age of 101. Although never an A-list celebrity, Winwood enjoyed a certain notoriety for her outspokenness, her four marriages, and her close friendship with the deliciously scandalous Tallulah Bankhead, of whom she was to remark, "I was the one person she could not shock."[16] Like many British stage actresses of her era, Winwood resisted the movies for as long as she could, and appeared in them sporadically—often openly admitting to participating only for the money. Both Elsa and Estelle Winwood were considered to be outspoken eccentrics, so when they first appeared together in *The Glass Slipper* (1955), Hedda Hopper anticipated fireworks, writing "Can't

---

12. *Los Angeles Times*, July 11, 1976.

13. *San Francisco Examiner*, September 9, 1979.

14. Higham, *In and Out of Hollywood*, 168.

15. *The New York Times*, June 20, 1976.

16. Hadleigh, *Leading Ladies*, 188.

you see Estelle and Elsa . . . trying to steal scenes from each other?"[17] Despite such speculation, filming of the MGM musical proved to be disappointingly un-newsworthy.

Elsa enjoyed her time on *Murder by Death*, and although she spoke fondly of all her co-stars and her director, she reserved her fullest praise for Winwood, claiming that they frequently gossiped together, catching up on the antics of mu-tual acquaintances and remembering times past. "Estelle is one of the few people as free-spirited as me," Elsa would say of her two-time co-star. "Her façade is very prim and even somewhat gothic, but she's a merry old soul, and we always laugh together. She has the most wonderful stories, not just about Tallulah Bankhead, but about everyone she's worked with or known."[18]

This may have been the truth as Elsa saw it, or it may have been a rose-tinted memory embellished for the interviewer, but either way, the "merry old soul" was not singing from the same hymn sheet. Interviewed by Boze Hadleigh in 1976, shortly after the completion of *Murder by Death*, Estelle Winwood did not hold back when asked her opinion about Elsa. "Not a friendly woman, and rather daft," was the unflattering conclusion. "Except when I saw her around her hus-band. Then she was simply dull. . . . If she'd stayed in England, she'd have starved. She came here and made a living playing English eccentrics. It wasn't talent—it's being herself, and she's got barmier with the years." In the same interview, Winwood also rather wonderfully described Truman Capote as "like Katharine Hepburn—arrogant. But not half so pretty, or thin."[19]

This was the kind of sniping cattiness that Hedda Hopper had hoped for on the set of *The Glass Slipper*—better two decades late than never! Winwood claimed that Elsa ignored her on the *Murder by Death* set, while reminding any-one who would listen about her associations with such famous "fossils" (Win-wood's term) as Charles Laughton and Isadora Duncan. Reports from others on the set—cast and crew—paint Elsa in a much more positive light, however, claiming that her extensive knowledge and spontaneous delivery of naughty lim-ericks had all within earshot in perpetual laughter.[20]

The film received some good notices, although many reviewers felt that the finished product did not deliver the quality promised by such an A-list cast. In the *Los Angeles Times*, Charles Champlin wrote that he found the film "amus-ing," then added, "why it is only amusing, and not hilarious, madcap, riotous, rip-roaring, or richly romping, I don't entirely know."[21] Elsa was rarely singled out in the reviews, and when she was, the opinion was often a negative one. An exception came in 2007, when author Axel Nissen commented that the scene

17. *Daily News*, April 15, 1954.

18. Hadleigh, *Leading Ladies*, 98.

19. Hadleigh, 196.

20. *Star-Gazette*, August 29, 1976.

21. *Los Angeles Times*, June 23, 1976.

where Elsa and Estelle Winwood's characters share a double bed "in nighties, robes, and nightcaps" was "one of the few high points of the film."[22] Indeed, much about *Murder by Death* makes for uncomfortable viewing today, particularly Peter Sellers's portrayal of a Chinese detective and several objectionable remarks about sexual orientation.

Although Elsa had voiced hopes that *Murder by Death* would lead to more offers—and perhaps even the chance to play the real Miss Marple—she was to be disappointed.[23] Nothing that sparked her interest was forthcoming, and she concentrated her efforts on interviews promoting Higham's book, before sinking quietly into retirement.

In 1978 Elsa allowed herself to be tempted into an onscreen television appearance in a British documentary about Charles Laughton for the BBC. *Hollywood Greats* (1977–85) was a series written and narrated by film critic Barry Norman, with each episode providing an in-depth profile of a movie legend. Charles's episode appeared in the second season of the show, in which the other stars featured were Joan Crawford, Ronald Colman, Jean Harlow, and Judy Garland. To tell each performer's personal and professional story, Norman conducted onscreen interviews with their surviving relatives, co-stars, and associates. Along with Elsa, Norman interviewed Paul Gregory, Christopher Isherwood, Billy Wilder, Lillian Gish, Charles Higham, Shelley Winters, and Tom Laughton, Charles's brother.

During her onscreen interview, Elsa discussed the most personal details of her unusual marriage, including the night that Charles confessed his sexual preference for men following the confrontation with a prostitute at their home. But Elsa also provided some lighter moments in the documentary. Discussing Charles's physical appearance, she remarked, "He was really better looking than a lot of good-looking people, that are so good-looking you could throw up, you know what I mean?" This typically blunt remark caused Barry Norman, seated off-camera, to let out an involuntary snort of amusement.

Elsa is also permitted to have the last word in the documentary, with the credits rolling immediately after her final statement. "I wish he'd been a happier man," she says in summary. "I know that I've become a more live, complete person since he died, but if I'd died first, I would say that Charles would be a more than tortured man, because we all think of what we might have done. I know he would suffer deeply from what he might have done."[24]

22. Nissen, *Actresses of a Certain Character*, 94.

23. Hadleigh, *Leading Ladies*, 99.

24. "Charles Laughton," *Hollywood Greats*.

31   Having Unloaded the Past

It is entirely possible that the general public only became aware that Elsa Lanchester had retired from acting when it was announced in December 1978 that she was making a comeback. This brief return—a television pilot and a movie—would be an unworthy climax to an illustrious career; indeed many prefer to consider *Murder by Death* her final cinematic outing.

The proposed sitcom, *Where's Poppa?*, was based on the 1970 film of the same name, concerning a man's increasingly frantic attempts to get rid of his eccentric elderly mother. While considered tasteless by many, the film was viewed by some as an outrageous farce, and it has built up a cult following in the decades since its release. For the sitcom pilot, which was filmed in early 1979 and aired in July, Elsa took the role played by Ruth Gordon in the movie, that of Momma; Steven Keats and Allan Miller were cast as her sons. Director Richard Benjamin said that Elsa was "more wonderfully eccentric than she ever was," and she certainly gave the part her all, relishing in the character's "delicious madness."[1] However, reviewers considered the premise of the proposed series to be in bad taste, with John J. O'Connor of *The New York Times* commenting that situations that were "perhaps tolerable in a film" became "curiously revolting in a situation comedy." O'Connor hated the pilot but loved Elsa, writing: "The producers have somehow managed to snare Elsa Lanchester. Unfortunately for them, Miss Lanchester is so cleverly wacky that most viewers are likely to root for saving her and eliminating the rest of the characters."[2] *Where's Poppa?* was not picked up by the American Broadcasting Company (ABC), and Elsa went on to work on the movie *Die Laughing* (1980).

The plot for *Die Laughing* involved a monkey, a wannabe pop singer, a secret formula, and a plutonium bomb, and starred teen idol Robby Benson. Upon its release, the film was justifiably eviscerated by the critics, with one writing "*Die Laughing* must have its sights set on being an entrant in the annual Worst Film

---

1.   *Los Angeles Times*, April 22, 1979; *Sacramento Bee*, July 17, 1979.

2.   *The New York Times*, July 17, 1979.

Festival. A movie this bad can't be entirely accidental."[3] It was not this critical panning, however, that made Elsa decide that she was finished with acting; after all, she had appeared in bombs before. Rather, her experience making *Die Laughing* was so disheartening and emotionally exhausting that it caused her to conclude that she no longer liked what show business had become, and that she wanted no further part in it. As is typical of Elsa, she did not keep these opinions to herself. While filming in San Francisco, she gave an amazingly candid interview to Marian Zailian of the *San Francisco Examiner*, in which she spoke at length about her situation. As an insight into Elsa's state of mind at the close of her career, it is heartbreaking:

> Getting up in the morning is getting less attractive. This film has really turned out to be, to me, a disappointment because the part was cut in half, and everything has gone to the speed, the youth, the jazzing, or whatever it's called. My character is of no interest whatever, really . . . it's awfully difficult to make something out of nothing. I'm doing my best, but it's a lot of waiting about. Sometimes I haven't been in a shot all day. I'm just sitting here. It's a form of discipline not to feel like you're in prison.
>
> I don't particularly want to work and I don't like acting, but everyone likes to keep their standard up—you know, the salary. There's no such thing as fun in acting. . . . I don't know what it is to get up in the morning and look forward to going to a studio to do a scene.
>
> As you get older people die or get married or something, and so you find yourself alone and have to start adjusting to being alone. I thought, coming here to San Francisco, there'd be a lot of people. But I have found myself *more* alone, and wondering, what does a prisoner do?[4]

Elsa had been saying for many years that she disliked acting, although in most interviews she clarified that what she really disliked was taking on small, cameo parts that gave her nothing to work with. When she was cast in a decent part—such as her work in *Then Came Bronson* or even *Willard*—then her love for the craft would often return, and she would discuss the enjoyment she felt in creating a character. But those parts were a thing of the past, and after being treated as unimportant and irrelevant on the set of *Die Laughing*, Elsa had had enough.

Her worsening health also played a part in her decision to retire. Since 1978, a hernia had meant that eating was difficult, and Elsa would struggle to keep food down. In 1979, author Gregory William Mank interviewed Elsa for his book *It's Alive! The Classic Cinema Saga of Frankenstein*, and found her "a kind and delightful good witch, ailing in her late seventies, yet still full of that sly humor."[5] When he visited her again in 1981, to present her with a copy of the book, she

---

3. *Sacramento Bee*, March 29, 1980.

4. *San Francisco Examiner*, September 9, 1979.

5. Mank, *Women in Horror Films*, 304.

was unwell, although she rallied enough to receive Mank. On this occasion, Elsa spoke to Mank as a fellow author, telling him about the book she was working on, which would be published in 1983 as *Elsa Lanchester, Herself: An Autobiography*.

Although her ill health and advancing age necessitated a slowing down at the beginning of the 1980s, Elsa still made use of the schoolroom at the Curson Avenue house, "rehearsing" three or four times a week with Ray Henderson. Elsa had no intention of performing again, but these musical sessions with Henderson—who was employed as a pianist in a top Los Angeles restaurant—were very important to her. Not only did they provide her with the regular company of a good friend, but the sessions seemed to Elsa to be "therapeutic and wonderful for breathing exercise."[6]

When *Elsa Lanchester, Herself* was published in May 1983, reviewers praised Elsa's frankness while bemoaning her lack of accuracy and insight. Ben Irwin—the public relations man who got to know Elsa when he worked for Charles Laughton—said that the prose style adopted in *Elsa Lanchester, Herself*, "at once original and bitchily observant," was an accurate representation of Elsa's conversational style: "such was her bent; compassion and the needle, all in one verbal thrust."[7]

In a pre-internet age, the full extent of the book's inaccuracies was not widely recognized, although Peter Hepple, writing in British theatrical newspaper *The Stage*, remarked that "few books can have more misspellings and errors of fact than this one, but all are readily forgivable in a story that is quite enthralling in its scope." Elsa was, Hepple declared, "a remarkable woman in her own right."[8] For other reviewers, the problem with Elsa's autobiography was not the accuracy of the facts that it did reveal, but the question of things that were left unsaid. Ellen Schlesinger praised the book for being "refreshingly lacking in hyperbole and self-promotion," but felt that Elsa's frank discussions on certain topics also served to emphasize her reticence in other areas. "Because she is more forthright and candid than most," wrote Schlesinger, "the omissions—and they are glaring—seem especially strange." She concluded: "Autobiography is in part an attempt to answer the question, How did I get this way? In Lanchester's case, the answer is still a mystery."[9]

Many readers will disagree with this assessment, on the basis that Elsa's unconventional upbringing and remarkable mother provide some of the answers that Schlesinger requires in her search for Elsa's personality origins. But if we consider the question from another angle, there is no doubt that Elsa is absent from lengthy sections of the book. In these she is describing events in which she played no part, some of which she witnessed firsthand, and others that she heard

---

6. Lanchester, *Elsa Lanchester, Herself*, 318.

7. *Los Angeles Times*, May 29, 1983.

8. *The Stage*, March 15, 1984.

9. *Sacramento Bee*, May 8, 1983.

about from those who had been there. In a way this is refreshing; celebrities frequently shoehorn themselves into events when recounting them, claiming a prominence for themselves that is not an accurate reflection of events. However, Elsa swings the pendulum too far the other way. As I suggested in the introduction to this book, this is possibly because Elsa was frequently asked about Charles Laughton. Elsa had written a book about Charles, she had been interviewed about him countless times, and she had cooperated with his biographer. She must have reasoned that Charles Laughton was what people wanted to read about, and so she gave the people what they wanted, perhaps ever wary of those 1938 reviews that accused her of too much self-promotion in *Charles Laughton and I*. She admitted that she "feared for any unwanted stressing of the 'I'" when the publisher suggested *Elsa Lanchester, Herself* as the title.[10] However, as Charles's fame faded over the years and Elsa became something of a cult icon for her portrayal of the Bride of Frankenstein, more recent readers of her autobiography have expressed confusion as to why Elsa dedicates so much of her autobiography to writing about someone else.

After the initial publication of *Elsa Lanchester, Herself*, Elsa appeared on several television talk shows to promote the book. But her age and declining health were taking their toll. After enjoying robust health for most of her life, and something of a new zest for life after Charles's death in 1963, Elsa found the ravages of old age particularly burdensome. She discussed her situation at the conclusion of her book, on the final page, which reads like a train of thought, disjointed and erratic, but somehow more genuine than polished prose might have been:

> I cannot tie up this ending with a pretty pink bow. Getting older is, to put it mildly, gruesome. And, having unloaded the past, memory is of course more localized now, though it seems to be a loyal machine, willing to serve if forced. So time is now up to its tricks with me—the Bitch! It's suddenly always Christmas again. Oh, I forgot, it's *Father* Time![11]

Elsa ends her autobiography by quoting a few lines from "The Last Leaf" by Oliver Wendell Holmes—a poem about aging and outliving one's contemporaries—before one final declaration, "Hold on, I'm still alive—this book is the evidence!" By the time she set her life down on paper, many of the characters in Elsa's story had passed away. Cave of Harmony contemporaries John Armstrong, Evelyn Waugh, Angela Baddeley, Harold Scott, and Tallulah Bankhead; former co-stars Boris Karloff, Ernest Thesiger, Buster Keaton, and Elvis Presley—all would die in the 1960s and 1970s. Iris Barry, a friend during some of Elsa's toughest times, died in France in 1969, at age seventy-four.

Elsa had already come out of retirement once, for a second act of her career, however ill-advised that had turned out to be. Now she was emerging from the

---

10. Lanchester, *Elsa Lanchester, Herself*, 318.

11. Lanchester, 318 (emphasis in original).

anonymity of retirement once again, this time with her life laid bare for her readers and a round of promotional interviews putting her before the cameras once more. But this final resurgence, this third act, was to be brief. In October 1983, less than six months after *Elsa Lanchester, Herself* appeared in bookstores, Elsa suffered a near-fatal stroke at home and was hospitalized at Cedars-Sinai Medical Center. A hospital spokesperson described her condition as "fair."[12] Ray Henderson, who visited Elsa at the hospital, said that although she was having difficulty speaking, she was regaining some movement in the left side of her body.[13] She was released from the hospital after nine weeks.

Although she was to live for another three years—surprising doctors with her strong will, according to a family friend—Elsa's condition declined dramatically during that time.[14] By the time Henderson died in 1984, Elsa needed regular medical attention and was largely unaware of what was occurring around her. She did not update her will, which left $250,000 to Henderson.

"I can only hope, and anticipate *your* own last year of life prove as harassed and unfriended as you caused your mother's to be."[15] That awful curse that Elsa's cousin had wished on her back in 1966 would come to pass twenty years later, although Elsa would thankfully be unaware of her solitude as by this time she had been in a comatose state for months.

She was cared for in her home by the Motion Picture and Television Fund, which became conservator of Elsa's person and estate in March 1986. The paperwork filed with this request described Elsa's condition as being confined to her bed after a series of strokes. She could no longer read, write, or speak, nor could she control her bladder or bowels. She was fed through a tube and had to be turned regularly to prevent bedsores. The heartbreaking documentation continued: "The conservatee has not spoken a word in many months. She gives no indication that she understands anything that is being said to her. . . . It is impossible to confer with her on any matter."[16]

Elsa Lanchester was admitted to the Motion Picture and Television Country House Hospital on December 17, 1986, and it was there that she died, from bronchopneumonia, on Boxing Day. She was eighty-four years old.

12. *Los Angeles Times*, October 19, 1983.

13. *Daily News*, October 20, 1983.

14. *San Francisco Examiner*, December 27, 1986.

15. Lanchester, *Elsa Lanchester, Herself*, 314.

16. Mank, *Women in Horror Films*, 316.

32 Afterlife

Obituaries appeared in newspapers all over the world to mark the passing of Elsa Lanchester, although they were frustratingly full of inaccuracies. Billy Wilder, who had directed Elsa in *Witness for the Prosecution* and also spent time with the Laughtons socially, paid tribute to her talent, as did her Turnabout songwriter Forman Brown. "Every role she undertook she made memorable," wrote Brown in a letter to the *Los Angeles Times*. "She was vivacious, she was witty, and she has assumed herself a lasting place in theatre history."[1]

Elsa's estate was valued at approximately $900,000, of which at least $500,000 went to the Motion Picture and Television Country House Hospital, with other amounts left to individuals such as her gardener and housekeeper, as well as to animal protection charities.[2] According to press reports, Elsa had "asked that no funeral be held and no information be released about the disposition of her remains."[3] There was some speculation that Elsa would be buried alongside Charles Laughton in Forest Lawn; however she had made her dislike of the cemetery clear in her autobiography—describing it as the "ogre of the Styx"—and had instead opted for cremation.[4] This was carried out by the Chapel of the Pines in Los Angeles on January 5, 1987, and Elsa's ashes were scattered over the Pacific.

With the body gone, the icon could take over. The Bride of Frankenstein is more popular now than she was when the film was released back in 1935. Like Dracula, the Wolf Man, Frankenstein's Monster, the Creature from the Black Lagoon, and other monsters brought to the screen by Universal, the Bride continues to exist in merchandise, with her face plastered on everything from clothing and makeup to action figures. As this book took shape in 2020, during the dark days of the Covid-19 pandemic, Universal Studios theme park in Orlando had a Bride of Frankenstein–themed scare maze for the Halloween season, and

1. *Napa Valley Register*, December 27, 1986; *Los Angeles Times*, January 8, 1987.
2. Mank, *Women in Horror Films*, 316; *Napa Valley Register*, January 7, 1987.
3. *Napa Valley Register*, December 27, 1986.
4. Lanchester, *Elsa Lanchester, Herself*, 300.

the stuffed toy company Build-A-Bear brought out a Bride Bear, officially licensed by Universal Monsters.

As a film, *Bride of Frankenstein* is now widely regarded as a classic, and as one of the few instances of a sequel outshining its predecessor. In 1998 it was preserved by the National Film Registry, which deemed it to be "culturally or aesthetically significant." It has also become the object of academic discussion and detailed critical analysis, something that would have shocked those haughty contemporary critics who claimed that it was very good . . . for a horror film. Some of this analysis has brought Elsa's private life into the discussion. Monika Morgan, for example, described the movie as James Whale's tribute to "the majesty and power of the homosexual creator." Her argument runs partially as follows:

> In addition to the director's well-known orientation, we have major characters played by gay or bisexual men: Ernest Thesiger, one of the most outrageous queens of '30s movie queendom, and the allegedly bisexual Colin Clive. Even the bride's (Elsa Lanchester) true-life husband, Charles Laughton, was a noted gay masochist, a fact that fits her nicely into the film's schema of camp assault.[5]

This interpretation is rejected by many—director Curtis Harrington powerfully described it as "pure bullshit"—but Elsa's links to gay men extend far beyond this film and her marriage.[6]

Elsa moved in bohemian circles before turning to the London theater scene and then on to Hollywood, so it is not especially remarkable that she would state in a 1970s interview that "most of my male friends have been gay."[7] Besides Charles Laughton, Elsa had close relationships with Christopher Isherwood, Michael Hall, Forman Brown, and Jack Grinnage. Some observers—most outspoken among them being Isherwood's longtime partner, Don Bachardy, who never got along with Elsa—felt that there was an unhealthy element to these friendships. Isherwood's biographer Peter Parker claims that the mutual enmity between Bachardy and Elsa was in part based on Bachardy's belief that Elsa "was half in love with Isherwood and on one occasion attempted to seduce him. She regarded Bachardy . . . as an obstacle to her own (wish-)fulfillment."[8] Bachardy himself would say that Elsa "was one of those women who gravitated towards queers—all the people she knew were queer—but she still wanted to be fucked by them and still imagined that she didn't like homosexuality."[9]

Whether a sexual attraction toward gay—and therefore unavailable—men was part of Elsa's psychological makeup is an interesting point to consider, but

---

5. Morgan, "Sexual Subversion."
6. Mank, *Women in Horror Films*, 309.
7. Hadleigh, *Leading Ladies*, 98.
8. Parker, *Isherwood*, 686.
9. Parker, 685–86.

there is little evidence that she ever tried to seduce Isherwood or formed any romantic attachment beyond close friendship to any gay men other than Charles.

Although interest in *Bride of Frankenstein* remained strong, interest in Elsa Lanchester waned over the years, and *Elsa Lanchester, Herself* went out of print. However, a "Reprint Elsa" campaign led by writer and performer Tom Blunt saw Elsa's autobiography published again by Chicago Review Press in 2018. Blunt's campaign began after he discovered an old copy of *Elsa Lanchester, Herself* in a thrift store. He was instantly drawn to the little-known live performance aspect of Elsa's career, and it was here he discovered common ground with the actress. "More than anything she achieved in film, Elsa felt her true calling was in cabaret singing," Blunt said. "And now here I was a century later, a struggling wannabe artist trying to create my own ridiculous scene, with drag queens and musicians and famous character actresses. She did everything first, and better. I was in awe."[10]

At the start of this book, I claimed that Elsa Lanchester would not have chosen to be remembered as just the actress behind the Bride of Frankenstein. So how would she want to be remembered? All must be conjecture now, decades after her death, but she was always proudest of her music hall/vaudeville-style stage routines, returning to them again and again over the years, from the Cave of Harmony in 1920s London, to the Turnabout Theatre in Hollywood twenty years later, to her one-woman tour in the early 1960s. A 1927 profile by J. T. Grein could therefore perhaps be read as a fitting epitaph:

> You remember Elsa Lanchester as a quaint person—something like a lanky marionette with limbs and frames run on wires. You remember her dancing unlike anybody else—something strange, humorous, almost *macabre*. You remember also a voice—nowise of a *prima donna*, but eccentric, strident; some of her notes pierce the atmosphere like an arrow. A Shockheaded Peter she is, with remarkable features: eyes like electric globes in glow, a *retroussé* nose, a sensitive mouth, almost a rosebud bursting into flower. If you look long enough, you discover a touch of Greuze: there dwells romance and eeriness in her countenance.[11]

10. Blunt, "From the Archives."

11. *Illustrated London News*, March 5, 1927.

Elsa in costume for her number "A Ballad of Balance" in the *Midnight Follies*, 1926.   *Pictorial Press Ltd. / Alamy Stock Photo*

References

Adler, Larry. *It Ain't Necessarily So*. London: Collins, 1984

Allen, Grant. *The Woman Who Did*. London: John Lane, 1895.

Baddeley, Hermione. *The Unsinkable Hermione Baddeley*. London: Collins, 1984.

Blunt, Tom. "From the Archives: Elsa Lanchester, Herself." Interview. *Haute Macabre* (blog). June 10, 2019. https://hautemacabre.com/2019/06/from-the-archives-elsa-lanchester-herself-an-interview-with-tom-blunt/.

Bradbury, Ray. "What Else but Elsa?" In *A Gamut of Girls*, by Elsa Lanchester and Forman Brown, 9–10. Santa Barbara, CA: Capra Press, 1988.

Brown, Forman. *Small Wonder: The Story of the Yale Puppeteers and Turnabout Theatre*. Metuchen, NJ: Scarecrow Press, 1980.

Callow, Simon. *Charles Laughton: A Difficult Actor*. London: Vintage, 2012.

Castelow, "No Vote, No Census—1911 Census Protests." *Historic UK*. Accessed May 24, 2020. https://www.historic-uk.com/HistoryUK/HistoryofBritain/No-Vote-No-Census-1911-Census-Protests/.

"Charles Laughton." *Hollywood Greats*, series 2, episode 4, written and narrated by Barry Norman. British Broadcasting Corporation, 1978. YouTube video, 48:34. Posted May 23, 2015 by Victor Jamison. www.youtube.com/watch?v=i2eCEbtxtyk.

Cockayne, Steve. *Master of the Marionettes: The Life and Work of Waldo Lanchester*. Glasgow: Scottish Mask and Puppet Centre, 2018.

Cockin, Katharine. *Edith Craig and the Theatre of Art*. London: Bloomsbury, 2017.

Croall, Jonathan. *John Gielgud: Matinee Idol to Movie Star*. London: Methuen Drama, 2011.

Curtis, James. *James Whale: A New World of Gods and Monsters*. Minneapolis: University of Minnesota Press, 2003.

Duncan, Isadora. *My Life*. New York: Liveright, 1927.

Gabler, Neal. *Walt Disney: The Biography*. London: Aurum Press, 2008.

Goldring, Douglas. *The Nineteen Twenties: A General Survey and Some Personal Memories*. London: Nicholson and Watson, 1945.

Guthrie, Tyrone. *A Life in the Theatre*. London: Readers Union, 1961.

Hadleigh, Boze. *Hollywood Lesbians: From Garbo to Foster*. Riverdale, NY: Riverdale Avenue Books, 2016.

———. *Leading Ladies*. London: Robson Books, 1992.

Hammond, John. *John Hammond on Record: An Autobiography*. New York: Ridge Press, 1977.

Hastings, Selina. *Rosamond Lehmann: A Life*. London: Random House, 2012.

Hershman, Gabriel. *Strolling Player: The Life and Career of Albert Finney*. Stroud: History Press, 2017.

Higham, Charles. *Charles Laughton: An Intimate Biography*. New York: Doubleday, 1976.

———. *In and Out of Hollywood: A Biographer's Memoir*. Madison, WI: Terrace Books, 2009.

Hirschhorn, Clive. *The Hollywood Musical*. London: Octopus Books, 1981.

Holmes, Rachel. *Eleanor Marx: A Life*. London: Bloomsbury, 2014.

Isherwood, Christopher. *Diaries*. Vol. 1, *1939–1960*. Edited and introduced by Katherine Bucknell. London: Vintage Books, 1996.

———. *Diaries*. Vol. 2, *The Sixties: 1960–1969*. Edited and introduced by Katherine Bucknell. London: Vintage Books, 2012.

———. *Diaries*. Vol. 3, *Liberation: 1970–1983*. Edited and introduced by Katherine Bucknell. New York: Harper Perennial, 2012.

Isherwood, Christopher, and Don Bachardy. *The Animals: Love Letters between Christopher Isherwood and Don Bachardy*. Edited and introduced by Katherine Bucknell. London: Vintage Books, 2014.

Kapp, Yvonne. *Eleanor Marx: A Biography*. London: Verso, 2018.

Lanchester, Elsa. *Charles Laughton and I*. London: Faber and Faber, 1938.

———. *Elsa Lanchester, Herself: An Autobiography*. 1983. Reprinted, with a foreword by Mara Wilson. Chicago: Chicago Review Press, 2018.

———. Introduction to *Charles Laughton: An Intimate Biography*, by Charles Higham, i–xviii. New York: Doubleday, 1976.

Lanchester, Elsa, and Forman Brown. *A Gamut of Girls*. Santa Barbara, CA: Capra Press, 1988.

Laughton, Charles. Introduction to *Charles Laughton and I*, by Elsa Lanchester, 7–8. New York: Faber and Faber, 1938.

Leigh-Bennett, E. P. "Lesser Lights: II—the Never-Mind-Where." *The Bystander*, September 24, 1924.

Lewis, Jeremy. *Penguin Special: The Life and Times of Allen Lane*. London: Viking, 2005.

Lord, Graham. *Niv: The Authorised Biography of David Niven*. London: Orion Books, 2003.

Loudermilk, A. "Elsa Lanchester Was Born to Defy Heteronormativity." *PopMatters*, October 31, 2018. www.popmatters.com/elsa-lanchester-herself-2614904290.html.

Low, Rachel. *The History of the British Film, 1918–1929*. London: George Allen and Unwin, 1971.

Mank, Gregory William. *Women in Horror Films, 1930s.* Jefferson, NC: McFarland, 1999.

Manley, Seb. "Comedy and Experimentation in British Alternative Film: The Funny Peculiar Case of Ivor Montagu's *Bluebottles.*" *Scope*, no. 10, February 2008. www.nottingham.ac.uk/scope/documents/2008/february-2008/manley.pdf.

Mantell-Seidel, Andrea. *Isadora Duncan in the 21st Century: Capturing the Art and Spirit of the Dancer's Legacy.* Jefferson, NC: McFarland, 2016.

Moffatt, Wendy. *Great Unrecorded History: A New Life of E. M. Forster.* New York: Farrar, Straus and Giroux, 2010.

Montague Browne, Anthony. *Long Sunset: Memoirs of Winston Churchill's Last Private Secretary.* Kent: Podkin Press, 2009.

Morely, Sheridan. *Odd Man Out: James Mason—A Biography.* London: Coronet Books, 1990.

Morgan, Monika. "Sexual Subversion: *The Bride of Frankenstein.*" *Bright Lights*, Fall 1993.

Napier, Alan, with James Bigwood. *Not Just Batman's Butler: The Autobiography of Alan Napier.* Jefferson, NC: McFarland, 2015.

Nash Information Services. "Annual Movie Chart—1971." *The Numbers* (website). Accessed February 20, 2021. https://m.the-numbers.com/market/1971/top-grossing-movies.

Nissen, Axel. *Actresses of a Certain Character: Forty Familiar Hollywood Faces from the Thirties to the Fifties.* Jefferson, NC: McFarland, 2011.

O'Connor, Barbara. *Barefoot Dancer: The Story of Isadora Duncan.* Minneapolis, MN: Carolrhoda Books, 2001.

O'Hara, Maureen, with John Nicoletti. *'Tis Herself.* London: Simon and Schuster, 2004.

Parker, Peter. *Isherwood.* London: Pan Macmillan, 2005.

Rich, Sharon. "Live Blogging *Naughty Marietta* (1935)." *Sharon Rich* (author website). April 17, 2018. http://sharonrich.com/2018/04/live-blogging-naughty-marietta-1935/.

———. *Sweethearts: The Timeless Love Affair—On-Screen and Off—Between Jeanette MacDonald and Nelson Eddy.* 20th anniversary ed. New York: Bell Harbour Press, 2014.

Rogers, Ginger. *Ginger: My Story.* 1991. Reprint, New York: HarperCollins, 2008.

The Scarlet Woman. Starring Elsa Lanchester and Evelyn Waugh. 1924. Silent film, 44 min. British Film Institute, https://player.bfi.org.uk/free/film/watch-the-scarlet-woman-1924-online.

Scott, Harold. *The Early Doors: Origins of the Music Hall.* London: Nicholson and Watson, 1946.

Server, Lee. *Robert Mitchum: Baby, I Don't Care.* London: Faber and Faber, 2002.

Sicherman, Barbara, and Carol Hurd Green, eds. *Notable American Women: The Modern Period.* Cambridge, MA: Belknap Press, 1980.

Sitton, Robert. *Lady in the Dark: Iris Barry and the Art of Film.* New York: Columbia University Press, 2014.

Sitwell, Osbert. *The Scarlet Tree.* London: Little, Brown, 1946.

Skal, David J., with Jessica Rains. *Claude Rains: An Actor's Voice*. Lexington: University Press of Kentucky, 2008.

Utley, Freda. *Odyssey of a Liberal: Memoirs*. Washington DC: Washington National Press, 1970. www.fredautley.com/OdysseyOfALiberal.htm.

Walker, Alexander. *Vivien: The Life of Vivien Leigh*. 1987. Reprint, London: Orion, 2001.

Wayne, Jane Ellen. *The Golden Girls of MGM*. New York: Carroll and Graf, 2004.

Wearing, J. P. *The London Stage 1920–1929: A Calendar of Productions, Performers and Personnel*. 2nd ed. Lanham, MD: Rowman and Littlefield, 2014.

Williams, Harcourt. *Old Vic Saga*. London: Winchester, 1949.

Wilson, John Howard. *Evelyn Waugh: A Literary Biography, 1924–1966*. London: Associated University Press, 2001.

Windeler, Robert. *The Films of Shirley Temple*. New York: Carroll, 1978.

Winters, Shelley. *Shelley: Also Known as Shirley*. London: Granada, 1980.

Witchard, Anne. "Sink Street: The Sapphic World of Pre-Chinatown Soho." In *Sex, Time and Place: Queer Histories of London, c. 1850 to the Present*, edited by Simon Avery and Katherine M. Graham, 221–37. London: Bloomsbury, 2018.

Wykes, David. *Evelyn Waugh: A Literary Life*. Basingstoke: Macmillan, 1999.

Filmography Index

Index

Note on abbreviations: EL—Elsa Lanchester; CL—Charles Laughton

CPSIA information can be obtained
at www.ICGtesting.com
Printed in the USA
LVHW080145031121
702327LV00012B/651

9 781629 338095